T0305242

FARM LABOR STRUGGLES IN ZIMBABWE

FARM LABOR STRUGGLES IN ZIMBABWE

THE GROUND OF POLITICS

BLAIR RUTHERFORD

INDIANA UNIVERSITY PRESS

Bloomington and Indianapolis

This book is a publication of

Indiana University Press
Office of Scholarly Publishing
Herman B Wells Library 350
1320 East 10th Street
Bloomington, Indiana 47405 USA

iupress.indiana.edu

Manufactured in the United States of
America

Library of Congress Cataloging-in-
Publication Data

Names: Rutherford, Blair A. (Blair Allan),
  [date] author.
Title: Farm labor struggles in
  Zimbabwe : the ground of politics /
  Blair Rutherford.
Description: Bloomington : Indiana
  University Press, 2017. | Includes
  bibliographical references and index.
Identifiers: LCCN 2016024512 (print) |
  LCCN 2016025126 (ebook) | ISBN
  9780253023995 (cl : alk. paper) | ISBN
  9780253024039 (pb : alk. paper) | ISBN
  9780253024077 (eb)
Subjects: LCSH: Agricultural laborers—
  Political activity—Zimbabwe. |
  Agricultural laborers—Zimbabwe—
  Economic conditions. | Land
  reform—Zimbabwe. | Land use—
  Government policy—Zimbabwe. |
  Agriculture and state—Zimbabwe. |
  Zimbabwe—Politics and
  government—1980-
Classification: LCC HD1538.Z55 R88 2017
  (print) | LCC HD1538.Z55 (ebook) |
  DDC 331.763096891—dc23
LC record available at https://lccn.loc.
  gov/2016024512

1 2 3 4 5 22 21 20 19 18 17

CONTENTS

ABBREVIATIONS

ALB	Agricultural Labor Bureau
CIO	Central Intelligence Organization
CFU	Commercial Farmers' Union
DA	District Administrator
DRC	Democratic Republic of Congo
ESAP	Economic Structural Adjustment Programme
FCTZ	Farm Community Trust of Zimbabwe
GAPWUZ	General Agriculture and Plantation Workers' Union of Zimbabwe
IFC	International Financial Corporation
ISO	International Socialist Organization
MDC	Movement for Democratic Change
NCA	National Constitutional Assembly
NEC	National Employment Council (for the Agricultural Industry)
NCR	Non-Citizen Resident
NGO	Non-Governmental Organization
RDC	Rural District Council
ZANU (PF)	Zimbabwe African National Union (Patriotic Front)
ZAPU	Zimbabwe African People's Union
ZAWU	Zimbabwe Agricultural Workers' Union
ZCTU	Zimbabwe Congress of Trade Unions

ZFTU   Zimbabwe Federation of Trade Unions
ZLC   Zimbabwe Labour Centre
ZNLWVA   Zimbabwe National Liberation War Veterans Association
ZRP   Zimbabwe Republic Police

PREFACE

A FORMER PROFESSOR of mine, Jim Faris, used to say that if you are ever completely satisfied with anything that you have written, then something is wrong, for it shows that you are no longer learning, no longer re-examining your conceptual tools and forms of analyses. This lesson, as it were, has made writing and finishing this book particularly difficult. As I was carrying out the research in Zimbabwe in the late 1990s and early 2000s that generated the material for this book, my own understandings and analysis were still developing. This was due in large part to the monumental changes occurring in Zimbabwe after February 2000, transforming the lives and livelihoods for the particular farm workers and former farm workers at the center of my analysis as well as elevating farm workers as a discursive category in Zimbabwe to the forefront of national and international debates and studies. Combined with engaging with the changing scholarly analyses of Zimbabwe and elsewhere, I struggled with my own analytical framing, finally focusing on what seemed to be a ubiquitous but relatively under-theorized topic: politics. By examining how the practices and power relations of electoral politics became entangled in the configuration of livelihoods and social projects of an extraordinary farm labor struggle, I hope that this ethnography contributes to wider understandings of farm workers, Zimbabwe, agrarian struggles and the importance of critically examining the ground of politics when advocating for social change.

For my learning for this book, I am heavily indebted to many. Foremost, I need to thank the Social Sciences and Humanities Research Council of

Canada which generously supported my research in Zimbabwe. The University of Regina and Carleton University both provided supportive institutional homes for me. Carleton's Institute of African Studies, for which I have had the privilege of being its first director from 2009 to 2015, has, in particular, been a source of fertile learning, with thanks in particular going to its overworked but very supportive administrator, June Payne, and my colleagues Linda Freeman, Susanne Klausen, Pius Adesanmi, Doris Buss, Louise de la Gorgendière, Aboubakar Sanogo, Chris Brown, James Milner, Audra Diptee, Moses Kiggundu, Nduka Otiono, Dominique Marshall, Christine Duff, Monica Patterson, and Paul Mkandawire, among many others based at Carleton or who have participated in various events organized by the institute over these years. I have also profited immensely from colleagues in the Department of Sociology and Anthropology and other departments and many of the excellent students at Carleton, some of whom critically read earlier drafts or segments of this book, including Holly Dunn, Gerald Morton and Heather McAlister, for whom I am very grateful. I also want to give a special thanks to Willie Carroll, who used his map-making skills to improve the map used in the introduction.

The manuscript that became this book initially took shape while spending a half year affiliated with the Institute de recherché pour le développement in Montpellier, France in 2007. The hospitality and insightful scholarship of Jean-Pierre Colin, Jean-Pierre Chauveau and Éric Léonard were greatly appreciated and influential in my own thinking.

I also greatly benefitted from my affiliation with the Institute of Development Studies at the University of Zimbabwe during this period. I have also benefited immensely from the critical thoughts, incisive analyses, and often warm friendships with many scholars who work on Zimbabwe or its diasporas, including (in alphabetical order): Lincoln Addison, Joss Alexander, Max Bolt, Patrick Bond, Joy Chadya, Ben Cousins, Suzanne Dansereau, Bill Derman, Sara Dorman, Marc Epprecht, Joost Fontein, Peter Gibbon, Allison Goebel, Zoe Groves, Munyaradzi Gwisai, Gertrude Hambira, Amanda Hammar, Andrew Hartnack, David Hughes, Diana Jeater, Léa Kalaora, Bill Kinsey, Norma Kriger, Rene Loewenson, Godfrey Magaramombe, Prosper Matondi, Murray McCartney, Jo McGregor, David Moore, Donald Moore, Toby Moorsom, Sam Moyo, William Munro, Phillip Munyanyi, Francis Musoni, Gift Muti, Anderson Mutemererwa, James Muzondidya, Thenji Nkosi, Brian Raftopoulos, Lloyd Sachikonye, John Saul, Richard Saunders,

Tim Scarnecchia, Ian Scoones, Juliet Sithole, Allison Shutt, Sam Spiegel, Marja Spierenburg, Irene Staunton, Evert Waeterloos, Richard Werbner, Luise White, Wendy Willems, Eric Worby, and Philan Zamchiya (amongst many others). Through workshop discussions, presentations at conferences, and through conversations and discussions with them in person and virtually, I have learned immensely about Zimbabwe, scholarship, and much, much more.

This book would not have taken shape without the help of Rinse Nyamuda, my longstanding friend, whose assistance in conducting the research in Zimbabwe was crucial, as well as the Zimbabwean farm workers and some commercial farmers who are at the heart of this book but who must remain nameless or be given pseudonyms to try to disguise them. My debt to my family, Laura Farquharson, Clara Rutherford, and Ry Rutherford, is also immense as they have had to accommodate too often my frequent travels, my distractedness, and my sometimes over-commitment to my scholarly and work pursuits. Finally, I need to greatly thank the three reviewers for their critical and highly relevant comments on the manuscript for this book, the expert and helpful team at Indiana University Press, and Dee Mortensen, my editor at Indiana, whose support and advice have been invaluable.

FARM LABOR STRUGGLES IN ZIMBABWE

INTRODUCTION

"AND, YOUR BOOK project . . . ?" I cautiously asked Tawonga,[1] knowing that in one of his infrequent e-mail messages from the previous year he alluded to a "story" about it.

"Ahh," Tawonga sighed with a wan smile. "After you so abruptly left that day ten years ago, there were so many anxieties and worries about being associated with you that the friend I was living with took all my papers and documents that were in any way tied to you, including everything I was accumulating for my book, and tore them up and threw them in the toilet." Glancing at his friend and fellow farm worker, Tapedza, Tawonga added that nothing ever did happen to them afterward because of me, although it was a "different time" then.

The conversation the three of us had in a downtown Harare restaurant that sunny October 2013 day was marked by a resigned acceptance of the precarious livelihoods they forged out of the new agrarian landscape that has emerged in Zimbabwe since the massive, and often chaotic, land redistribution exercise that began in 2000. Although still working for one of the few remaining white farmers in the country, Tawonga and Tapedza were infrequently paid and depended on a wide range of livelihood strategies to seek sustenance and to strive as best they could toward a better future for themselves and their families. These precarious livelihoods were shared by most, if not all, of those now working for the large-, medium-, and small-scale black farmers on what had been officially called the "large-scale" commercial farming areas during the first two decades of Zimbabwe's independence, from 1980 to 2000. During that period, most of these farms were predominantly owned and operated by white farmers, the majority of whom were Zimbabwean. The year 2000 marked the start of wide-scale occupations of white-owned commercial farms by black Zimbabweans, spearheaded by veterans of the anticolonial war of the 1970s, with organizational support from the ruling Zimbabwe African National Union (Patriotic Front), also known as ZANU (PF), political party and various branches of the state, particularly the security services. With policies and laws trying to catch up with the events on the ground, these occupations and farm invasions were formalized on paper and in haphazard bureaucratic and political practices as the "Fast-Track Land Reform" program, which has seen the compulsory redistribution of nearly eleven million hectares from about four thousand white farmers—half of which has been transferred to over one hundred fifty thousand black citizens.

Tapedza and Tawonga were part of, and helped to lead, a historic farm labor struggle that stretched out for more than a year and a half, which overlapped with the buildup to and start of the mass takeover of white-owned farms. It was a farm labor struggle that explicitly aimed to be a catalyst to improve the rights and livelihoods of farm workers on a wider, if not national, scale. Its durability and ambitions were fueled and sustained by its entanglement in national-scale politics.

In October 1998, a major Zimbabwean agribusiness company, which I call Zimfarm, fired 879 farm workers on one of their horticultural farms, which I call Upfumi, for taking an unlawful industrial action. The management of Upfumi farm claimed the workers refused to work without cause, and after going through their company's industrial relations processes, they dismissed virtually the entire workforce.

Although many of the fired workers ended up either leaving the farm to seek livelihoods elsewhere or to return to work under more precarious contract conditions, most of the fired workers declared it an unfair dismissal, the culmination of what their leadership claimed was a series of attempts by the new management to roll back gains that their workers' committee had earlier achieved for the workforce under the previous management. Hundreds of mainly women farm workers challenged their dismissal through the company's labor relations appeal mechanisms and then through the state's justice system. They finally won some compensation from Zimfarm in June 2000 through the Labor Tribunal, the highest national judicial body responsible for labor disputes.

A core of the workers involved in the struggle had remained on Upfumi farm after they were fired and then had camped next to it after they were evicted by state authorities in July 1999, until they received the compensation awarded to them by the Tribunal eleven months later. The payout was much less than anticipated by these workers, and their victory, as it was, was now overshadowed by the land occupations and politicized violence occurring on many of the commercial farms and elsewhere in Zimbabwe.

During the farm occupations that began in February 2000, farm workers found themselves positioned between the politicized land occupiers and their white bosses. As Zimbabwe began to receive worldwide media attention in 2000, so did farm workers. "Farm workers in Zimbabwe" had now become a very politicized topic. But much of the discussion of farm workers and politics was very different from how politics had been used in the Upfumi struggle.

This book examines the ground of politics in regard to farm workers in Zimbabwe in two distinct ways: how farm workers have been framed by much of the bifurcated politicized commentary on Zimbabwe post-2000 and, at the same time, how a particular configuration of politics enabled the relative success of the Upfumi labor struggle while also constraining it. I thus examine how farm workers in Zimbabwe have been grounded in dominant discourses concerning the politics of Zimbabwe as well as the specific ground of politics that nurtured the Upfumi struggle. I argue that the former grounding misses the varied and sometimes contradictory ways in which Zimbabwean farm workers would engage with politics, let alone be engaged by it. I suggest that when examining how political action can energize and be energized by concerns emerging from everyday practices and struggles of livelihood, one learns about a grounding of politics in Zimbabwe that is very different from that discussed in dominant analyses of Zimbabwean politics—both those analyses that laud the massive land redistribution on social justice grounds and those that condemn it on the grounds of its violence and violation of a range of human rights. An in-depth exploration of the Upfumi farm labor struggle is an excellent illustration of the contradictory grounds of politics for farm workers in Zimbabwe and, to extrapolate, of wider labor struggles.

I begin my own book by noting Tawonga's aborted effort to write a book about their struggle in order to highlight how the task of writing can become entwined with wider events. Conducting research and writing about struggles that are motivated by claims of justice and rights can almost inevitably draw one into the campaign. I found myself in sympathy with the Upfumi farm workers, their mobilization of political support, and their ambitions for improving the rights of all farm workers. But the wider politics that engulfed them and Zimbabwe at large after February 2000 have made me more critically reflexive of the framing of politics itself, both as a source of support in struggles such as those of the Upfumi workers and in terms of scholarly analyses such as this book. Scholarship can adopt the dominant framing of different struggles and, in so doing I suggest, miss the actual ground of politics in specific localities and struggles.

It has been difficult to write about Zimbabwe after 2000 without being influenced by the larger grounding of "politics in Zimbabwe," which is dichotomized between those "for" or "against" the ZANU (PF) government's actions. Much of the writing that has focused on farm workers after 2000 tends to follow one side or the other of that framing, but in so doing glosses over the specific possibilities and perils that electoral politics provided to differently situated Zimbabweans. By discussing the particular grounds of this farm worker labor struggle, which took place during a momentous time in Zimbabwe's history, I hope this book opens a new perspective on Zimbabwean politics—one that is different than the two dominant viewpoints of it.

Two very different views of Zimbabwean politics emerge through opposing narratives commonly used to examine the country after 2000: politics as liberatory, as asserting the sovereign rights of a people to claim back its resources from a colonial past, is the theme found in analyses supportive of the massive land transfer carried out by the Zimbabwean government; or politics as oppression, as emphasizing the violence found in actions by the state and those operating in the name of the state in Zimbabwe to point toward the need for establishing a political system that respects human rights, is the theme promoted by those who are critical of the Zimbabwean government. Both positions have long international and national genealogies and come across as universal grounds to evaluate Zimbabwe and to intervene, or to propose interventions, in the lives of farm workers in Zimbabwe. A common example of the former is the claim that farm workers need to join the latest phase of the liberation struggle of which the state-abetted takeover of white-owned farms is the latest manifestation; whereas, an example from the latter narrative is the argument that farm workers' individual human rights need to be protected from oppressive state politics. Yet, such politics and interventions take on a different complexity, beyond the either-or propositions in which they are often grounded, when one examines them through the particular struggles of farm workers.

This book is thus about the particular place of politics that emerged through an extraordinary farm worker labor struggle (in which Tapedza and Tawonga were involved) as a way to provide more insight into postcolonial politics as well as struggles for workers' rights and agrarian livelihoods in Zimbabwe and in Africa, more broadly. The two dominant narratives used in analysing politics in Zimbabwe—politics as liberatory and politics as oppression—were both relevant in this labor struggle, but their meanings and consequences were varied as the struggle unfolded within a rapidly changing national and international context.

The Upfumi labor dispute was an extraordinary effort given that farm work has been marked as one of the most devalued, lowest-paying, and servile jobs in the country, like elsewhere in the world (Gibbon, Daviron, and Barral 2014). Their struggle was sustained by a relatively militant workers' committee, of which Tapedza was the nominal leader. It was mainly driven, however, by Chenjerai, the vice chairman of the workers' committee who actively sought political support for their labor struggle. He did so by entangling the Upfumi labor dispute in the wider events regarding electoral politics and national policies occurring in Zimbabwe at that time. While these connections to political networks, institutions and the symbolic capital of electoral politics itself—the power that can be invoked and come from being involved in national political processes or interacting with people who are part of them—were key factors in sustaining the farm worker struggle, not everyone who was part of it necessarily supported this wider involvement— then or in hindsight.

The weight politics carried in this labor struggle, and the ambivalence directed toward it, came through in the conversation I had with Tapedza and Tawonga that October day. Tapedza was very critical of Chenjerai for his devotion to politics. As he declared, "Even now, Chenjerai lives by working for the various politicians. But he hasn't moved up in the ZANU (PF) hierarchy at all," suggesting that it was a futile dedication. In response to my inquiry about whether Chenjerai was always like that, Tawonga commented, as Tapedza nodded in agreement, "He was always political, but he initially was very much focused on farm workers' rights, on our struggle. Then, he was a good leader."

The ground of politics, and the ground that politics provided, had shifted substantially in Zimbabwe in that nearly fifteen-year period. In August 1999, when I first met and began researching the farm workers involved in the Upfumi struggle, I was struck, and frankly excited, by how they drew on wider claims as "workers" and "citizens"; and how they were creating links to national-scale political parties, their trade union, and other groups based in Harare, to sustain their labor dispute. It was a vibrant and audacious struggle in contrast with what I had learned during my 1992–93 doctoral research on farm workers in Zimbabwe, which showed that farm workers rarely contested the grueling conditions and meager compensation; or, only did so through the lineaments of the farm authority relations, which highly favored management (Rutherford 2001a). The Upfumi struggle was energized by the entanglement of its leaders, particularly Chenjerai, in national-scale politics and their political imaginations during the contestation and antagonism of ZANU (PF)'s rule in the second half of the 1990s.

Tapedza's ambivalence toward politics thus marks, in part, the different periods of time in Zimbabwe: the late 1990s was a time when there was more public talk and visceral affect about the need for "greater democracy" in the country. In 2013, there was very little public talk, let alone, support for electoral politics, save for events engineered by ZANU (PF). But it also points to how, from the perspective of these two farm workers, electoral politics both enabled their labor struggle and hindered it.

In order to put this Upfumi struggle into context, let me begin by examining the positioning of farm workers in the wider political economy of Zimbabwe in the late 1990s.

Farm Workers: Livelihoods and Contestations

To understand the broad situation of farm workers in Zimbabwe, one needs to start with the key spatial distinctions that have been instrumental to statecraft and politics in the country (Worby 1994; Munro 1998; Hammar, Raftopoulos, and Jensen 2003; Moore 2005). In addition to the larger, and common, division between urban and rural, there have been important distinctions in Zimbabwe made between communal lands, commercial farms, and resettlement farms (see map I.1). These categories of land use have not only been legal and administrative categories but they have also helped

FARM LABOR STRUGGLES IN ZIMBABWE

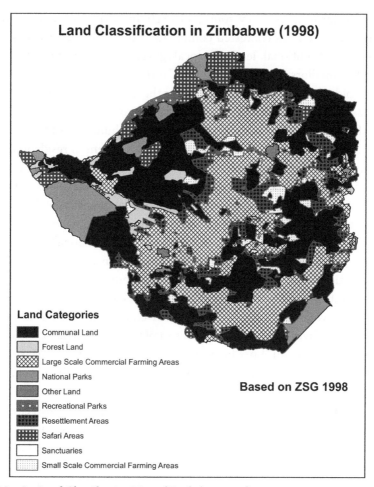

Map I.1. Land Classification Map of Zimbabwe, 1998[2]

define particular relations of authority, political subjectivities, and economic practices on the local, national, and international scales. There have
been a range of livelihood practices carried out through unequal relations in
each of these land use categories.

"Communal lands" are the former colonial native reserves, typically
located in agriculturally marginal lands, into which Africans defined as
indigenous were shoehorned (Phimister 1988) as "native tribesmen." Since
independence, households living in these areas have been mainly characterized as "smallholder farmers," often relying on a mix of subsistence and

cash-crop farming as a key source of livelihood; they are administrated through a sometimes contested combination of authorities, such as those defined as "traditional leaders," local government administrators, and elected councillors. "Commercial farms" is the post-1980 name for land held in freehold tenure, reserved until 1979 for those defined as European. Until the massive land redistribution that began in 2000, they were still largely owned and operated by white farmers, and many hundreds of thousands of farm workers and their dependents also lived on them in residential compounds. "Resettlement farms" refer to land, typically white-owned commercial farms, purchased or taken over by the government after 1980 and distributed to black Zimbabweans, who use the land mostly for farming.

"Farm workers" in Zimbabwe refers to the men and women (and occasionally children) who work, or had worked, on commercial farms. In the colonial period, these were known as European farms, and working and living conditions were so harsh that the farmers tended to rely on (putatively) more pliant migrant workers from colonial Malawi, Zambia and Mozambique. The workers tended to live in labor compounds on the farms and much of their lives were under the control of the white farmers, their white managers and African "boss-boys" as legally they fell under the Masters and Servants Act rather than labor legislation (Clarke 1977; Rubert 1998; Rutherford 2001a). Although many of the immigrant farm workers returned to their countries of origin or made their way to work opportunities elsewhere in colonial Zimbabwe and apartheid South Africa, many remained on the European farms—and their families and descendants also ended up working there.

Even with the transition from colonial to postcolonial Zimbabwe, farm workers as a community were largely marked in Zimbabwe as cheap laborers, foreigners, and under the control of white farmers. Just before independence in 1980, farm workers became legally recognized as "workers" rather than "servants." They were also permitted to vote in the contentious 1979 Rhodesia-Zimbabwe elections and the first independence elections of 1980, regardless of their actual citizenship; a move that critics saw as a way to increase the votes for the candidates approved by white farmers given the amount of control farmers had over farm workers' lives (Palley 1979, 10–13, 25). After independence, legislation increased their new status as "workers" by providing a minimum wage and introducing a labor relations machinery. This facilitated an improvement in real wages as well as some tentative attempts at organizing them by trade unions and political activists in the early 1980s (Rutherford 2001b). Although the new government expanded social services to much of the population, very few schools or health clinics were built in commercial farming areas (Loewenson 1992), because ZANU (PF) continued to rely on the colonial assumption that the onus of farm worker care ultimately rested on the predominantly white farm owners in a number of its policies (Rutherford 2001a).

For example, upon independence in 1980, the ZANU (PF) government launched an ambitious land resettlement program, with donor support, to rectify the racially skewed land imbalance inherited from the colonial period. It aimed to transfer land on a "willing buyer, willing seller" basis from white commercial farmers to Africans who would take up smallholder farming in resettlement schemes (Moyo 1995; Kinsey 1999; Alexander 2006). Whereas farm workers were explicitly included as a population who could potentially participate in the first years of land resettlement, the government, under pressure from donors, changed its criteria and focus in the late 1980s to select those with a putatively more "commercial" orientation (Moyo 1995, 44ff.; Palmer 1990; Ranger 1993; Alexander 2006). Assuming that farm workers "belonged to the (white) farmer" and, in general, had questionable citizenship status (given the history of foreign labor migration to the farms), government officials felt it acceptable to exclude them. Officials thus viewed farm workers as unsuitable candidates for resettlement, based on assumptions that they all were "foreigners," and assumed farm workers also lacked the proper development ethos to work for themselves. Such an evaluation flowed from the assumption that farm workers were so accustomed to working for a (white) boss, that they lacked self-motivation (Moyo, Rutherford and Amanor-Wilks 2000; Waeterloos and Rutherford 2004).

The heritage of colonial representation continued to shape public perceptions of farm workers. By the late 1990s, more than 70 percent of farm workers were born in Zimbabwe (Sachikonye 2003, 66). Yet, the modalities of acquiring official recognition of that status made it difficult for many farm workers to acquire evidence of their legal citizenship to Zimbabwe (Sachikonye 2003, 18). Moreover, the category of "farm worker" was marked as foreigner in Zimbabwe even if on some farms, like Upfumi, the majority of the women workers were Zimbabwean by birth and descent.

Like most other Zimbabweans, commercial farm workers saw their standard of living fall after the adoption of the donor-prescribed Economic

Structural Adjustment Programme (ESAP) in the early 1990s, in spite of increased profitability in the agricultural sector (Bond 1998; Moyo 2000). Starting in 1992, their real average wages dropped below 1980 levels. This disparity included a growing gap between commercial farmers (and shareholders) and farm workers as the former took a greater share of the profits through the 1980s and 1990s (Kanyenze 2001). As a 1998 report for the International Monetary Fund put it, commercial "farmers gained almost all the share [of the GDP] that wage earners lost" (quoted in Brett 2005, 10).

Given these wider economic and political changes, I noticed a clear shift in attitudes between the time of my initial research on farm workers in 1992–93 (Rutherford 2001a) and my later research starting in 1998. During the late 1990s, "rights" had become a growing topic of conversation for many farm workers, particularly younger men, which, on farms like Upfumi, saw them challenging a form of governance that I call "domestic government" (discussed below). These young workers were often better educated than older workers, having taken advantage of relatively more educational opportunities since independence; at the same time, they often felt "stuck," forced to work on farms due to lack of other job opportunities for school-leavers. Many recognized the discrepancy between the labor relations laws and what actually occurred on many, if not most, farms. The vast differences of material wealth between farmers and workers reinforced their sense of inequality and injustice.

Actions on the national scale helped to nurture this interest in rights among farm workers. A political imaginary of democracy and human rights, including labor rights, was resonating for many throughout the urban areas and countryside in Zimbabwe, like elsewhere in the world in the 1990s. Combined with increased donor support of governance and human rights agendas and the growth in the number of nongovernmental organizations (NGOs) in the Global South (Abrahamsen 2000; Englund 2006), the growing economic immiseration under ESAP, and concern over ZANU (PF) rule, the number of protests and stay-aways in Zimbabwe grew as the 1990s progressed, particularly in urban centers. A number of groups, including trade unions, churches, students, civil society activists, and ex-combatants from the guerrilla armies (affiliated with the African nationalist groups that fought for liberation against the white settler regime in the 1960s and 1970s) began contesting both the economic policies (and their largely negative consequences on the livelihoods of the majority of Zimbabweans) and the lack of political space and constitutional provisions for a wider democratic polity to emerge (Raftopoulos 2001; Sachikonye 2012). These protests and this political imagination contributed to and were promoted by the launch of the Movement for Democratic Change (MDC) in September 1999, a new political party that emerged out of these civic groups—particularly the trade union movement, which had become more mobilized during this decade.

The enhanced donor interest in good governance also led to increased support of the General Agricultural and Plantation Workers Union of Zimbabwe (GAPWUZ), the main trade union representing farm workers, and a relative growth of NGO interest in farm workers in the 1990s. GAPWUZ and the NGOs had a variety of programs, with differing effects on and responses from farm workers and farmers (Rutherford 2004; Sadomba and Helliker 2010; Hartnack 2015). For some workers and farmers, for very different reasons, these organizations helped to cultivate a sense of being part of a social project of "change" which was wider than the individual farm; this is demonstrated by the following three examples.

In September and October 1997, there were a series of wildcat strikes by thousands of farm workers. Surreptitiously fanned by GAPWUZ to deal with its deadlocked collective bargaining negotiations with the employers' organization, the Agricultural Labor Bureau (ALB), these strikes spread to many parts of the country. They resulted in blockades of highways, destruction of farm property and, on a few occasions, the chasing of farmers from their homes (Tandon 2001).

Secondly, farm workers began to emerge as a recognized electorate. In 1997, farm workers enjoyed the franchise for the first time, in local government elections, which meant it was no longer just property-owners or lease-holders in commercial farming wards who could vote to elect their councillor for the Rural District Councils. Although farm workers were ignored and few voted in many wards, in others, candidates actively sought their votes, viewing farm workers as a potential political constituency.

The third example is the reception of the government's Constitutional Commission among many farmers and farm workers. In early 1999, as a way to try to co-opt the mobilization (by an umbrella group, the National Constitutional Assembly [NCA], for a new constitution, which was gathering momentum among trade unions, professional groups, NGOs, and churches [Dorman 2002, 2003; McCandless 2012]), the government established a Constitutional Commission to travel the country to collect Zimbabweans' views of a new constitution. Although strongly criticized by the NCA, because the ZANU (PF) government dominated the processes of selecting its members and ultimately crafting its draft constitution, nevertheless the Constitutional Commission hearings unleashed a series of public criticisms of the ZANU (PF) government, its constitution, political practices and economic policies (Dorman 2003, 853). A number of its 4,321 public meetings were held in commercial farming areas, and were attended by farmers and farm workers alike. Given the many criticisms raised during these meetings, and the lack of government retribution against the critics, some farm workers and white farmers became emboldened by the new situation and actively took part in campaigning for the successful "No" side in the February 2000 referendum on the government's draft constitution (McCandless 2012, 67)—the first national electoral defeat of ZANU (PF). Moreover, many white farmers and farm workers began supporting the MDC, the new political party led by Morgan Tsvangirai, who had been the secretary general of the Zimbabwean Congress of Trade Union (ZCTU) as well as the NCA chairperson.

These changes and events played out differently on individual commercial farms. Although many farm workers and white farmers explicitly refused to take part in politics (Hughes 2006, 282–283), some did and, by early 2000, there was a new visibility of farm workers and white farmers in public life in Zimbabwe. The visibility of whites in the MDC mobilization led to claims by ZANU (PF) that the MDC was serving "colonial interests" and eventually fed into growing divisions in the opposition party (Raftopoulos 2006, 18–19). The ZANU (PF) government and its cadres also used this to draw on the established attributes of farm workers as foreigners under the control of white farmers. ZANU (PF) tried to use the campaign leading to the constitutional referendum as a debate over land reform, and characterized the new MDC party as supporting "white settlers" (Dorman 2003, 853–854). As President Mugabe threatened just before the referendum, "white farmers urging their employees to vote 'No' would be treated to a display of the government's 'true colours'" (quoted in Muckraker 2000). These "true colors" were revealed a few days after the defeat of the government's draft constitution in the February 2000 referendum, when the occupation of commercial farms led by members of the Zimbabwe National Liberation War Veterans Association (ZNLWVA) began. Shortly afterward, land occupations became explicitly intertwined with the political goal of ensuring ZANU

(PF) victories in upcoming elections. And so began *jambanja*—a word that connotes the violence and uncertain times associated with the post-2000 land occupations.

Farm workers became even more of an object of concern, inquiry, and debate for politicians, national and international media, donors, NGOs, and scholars as the land occupations and forcible land redistribution placed them squarely in the middle of the momentous politics in Zimbabwe. In a number of the land occupations, farm workers faced violence from the occupiers and had their property confiscated or destroyed, while many were also chased away from the farms. At times, some farm workers tried to evict the occupiers. At other times, some farm workers joined the occupiers and attacked the white farmers. In many instances, farm workers sought to avoid the conflict but saw their jobs disappear as farmers cut back production, were evicted, or they decided to leave employment given the uncertainty and conflict. Over time, the changing agricultural structure and landscape as black smallholder farmers and black landholders replaced white commercial farmers saw a transformation in the type and quantity of farm labor, remuneration, and working and living conditions (Chambati 2011; Rutherford 2014; Hartnack 2015). The largely dichotomizing debate in the appraisal of the land occupations and the Zimbabwean state has played out in terms of appraising farm workers.

Farm workers have thus become one of the rhetorical battlefields in the debate between these two dominant narratives, as different studies focus on which side the workers were on during the farm takeovers, their participation or lack thereof in the subsequent land resettlement process, and the change in their livelihood opportunities, remuneration and social welfare after the dramatic transformation in the agrarian landscape since 2000. Most commentators appraise their changed situation by grounding their analysis through one of the main viewpoints of Zimbabwean national politics.

Methodological Moves

Brian Raftopoulos, a leading Zimbabwean scholar and public intellectual, has consistently written about the need to go beyond the tendency to either focus on issues of historical social justice and economic rights or the "structural legacies of inequality," or to draw on human rights perspectives with the aim to consolidate and expand democratic practices. In his essay critically examining this schism among "the left" in Zimbabwe and beyond, he noted how this division has become replicated and deepened through the political divide since 2000. ZANU (PF) and its political and intellectual backers stress the structural legacies of inequality, while the MDC and its political and intellectual supporters emphasize civic, political, and human rights (Raftopoulos 2006).

This polarization has been strongly apparent in the academic literature, particularly as scholars and activists tended to analyse Zimbabwean events and activities since 2000 through the lens of the political clash between ZANU (PF) and the MDC (for a wider discussion, see Raftopoulos and Phimister 2004; Moore 2004, 2007; Moyo and Yeros 2005). In regard to farm workers, the two opposing dominant narratives have sought to suture shut any space that would provide an alternative analysis of their livelihoods and diverse tactics grounded in the particular power relations and social hierarchies shaping their lives. Accordingly, the consequences of the post-2000 land redistribution for farm workers have tended to be evaluated through this dichotomous analytical lens. On the one hand, in what I term the "politics as liberation" narrative, farm workers become those who may have suffered hardships yet their loyalties were misplaced since the land occupiers and ZANU (PF) government saw them as trying to prevent the redress of the colonial inequalities as they supported their white bosses. From this perspective, only those farm workers whose consciousness was properly revolutionary would recognize that their real interest lay with freeing themselves from white farmer control (see, e.g., Chambati and Moyo 2003; Chambati 2011; Hanlon, Manjengwa, and Smart 2012). On the other hand, in what I call the "politics as oppression" narrative, farm workers have been portrayed as people who have been victimized, whose human rights were ignored (as many were attacked by the land occupiers), on the assumption that they were allied with the white farmers. Moreover, this analysis continues, farm workers lost their source of livelihood through the forced transfer of white farms, with the assumption that white farmers had properly looked after and assisted farm workers (e.g., ZCDT 2003; JAG and GAPWUZ 2008).

In both narratives, "politics" is understood as either liberatory or authoritarian, depending on the analytical perspective. Moreover, farm workers' actions since 2000 became scripted in these narratives based on their relationship to white farmers: necessary victims (until their consciousness was raised) or oppressed victims.

In contrast to grounding the analysis in these national-scale narratives, my analysis of the Upfumi farm labor conflict problematizes them, troubling the easy division between sovereignty and redistributive justice versus democracy and human rights, which animate these rival narratives of Zimbabwean politics. Moreover, this book examines how both such narratives of politics became part and parcel of the Upfumi struggle, discursive resources deployed for varied ends and at different times. By grounding the practices made in the name of these important political and legal imaginaries in the power relations and gendered and racialized social hierarchies shaping livelihoods and the labor struggle itself, I suggest one is able to better understand how connections to institutions and individuals that are part of national electoral politics initially assisted these farm workers and then, ultimately, overdetermined their struggle. I shift the perspective from grounding the analysis in demands for sovereignty or rights to how such demands can inspire, limit, and become entangled in a matrix of social and power relations within specific sites during particular historical moments. This requires understanding the specific livelihood practices and their hierarchical relations of dependency and power relations, which form the ground of politics, when activities and struggles become politicized.

This book builds on a running theme in recent scholarship of Zimbabwe to ground analyses in the lives of historically and spatially situated Zimbabweans (e.g., Worby 1994; Munro 1998; Hughes 2004; Alexander 2006; McGregor 2009; and especially Moore 2005). As Donald Moore skillfully demonstrates in his rich ethnography of the politics of land in eastern Zimbabwe, *Suffering for Territory*, to better understand relations of rule, techniques of governmentality, and hegemonic discourse one needs to examine how they become "entangled" in the cultural practices, social relations, and struggles within people's lives in particular places. His book aptly shows how these "places" are produced, in part, through an interaction of wider scale institutions, translocal networks, and micropractices that engage with them, drawing on current and historically layered meanings, body habits, and social practices: "Place emerges as a distinctive mixture . . . a nodal point where these translocal influences intermesh with practices and meanings previously sedimented in the local landscape" (Moore 2005, 20). At the same time, Moore cogently illustrates that this sense of "place" is not necessarily uniform or shared by all: "Axes of inequality, differences of identity, and power relations make places subject to multiple experiences, not a unitary, evenly shared 'sense.' Within any one place, social actors become *subjected* to multiple matrices of power" (Moore 2005, 21, italics in original).

Drawing on Moore's suggestive analysis, I examine the ground of politics within the Upfumi farm worker struggle through a series of concepts to understand the particular "place" of commercial farms, the hegemonic portrayal of farm workers in the Zimbabwean body politic, and the particular set of meanings and practices of electoral politics in Zimbabwe. This conceptual grounding, I propose, provides a richer understanding of the entanglement of electoral politics and the Upfumi struggle, and, more broadly, the possibilities and limits of labor struggles in Africa and beyond, than analysing it through a national-scale lens of politics (be it as liberation or as oppression).

"Belonging" is a concept used more and more in recent Africanist scholarship to refer to the politics over citizenship, autochthony, foreignness, and claims-making more broadly (see, e.g., Nyamnjoh 2006; Geschiere 2009; Lentz 2013). It provides an analytical lens into the power relations shaping the ways in which different categories of people are able to make claims to different resources in their work, forms of accumulation, and other livelihood strategies, including wages, housing, social welfare, land, and land-based resources.

I focus on different, at times competing, scales of belonging that are grounded in particular social territories, what I have called "modes of belonging," defined as "the routinized discourses, social practices, and institutional arrangements through which people make claims for resources and rights, the ways through which they become 'incorporated' in particular places" (Rutherford 2008, 79; see also Hammar 2002). I have called the dominant mode of belonging that operated on white-owned commercial farms "domestic government," as a gendered, raced, and classed configuration of power and hierarchical social relations that promoted the rule of the farmer over state officials while "valuing paternalistic relations between male workers and their families and between farmers and 'their' workers" (Rutherford 2001a: 14).

The convergence of colonial state policies and advocacy by white farmers ensured that much of farm workers' lives fell under the state-sanctioned authority of white farmers. Whereas by the 1930s there was growing state interventions in the lives of African peasants in the name of conservation or, later, development (Munro 1998; Moore 2005), white farmers sought to keep outside agencies and their forms of governmentality away from "their" farm workers. It was gendered in that white farmers generally employed African men as permanent workers and then relied on them to recruit their spouses and children to work as seasonal labor when needed (Rutherford 2001a). I will show that this was still the main form of governance found on commercial farms in the early 1990s, including on Upfumi.

Modes of belonging have particular cultural politics regarding the recognition of rights, claims, and responsibilities in very specific localities, including building and policing the boundaries of rule themselves. Yet, they are always entangled in translocal processes and histories, including state administrative and legal practices. These practices generate what Kelly and Kaplan (2001, 22) call "represented communities"—"'communities' renewed in their existence not only by representations in the semiotic sense, but also by representations in the political, institutional sense," through state formation via governmentality, hegemony, and practices of citizenship, including mass-mediated narratives and academic analyses of such social "identities."

These represented communities acquire certain characteristics, institutional forms, and political possibilities on the scale of the "nation" and on more localized or transnational scales. I use the term "scale" to denote the scope of action and audiences envisioned by various social practices and possibly entailed by them, rather than assuming that, say, "national level" institutions automatically have a particular and uniform effect on the national territory (Ferguson 2006). The wider represented communities of "farm workers" and "white farmers," for example, had informed, but not determined, the contours of the modes of belonging that had operated on Zimbabwean commercial farms.

I implicitly draw on the works of Michel Foucault to understand the power relations shaping both the contours of the modes of belonging and the social hierarchies within them. On commercial farms, Foucault's disciplinary power is heuristically useful—the discursive practices, including policies, and arrangement of space and objects that aim to train bodies in particular ways, defining "how one may have a hold over others' bodies, not only so that they may do what one wishes, but so that they may operate as one wishes, with the techniques, the speed and the efficiency that one determines" (Foucault 1979, 138). Farmers and their managers often deployed disciplinary power within farms as they sought to mould farm workers in particular ways. Moreover, the contours of domestic government and the represented communities of "white farmers" and "farm workers" emerged largely through what Foucault called "governmental-ity"; that is, national-scale attempts to shape the conduct of both farmers and workers through laws, policies, and programs by state and nonstate actors and agencies in the colonial and postcolonial periods as part of the wider biopolitical aim of securing the "welfare of the population, the improvement of its condition, the increase of its wealth, longevity, health, et cetera" (Foucault 1991, 100).

Yet, there is a more of a Foucauldian sensibility to my analysis rather than a strict application of some version of his rich oeuvre of analytical methodologies. This is in part due to a tendency, in at least Anglophone social sciences, of making governmentality into another analytical model to be applied to a set of empirical phenomenon, which leads to a dry analysis of policies and programs on the presumption that their power-effects are straightforward (Walters 2012). Rather, I aim to ethnographically examine "the multiple forces configuring the sets of relations with which government is engaged" (Li 2007, 279), showing that the intentions of planners do not necessarily translate into reality. Rather they become "grounded" in the authority relations and social projects within different social spaces.

Accordingly, in my analysis, modes of belonging are not reducible to these wider forms of governmentality. Rather, modes of belonging emerge from, energize and are entangled with "social projects," which are orga-nized aims and efforts of action. When such social projects become rou-tinized forms of control over specific localities, they can become modes of belonging themselves. In turn, new social projects are invigorated by, cross through, or even oppose such modes of belonging at various, poten-tially overlapping, scales of action. Such social projects themselves are often entangled in assertions of leadership, aims to bolster, affirm or create public authority.

Questions of public authority raise issues of sovereignty. Territorialized modes of belonging imply positions of authority that claim, or seek to claim, sovereignty over people in a bounded site. Many scholars have challenged the isomorphic assumption that sovereign power solely rests with terri-torialized states, examining such a nexus both as historically constituted and empirically variable. Rather, for them, sovereign power is a "tentative and unstable project" predicated "on repeated performances of violence and a 'will to rule'" (Hansen and Stepputat 2005, 3). Hansen and Steppu-tat note there is both legal sovereignty grounded in law, state practices, and enduring discourses concerning "legitimate rule" as well as de facto sovereignty "grounded in violence that is performed and designed to generate loyalty, fear and legitimacy" (Hansen and Stepputat 2006: 297). Both forms of sovereignty define authority over people and space at different scales of action, which sometimes reinforce each other, other times clash, and yet other times coexist, as the terms and scope of public authority are never stable (Lund 2006). As Moore skillfully illustrates, intertwined histories of precolonial political dynamics, colonial administrative rule and installations of settler enterprises, and strategies of liberation armies, have all added layers of sovereignty that have become rearticulated through postcolonial administrative efforts and varied and competing social projects in various places: "Postcolonial rule ... emerged from sediments of sovereignties in the plural" (Moore 2005, 224).

Whereas Moore and others have insightfully examined such competing practices of sovereignty and other assertions of public authority between chiefs, administrators, rainmakers, nationalist and ethnic mobilizers, among others, in various rural territories in Zimbabwe (e.g., Worby 1994, 1998; Munro 1998; Maxwell 1999; Spierenburg 2004; Hughes 2006; Alexander 2006; Fontein 2006; Hammar 2008; McGregor 2009; Zamchiya 2013), there has been less attention to how these projects have played out on commercial farms (although, see Hartnack 2015). Although there have always been a range of sources of authority shaping the lives of farm workers on farms—generational, patriarchal, kin-based, religious, and so forth—these are ultimately subordinated to the territorialized sovereign authority of the commercial farmer and his or her *mitemo yepurazi* (rules/laws of the farm). By exerting control through these rules and seeking to shape the conduct of farm workers through racialized and gendered power relations, there was a specific and distinct power/sovereignty dynamic operating through domestic government.

Electoral politics brings the possibility of tapping into a greater sovereign authority with its arsenal of tools of compulsion—that of the state. This does not refer only to actual state institutions, which have many techniques of coercion and consent that have been explicitly used in state-making "projects of rule" in colonial and postcolonial Zimbabwe (Munro 1998); it also refers to the tactics of violence and persuasion, which have been part and parcel of mobilization mechanisms deployed by all parties in the conduct of electoral or anticolonial politics in Zimbabwe, including in the colonial period (e.g., Kriger 1992; Moore 1995; Kesby 1996; Scarnecchia 2008; Alexander and McGregor 2013).

National-scale electoral politics can become entangled in particular labor struggles, though the consequences depend on both the wider historical circumstances and the specific ground of the place in which they occur. As I will show, electoral politics, or *poritikisi* in ChiShona, was a crucial dynamic for trying to assert labor rights and, in so doing, challenging some of the inherent inequalities on commercial farms for the Upfumi farm workers. Their leadership drew on some techniques, organizational support, and, ultimately, the strength, including violence, associated with electoral politics in Zimbabwe to sustain their labor struggle and, after that, to participate in the new post-2000 context in rural Zimbabwe. As this was a time of momentous politics in the country, the labor strife provides a unique insight into some of these wider dynamics that have been occurring in Zimbabwe since the late 1990s.

Interrelationships between modes of belonging, represented communities, and social projects and their range of different types of power relations determine the specific "effective articulations" (Moore 2005; 25) of rule; what is effective in one locality and at a certain time may not necessarily work elsewhere or at a different moment in time. This research analytic, I propose, also enables one to better examine the strategies and effects of political mobilization and immobilization. It allows one to understand how groups can work with, subvert, and challenge the particular forms of rule to which they are subjected.

The focus on mode of belonging also emphasizes the relations of dependency through which many livelihoods are forged. Economic livelihoods in southern Africa, like elsewhere, have long been constituted through dependency relations, be they through generational and gender hierarchies, pawnship relations, or class and racially defined hierarchies (e.g., Kesby 1999; Hughes 1999; Englund 2004). James Ferguson argues that there is a strong history in the precolonial, colonial and apartheid eras of people in southern Africa pursuing their own subordination and involved in relations of dependency, as a way for some to improve their situation; as Ferguson pithily puts it, "*being* someone continued to imply *belonging* to someone" (2013, 228, italics in original). The demand for cheap black male labor in apartheid South Africa provided different pathways for many African men, although through exploitative and hierarchical relationships.

As South Africa, like much of Africa, if not elsewhere, has seen massive shedding of formal sector jobs and has entered into a period of "jobless economic growth" over the last twenty plus years, Ferguson argues that, given this difficulty of finding permanent jobs, the livelihoods of many in South Africa rely on becoming intermeshed in relations of dependency (and interdependency), often with other poor people, as a way to make claims on support and opportunities, limited as they may be. Such a shift, as I will show, has also increasingly occurred in post-2000 Zimbabwe.

Gender is a key dimension in many social and power relations and it is an important dynamic in agrarian relations. It was also a key dimension in this labor struggle at Upfumi farm. Gender ideologies and spatial configurations have informed power relations, privileging the masculine over the feminine in households, work situations, and other public spaces. There is also a long history in Zimbabwe of resistance and contestation over gender relations, as well as women leaving homes to other areas to escape from certain forms of male authority (such as that of their male relatives or husbands); although, they then become reinscribed into new power relations and forms of authority (see, e.g., Schmidt 1992; Jeater 1993; Kesby 1996, 1999; Goebel 2005). Commercial farming areas have been such spaces of escape for some women.

Through an in-depth understanding of a significant labor struggle on a commercial farm, this book aims to also contribute to providing greater understanding of agrarian dynamics and worker struggles in Africa. There is generally a shortage of careful examinations of rural labor dynamics in Africa, an oversight common to "both proponents and critics of large-scale agriculture" (Gibbon, Daviron, and Barral 2014, 166). Although there tends to be less of a focus on the figure of "workers" compared to a focus on "peasants," "smallholder farmers," or "rural entrepreneurs," this book shows the centrality of labor to large-scale agriculture in general and, during particular instances, wider politics. The Upfumi struggle also contributes to the relatively scant literature on organized workers' struggles in Africa. Its attention to the dynamic interactions between the organization of the workplace, national unions, and local and national level party politics contributes to the important literature that examines labor movements and the wider political economy in different postcolonial African countries.

A very important recent contribution to this literature is Pnina Werbner's ethnography (2014) concerning the complex interplay between the largest public service union in Botswana (the Manual Workers' Union), political parties, the legal system, the social identification as workers, and projects of nation-building. Her analysis builds on both E. P. Thompson's (1963) classic study of the formation of the English working class and the literature on African trade unions and workers (e.g., Grillo 1974; Peace 1979; Cheater 1986; Cooper 1987, 1996; Raftopoulos and Phimister 1997; Ferguson 1999; Larmer 2007; Beckman, Buhlungu, and Sachikonye 2010; Barchiesi 2011). Werbner locates her study in the varied urban and rural livelihoods of these lowly paid civil servants, their daily lives, and national and transnational scale aspirations and legal instruments. She expertly examines the use of law cases as a strategy of social mobilization that, along with performative dimensions by the union leadership, workers, and the media during a national public service strike in 2011, helped to craft a sense of social justice and progressive social change for these workers and others in Botswana, against an intransigent government (which also happens to be their employer). Werbner concludes her ethnography on an optimistic note based on her detailed analysis of this significant civil society actor in Botswana, which reaches "to the far corners of the land, encompassing town and country, transcending ethnicity, so that even in its conflicts with the government, the employer, the union simultaneously contributes to nation-building. As a powerful dissenting voice it embodies, performatively, values of democracy and freedom of speech. As an organisation able to mobilise sufficient funds to challenge the government effectively through judicial review, it tests the independence of the judiciary. In alliance with other unions, it joins workers in solidarity across class and educational status" (Werbner 2014: 254).

This vision of social change paralleled to a degree the image that animated the leaders and many of those involved in the Upfumi strike in 1999. But the Upfumi labor dispute was driven by the workers and not GAPWUZ. Moreover, farm workers were in a structurally different position materially and discursively within Zimbabwe than public servants in Botswana. Finally, the cultural politics of politics in Zimbabwe are quite different from that in Botswana (e.g., R. Werbner 2004; Gulbrandsen 2012), which enabled the relative successes of the Upfumi labor struggle and ultimately overdetermined it and Zimbabwe at large after February 2000.

In terms of the research process, the information for this book comes principally from my participant observation and interviews of various

Zimbabweans as well as by interviews carried out by Zimbabwean research assistants. My interviews were conducted mainly in English, though some also in ChiShona (which I translated back into English). My research assistants carried out interviews in ChiShona and translated them into English. I also tape-recorded some of the events in which I participated and I had a research assistant transcribe and translate into English. I conducted research in Zimbabwe for four months in 1999 and for shorter periods in the years 1998, 2000, 2002, and 2003.

I do not give too many details about the ownership structure of Upfumi farm as a way to provide some anonymity to the participants of the struggle. I also had limited opportunities to interview members of the management, as they saw my spending time with the workers engaged in the labor dispute as a sign of where my loyalties lie. The focus instead is on the ways this group of farm workers conducted their labor struggle.

As will be noted throughout the ethnography, I was often positioned in particular ways by my own actions as well as those of others, which shaped responses by my interlocutors and my ability to talk with certain individuals. Given the fraught times during the labor struggle and then the wider national politics post-2000, both which hardened lines between opposing groups, my sympathies toward "farm workers" and being raced and gendered as a "white man" opened up some doors and closed many others. I tried to negotiate these shoals of particular expectations to the best I could; however, that was not always sufficient in some contexts.

I have used pseudonyms and have disguised as best as I could the individuals involved in the labor action as well as the name of the farm and surrounding farms. I have also not named my research assistants, save for my good friend, Rinse Nyamuda, who has long worked with me on various research projects. I have not disguised the name of public figures who were involved in it, as none of the actions they took in this struggle are contrary to other public actions for which they are known in Zimbabwe.

Outline

The Ground of Politics is a book about a remarkable farm labor struggle, which aims to go beyond the two dominant narratives used to situate Zimbabwean politics since 2000: either Zimbabweans taking "back their land," through the support of ZANU (PF)'s liberatory politics, or of ZANU (PF) oppressing the rights of its citizens through compulsory land redistribution

and politicized violence against the MDC and its (real or putative) supporters as a way to remain in power. Both narratives tie farm workers to these
overarching themes, making it difficult to analyse not only the specific play
of politics in particular instances, including those driven by some farm
workers, but also the livelihood insecurities of farm workers both before
and after 2000. This book shows how farm worker lives and livelihoods in
both periods have been informed by a precarious gendered and conditional
belonging on farms, which govern their access to land and labor forms. Such
precariousness has been reinforced by national-scale laws, policies and discourses situating farm workers as particularly suspect citizens. While showing the affective resonance of the language and practices of "rights" which
grabbed many of the women and men farm workers involved in this labor
struggle as in the wider struggle for democracy in Zimbabwe, *The Ground
of Politics* also indicates how such struggles cannot be divorced from both
the historical practices of electoral politics, which, in Zimbabwe, frequently
entails the threat of (gendered) violence and the social relations of dependency shaping livelihood practices.

The first chapter introduces this Upfumi labor conflict by outlining
the dominant mode of belonging of domestic government that operated on
white-owned and operated commercial farms at that time. In particular,
it discusses in detail the particular gendered and raced relations of dependency, power, and sovereignty constituting the dynamic of domestic government on Upfumi farm and its performative practices from which this
labor struggle emerged and that it squarely challenged. It then introduces
the start of the labor conflict by showing how the particular dependencies of
the mode of belonging on Upfumi began to face challenges through a combination of changing management styles and a new leadership among the
farm workers. This leadership drew on translocal resources and networks
that were caught up with the exciting ferment of "change" at the national
scale, particularly through the idiom of *maraiti*, "rights" in ChiShona.

Chapter 2 examines the first year of the dispute on Upfumi farm—the
mass firing of the workers, the maneuvering and tactics of the company,
and, in particular, of the fired workers, including their leadership's decision to legally and politically challenge their dismissal. Great attention is
paid to the entanglement of this struggle within the expanding mobilization in the name of "democratization" on the national scale. Its entanglement in poritikisi provided new dimensions and possibilities for the labor

struggle. By interweaving analyses of the particular actions and events on Upfumi farm with examinations of national-scale events regarding constitutional consultation and the launch and expansion of the new opposition party, the MDC, this chapter brings the book's narrative up to the end of 1999, when great excitement and anticipation over the promise of political "change" to ZANU (PF) were widespread in the lives and actions for many Zimbabweans.

The third chapter looks at the fraying within the struggle, in part due to its entwinement with some of the cultural practices associated with electoral politics, and the livelihood practices and growing anxieties and suffering of those involved in the labor dispute. The suffering was not mere words, but was deeply etched into many of their lives and took on distinctive, gendered forms. As farm workers, the vast majority were accustomed to having limited resources and arduous livelihood practices. Nonetheless, being involved in this prolonged labor dispute put many of them into an even more precarious situation, which was a hardship to endure; such a tenuous condition, which the vast majority of all farm workers—let alone many other Zimbabweans—were soon to experience even more intensely as national-scale politics erupted into the land occupations that started in February 2000. Out of this tumult, conflicts within the struggle deepened. This chapter concludes by discussing two events in June 2000: the partial legal victory of the Upfumi workers in the Labor Tribunal and the disputed parliamentary electoral victory of ZANU (PF).

The fourth and final substantive chapter examines how the political violence associated with the land occupations—what Zimbabweans popularly call *jambanja* (militant confrontation during the land conflicts)—targeted farm workers and dramatically shaped their claims of belonging and relations of dependency, whether or not their particular white employer was chased away. This chapter centers on the dramatic changes to livelihood possibilities as the territorialized mode of belonging of domestic government has been replaced on most commercial farms with competing forms of territorialized power in the form of different and overlapping land-giving claimants and authorities striving for some form of sovereignity. Concentrating on the competing claims to Upfumi farm and surrounding farms from June 2000 to June 2003 made by war veterans, current farm workers, and farm workers who had been fired—as well as the diverse economic activities of former farm workers—it explains the precarious forms of livelihoods and the modes of power through which they operate. It shows how farm workers' previous conditional belonging to farms through domestic government was made even more uncertain and unforgiving as the wider economic crisis and politicized violence impinged on their claims to land-based resources.

The book concludes by explaining how this study speaks to current debates about rights, democracy, and social justice—about, that is, citizenship and belonging, electoral politics, and livelihoods. In so doing, it intertwines an analysis of current land and rural labor dynamics in Zimbabwe with a discussion of the politics of ethnographic research, more broadly, and among marginalized populations during times of heightened and mass-mediated attention, more specifically. The latter discussion suggests how research itself is informed and shaped by the convergence or divergence of varied social projects of interlocutors. Such reflexive analysis locates the anthropologist and other analysts of Zimbabwe and promoters of "democracy" or "social justice" firmly within the politics of representation and the particular traditions of electoral politics that place very different consequences and risks for varied participants positioned by their location in a wider political economy. The "ground of politics" can incorporate the researcher as she gets entangled in the particular struggle under study.

CHAPTER 1

OPPRESSION, MARAITI, AND FARM WORKER LIVELIHOODS: SHIFTING GROUNDS IN THE 1990S

October 20, 1999
Harare
Office of ZimfarmEast

I MET WITH Mr. Chapunga at his company's headquarters on the edge of the manufacturing district in south-central Harare. It was not until near the end of this interview that he came closest to the topic he had told me he would not broach—the ongoing labor dispute on Upfumi farm, which was the very topic I had arranged to meet Mr. Chapunga about in his capacity as acting group human resources manager of ZimfarmEast. The farm's pack-shed and agricultural operations were owned and run by ZimfarmEast, which was then the agro-based division of Zimfarm Limited, the highly profitable Zimbabwean agro-industrial company.

Looking at me directly, his tone serious, he said, "There are two English sayings that are pertinent here: 'blood is thicker than water,' and 'home is best.'" Keeping his eyes on me, he said no more. After a few awkward seconds, I asked for clarification. Somewhat contemptuously, he said that I should recognize what he was saying. "Even if you move and your dad dies," he said, "you still remain identified with your home. If someone as white as you are says, 'Stay on, you will win,' it is Dutch confidence." I asked for further clarification, and he explained that the phrase "Dutch confidence" refers to the tendency of "the Dutch to drink before they go to a war they can't win to give them courage. You should conclude what this means," he said abruptly, folding up papers on his desk, signaling the interview's end, "on your own."

"As for the second saying?" I pushed further, as I hastened to gather up my notebook and bag.

"That simply means," he commented firmly but more quietly as he escorted me to the door, "people will say that some people belong to this area and some don't. Remember the old days when we fought against whites."

As I left the ZimfarmEast office and emerged into the humid, busy streets of midday Harare, I knew I had just been told to butt out of this labor dispute. I understood that my occasional visits to the fired Upfumi farm workers who were staying at the *musososo*—the not-so-temporary camp next to the short gravel road leading to Upfumi farm on the Harare–Mutare highway—during the previous two months, were being watched and assessed by the company's point man in this dispute. And moreover, I knew that racial identification and belonging were factors in how Mr. Chapunga saw me. Yet I did not fully understand his somewhat cryptic remarks, the illocutionary force of his discussion of the "two English sayings." By noting the "Englishness" of these phrases, he clearly wanted to suggest a familiarity with what he perceived as my "world," indexed by my racialized coding as "white" and my first language of English more than by my Canadian citizenship. Nonetheless, since the main managers of Zimfarm and of Upfumi farm itself were, at that time, white Zimbabweans, it was unclear how he saw his own positioning as a black Zimbabwean working under this order, given his invocation of race and belonging as a bedrock of identity. Subsequently, the fired farm workers staying at the musososo and I discussed this interview several times, conjecturing different possible meanings. Although we never settled on a single explanation of its semantics, we agreed that the aim of Mr. Chapunga's "English sayings" was to warn and unsettle me.

The ambivalence and lingering unease of this interview was an incidental example of the marked uncertainty of discursive intent and audiences, mingled through assertions and sentiments of defining who belongs and who does not. This lengthy labor dispute was intertwined with a diverse range of social forces, including electoral politics, gendered regimes of labor, legal domains, preternatural realms, and icons of potential power from Harare to Marondera, Europe to Canada. These are just some of the divergent threads that entangled these farm workers. It was an unease that became increasingly visceral and volatile for these mainly women farm workers, located as they were in precarious livelihood activities, as this twenty month labor dispute drew to a close in June 2000. The labor battle was energized by the momentous, charged, and highly ambivalent political and economic struggles vigorously agitating on the national scale in the late 1990s, with audiences and networks ranging from very local to international, and with a number of economic, social and bodily repercussions. The ongoing uncertainty of the labor dispute often meant that the farm workers involved in it were not always certain of the ongoing status of their case, let alone what the presence or changing intensity of one of these social forces meant for them.

The manager's reference to "war" was commonly deployed by the farm workers engaged in the dispute and by many of those who offered support as well. Many even referred to the camp where some of them stayed outside of Upfumi, the musososo, as "DRC," (Democratic Republic of Congo, the central African country that was in the midst of war at that time and to which Zimbabwean troops were controversially sent in August 1998 to help prop up its new government).[1]

"War" was also an appropriate metaphor as these farm workers drew on a repertoire of songs and other signifying practices associated with the liberation struggle of the 1970s. This struggle had acquired importance on the national scale as ZANU (PF) had sought to legitimize its rule and power since winning the 1980 national election, and every subsequent one until 2008 by, in part, privileging the "patriotic memories" and citizenship claims of those who were part of the guerrilla armies during the 1970s war over those of other Zimbabweans (Werbner 1998; Kriger 2006; Ranger 2004). These Upfumi farm workers were apt to view their labor struggle as having momentous consequences for others. They were buoyed by generally supportive, although infrequent, national media coverage, the occasional interest of international groups and individuals, and by recognizing their own endurance for taking part in such a lengthy labor struggle, extraordinary in its duration in the history of agricultural labor relations in Zimbabwe.

As I spent time with them in the last half of 1999, these workers increasingly saw their struggle, their war, as having import on the national scale. They viewed it as part and parcel of the wider mobilization occurring in the name of workers and change signaled by the widespread strikes and stay-aways, occasional urban riots as well as the contentious processes of constitutional change playing out in the late 1990s up to February 2000 (Raftopoulos and Sachikonye 2001; Raftopoulos and Mlambo 2009). The focal point of this mobilization was the emergence of the Movement for Democratic Change (MDC), which many initially saw as a "workers' party" (e.g., Alexander 2000a). Formally launched in September 1999, this new political party was strongly associated with the main national trade union congress, the Zimbabwe Congress of Trade Unions (ZCTU), through its organizational role in the party's formation and because its secretary general since 1988, Morgan Tsvangirai, became the MDC's leader. The ruling ZANU (PF) party itself was not untouched by these debates for democratization and change in 1999, in part as younger members were calling for a greater role in the decision-making of the ruling party and questioning the wisdom of their aging leaders.

During speeches at rallies and in conversations they had with each other and with me, those in this labor struggle frequently drew on narrative forms and signs that are found in the dominant Zimbabwean nationalist repertoire such as those coming from Marxist and Christian traditions (e.g., Brand 1977; Sylvester 1991; Ranger 1995; Scarnecchia 2008). Such tropes were clearly drawn upon in a speech made by Councillor Banda, the then ZANU (PF) councillor to the Goromonzi Rural District Council for the ward in which Upfumi was located. He gave it during an August 1999 rally held at the musososo and attended by more than one hundred people; participants who by their sheer numbers helped to signal the sense of national import assumed by many. Although the majority at the rally were predominantly the women farm workers involved in the labor dispute, there were also the male executives of the workers' committees of neighboring farms, and Harare male representatives of International Socialist Organization (ISO) of Zimbabwe, who were mobilizing for the launch of the MDC, and of the Zimbabwe Federation of Trade Unions (ZFTU) , a rival trade union federation to the ZCTU supported and promoted by ZANU (PF). Facing this politically diverse audience, the ZANU (PF) councillor declared:

> I think the time has arrived for you workers of Upfumi to be the light of the workers on the farms in Zimbabwe. Your story is being broadcast in the newspapers, so your story is being understood everywhere. You are like Christians who were told in the Bible that you are the light of the world, so you must light

the whole country. . . . Comrades, the time has come so that you can liberate your fellow workers, and you too, must liberate yourselves when you are liberating others. You are hearing people saying that you are so oppressed, you are not supposed to be here [at this type of meeting], yet by being here shows that you know your rights [*maraiti*] and where you are going!

The discursive background, the unsaid, with which Councillor Banda engaged in dialogue, was the assumption that farm workers do not agitate for their rights, do not attend union meetings, and thus are passive and simply subject to the will of their (white) employers. It was one of the assumptions examined in my earlier work on farm workers in Zimbabwe (e.g., Rutherford 2001a, 2001b) and also by the other limited work focusing on farm workers in the 1980s and 1990s (e.g., Loewenson 1988; Mugwati and Balleis 1994). It was also a key entailment of the representation of farm workers as a "community" in national-scale discourses.

How did these maraiti come to mean so much to the farm workers? Why did they imagine their struggle to have national import? How was this struggle predicated on, yet worked against, the conditional mode of belonging that situated the vast majority of commercial farm workers since the colonial period? Why were representatives of both organizations that were soon to be visibly against each other in a very violent political contestation (as ZANU [PF] sought to crush the MDC starting in early 2000), and with varying levels of involvement during the Upfumi struggle, present at this rally? How did gender inform the dynamics of this struggle, given that the leaders in this struggle—including most of those on the Upfumi workers' committee who were leading the workers in this war, the management team of Upfumi and Zimfarm, the lawyers, politicians, as well as interveners like myself—were men, yet the vast majority of the Upfumi farm workers were women? In what ways did this struggle resemble the heroic plotline portrayed by the councillor and the media of the oppressed being conscientized into action in the name of their rights; a plot that resonates in many social science narratives as well as political discourse elsewhere? And how did I understand and contribute, in very modest ways, to this struggle, so that Mr. Chapunga felt obliged to obliquely, but firmly, declare that I need to disengage as I did not belong to the farm, let alone to Zimbabwe?

This chapter outlines the dominant mode of belonging that existed on Upfumi farm until the mid-1990s, when its particular dependencies began to face challenges through social projects of localized leadership. This leadership drew on translocal resources and networks that were caught up in the exciting ferment of change on the national scale, particularly through the idiom of rights. Since this was a struggle that drew on performative styles and narratives that resonated widely, but also had to assist in the social mobilization of the workers, audiences were key. Examining how this labor dispute found traction among different constituencies and how it became entangled in multiple and competing scale-making projects with varied effects is, however, the aim of the following chapters. In this chapter, I lay out the particular gendered power/sovereignty dynamic of the dominant mode of belonging and its performative practices from which this labor struggle emerged and that it squarely challenged, thus contributing to a fraying of the authority relations that had already begun.

"You Are No Better than Dogs": Domestic Government in Independent Zimbabwe

All workers who had been working on the farm before Zimfarm purchased it in February 1997 described the mode of belonging, similar to "domestic government" as discussed in the introduction: a territorialized project pivoting on racialized and gendered rule and performative styles implemented through bodily disciplining techniques of surveillance, work rhythms, rewards, and, on occasion, corporal punishment. Racialized and gendered codes of respect for the farmer and his management hierarchy were the most relevant bodily styles workers needed to learn as a way to minimize problems for themselves and acquire whatever resources were permissible for them to acquire (e.g., wages, rations, fields to grow food, credit).

Until 2000, commercial farms were, for the most part, an effective and largely profitable form of territorialized power for the owner(s)—a means of seeking to act on the actions of others by delimiting and asserting control over a geographical area. Given the racialized colonial history of these farms, many analysts concentrate on particular attributes associated with the resulting identification of the owners and workers. This focus is typically the whiteness of the farmers, which putatively marks either the modernity and capitalist orientation of the enterprise or as a sign of colonial brutality and privilege over the blackness and relative poverty of the workers (see Rutherford 2001a; Selby 2006; Hughes 2010; Pilossof 2012). But there tends to be less attention paid to how commercial farms have operated as a form of governance, how control over land has also meant particular forms of control over people who have worked and often have lived on it, and how labor relations cannot be separated from a range of dependencies and identifications that shape life during and outside working hours; that is, how landed property here as elsewhere[2] entailed forms of power over people that have been closely imbricated in the state formation of the colony and the nation-state.

In regards to landed property in British-controlled Egypt, Timothy Mitchell (2002) has observed that European legal theory commonly has contrasted the right of property with sovereignty, or rule over people. Yet, in practice, state arrangements in Europe and European colonies have frequently made landed property a "realm of exception, within which power operated without rights" as the "architecture that formed the enclosed agricultural colony, a microcolonialism within a larger colonial domain, went hand in hand with a legal architecture that constructed territories of arbitrary power within the larger space of legal reason and abstraction" (Mitchell 2002, 70–71).

Commercial farms in colonial and postcolonial Zimbabwe formed a microcolonialism that entailed a range of power relations particular to its territorialized domain—as well as those that cut across it—defining comportment, rule, and claims. In other words, it entailed a particular "mode of belonging" where forms and modalities of recognition other than rights operated on the farm, although white farmers and their associations had previously cited property rights in their typically efficacious claims for assistance and other forms of recognition by institutions and organizations at national and international scales of action. It was a mode of belonging deeply resonant with racialized practices and sentiments.

White farmers had long used their status as the archetypical "settler citizens" (Mamdani 1996, 2001) in the (Southern) Rhodesian nation to acquire a range of governmental support for their production and marketing, including ensuring a cheap and relatively pliable workforce (Clarke 1977; Rubert 1998; Rutherford 2004). Their rights relied on the absence of workers' rights. Colonial legislation such as the Masters and Servants Act provided the legal architecture, while the routinized social projects imbricated in state practices of racial rule aimed at establishing an economically productive and civilized colony for white settlers helped to lay out the contours of social and power arrangements of what Rhodesian nomenclature defined as "European farms." In these social territories, many of those recognized as European farmers became adroit at forming organizations to demand and build on their racialized rights at varied scales of action—from localized to national to international—including ensuring a cheap labor force with no rights recognized by governmental authorities (e.g., Clarke 1977; Phimister 1988; Rubert 1998; Selby 2006). The success of these practices, however, was not guaranteed.

Domestic government was not a seamless colonial process because its politics of recognition were influenced by political and economic conjunctures, including state policies, markets, and accumulation dynamics. Broader competing factions of capitalist entities (manufacturing, mining, etc.), agricultural sectors, regions, missionaries, varied governmental policies, the British colonial office, gendered notions of self and respectability, ethnicity, farming practices, and kinship—to name but a few of the key social dynamics—all interacted in shaping these broad contours and the particular constellation of power and possibility on individual farms at different points in time. Nonetheless, there were a number of common features.

The mode of belonging on these white-owned commercial farms, this domestic government, pivoted around the farmer. For many of the white farmers, it generated an identification with an environmental belonging to the landscape (Hughes 2006), a strong sense of the propriety of private property, and a paternalistic responsibility over the comportment, if not edification, of the farm workers (Rutherford 2004; Hartnack 2015). The mode of belonging generated a series of dependencies in which workers had to comport themselves properly, in a gendered and racialized way, to the farmer and management—for example, being obsequious and waiting for an acknowledgement before speaking to the boss or madam, circumscribed in the spaces they can travel and the times in which they can be seen—in order to raise any questions, seek any favor, or provide any explanations. Such dependence was nicely summed up in what a farmer near Upfumi reportedly used to tell his workers. As recalled by a worker who had left work on that farm in August 2000 and was living beside Upfumi in 2001, this neighboring farmer "sometimes told us [farm workers] that we are dogs and do not deserve any bonus on this farm. He said that we are dogs because he is looking after us—looking after us by giving us the work to do while listening to and occasionally attending to our requests and complaints." His was a power that operated without rights. Rather, it rested on forms of recognition resting on the hierarchical dependencies anchored around the sovereign commands and actions of the white farmer and his or her management workers, of the operations of what can be seen as a distinct power/sovereignty nexus in the microcolonialism.

As a type of microcolonialism, commercial farms largely operated as a very circumscribed public space for those living and working there. On commercial farms the authority of commercial farmers was very much a territorialized power, enabling their claims over and actions on the workers' actions in the living and working spaces. The extent and depth differed from farm to farm and, over time, with the farmer's power on some farms being more intimately involved in workers' lives than others. The workers and those who lived with them recognized that this paternalistic power was a form of rule (Du Toit 1993), *mitemo yemurungu* or the "rules/laws of the farmer," and that transgressors could be, and often were, judged by the farmer or by those he (or, less commonly, she) delegated. This domestic government continued after Independence, although modulated at times by changing national-scale dynamics.

Playing the role as crucial intermediaries in these dependencies were black workers in management positions such as foremen, clerks and, as the 1980s progressed, more and more as managers themselves, replacing white men who had dominated these positions on farms during the colonial period and the first decade or so of independence. As workers would tell me, these black management workers could make life too difficult for the workforce, because it was "black versus black." In the words of Patience, a woman involved in the Upfumi war, "Those people who are promoted are harsh to those who are at the lower positions." And in the workers' recollections of the territorialized forms of power operating on Upfumi before Zimfarm bought it, it was this black versus black dynamic in particular that was emphasized.

The mode of belonging that operated on Upfumi before 1997 was typical of that operating on Mashonaland commercial farms, particularly horticultural ones, at that time; although, Zimfarm's emphasis on explicitly established labor relations processes differed from what had occurred on the farm before they purchased it. Indeed, this emphasis on explicit labor relations was less common on the majority of farms, which were not owned and operated by an agribusiness company.[3] I concentrate here on gender dynamics and social practices concerning national citizenship, two important features of the domestic government operating on Upfumi then that were also found on many commercial farms more broadly (Rutherford 2001a). Even if the majority of the Upfumi farm workers in the 1990s were Zimbabwean by birth and descent, they were viewed as foreigners by virtue of the hegemonic view of farm workers as a represented community in Zimbabwe. These features of gender and national citizenship, like governance of labor relations more broadly, all were informed by translocal dynamics and other forms and scales of territorialized power informing livelihood possibilities. They took on particular attributes as they became entangled in the particular power/sovereignty cluster on specific farms and engaged with wider events and varied social projects occurring during specific historical conjunctures.

Here I discuss dominant tendencies in the governance of labor relations on Upfumi before Zimfarm purchased it in February 1997. This shows the key features of domestic government on the farm, the operation of power without rights. This configuration of power was not unchanging and, as I will show, it was also challenged in the first years of Independence in the early 1980s as the ruling political party, ZANU (PF), became a new source of authority in the country, providing early glimpses of how electoral politics had considerable weight that could bear down in spaces and social fields ostensibly independent.

"Upfumi Girls High School": Women Farm Workers and Domestic Government

Mr. Botha, the farmer who owned Upfumi from 1991 to the time when Zimfarm bought it in February 1997, replaced tobacco production with vegetable and some fruit production and set up a pack-shed to grade and package the harvest largely for export. He was taking advantage of the expansion of horticultural markets and more favorable credit for Zimbabwean farmers that began during that decade with structural adjustment (Moyo 2000). The workforce expanded dramatically, particularly in the hiring of women workers. By 1997, workers estimated there were 400 to 600 women working at Upfumi and perhaps fifty to seventy-five men, who were mainly working on irrigation in the fields and as senior foremen.

Most of the women were single and young—either coming when they finished school or single mothers or both. Single mothers made up the majority. These women commonly left any young children with their grandmothers or other relatives at a *musha* (rural home), while, following the patrilineal claims to offspring common in Zimbabwe, any older children often were looked after by their fathers or their female relatives. At the end of August 1999, I talked with five women staying at the musososo about how they had started work at Upfumi and their family circumstances at that time. There was a broad overlap in their personal trajectories. Arianna said she learned about the job through a notice at an employment exchange in Harare. She and about thirty other women started at Upfumi then. She needed money to look after her two kids who were living with her mother at her father's musha. Faith agreed, saying she also needed money for her children; she had six of them living with her relatives and their father's relatives. She found the job at Upfumi after visiting her sister who was working at the farm. Netsai related how she had been living in Harare but when her husband died, she returned to her parents' musha. "As I had a child to look after, I was looking for employment and my brother told me my relative was working here." Another woman was divorced and was living with her children at her parent's musha about twenty-five kilometers away, and she jumped in a truck that Upfumi had sent to the communal land[4] looking for workers. Rudo said she was divorced and had been selling clothing to farm workers in the area to raise money to look after her children when she heard Upfumi was hiring. None of these women, like the vast majority I met, had a male partner when they sought and found work at Upfumi. As Pedzi observed, while she was washing her clothes at the musososo and I was talking with the other women, "When we women are on our own we discuss mostly the issue [nyaya] of our children which we cannot look after. Most women here have children who are being looked after by relatives because the men of most of the women who have worked at Upfumi have divorced them, separated, or passed away." This nyaya led them to farm work and marked them in particular ways.

For them, finding any job was what mattered. These women had little money to start with and found it difficult to receive any resources, at least on a regular basis, from the fathers of their children. Family maintenance laws exist in Zimbabwe, but either these women were unaware of them or, more commonly, they did not have the knowledge, resources, or inclination to pursue the issue through the courts (e.g., Stewart 1987). As single mothers, they also had problems receiving livelihood resources from their family, at least in terms of residing with them for a long time, particularly those who were neither married to the father of their children nor had their family-initiated bridewealth negotiations with him and his patrilineal relatives.

They talked about how their families saw them as morally suspect, as women who irresponsibly played around (*kupinda-pinda*) with men or boys who refused to marry them. As one of the women, Rita, explained, "Our parents drive us away from the musha, saying we are contaminating the reputations of our younger sisters and possibly making it difficult for them to find a man to marry who will pay *roora* [bridewealth]."

Their family elders—including their fathers and his brothers and sisters, their mothers, and their own brothers—were making gendered calculations over the bundle of respectability, parenting, and resources that has formed the politics of marriage in Zimbabwe in the contemporary accounting of the precolonial cultural logic of "wealth in people" common in sub-Saharan Africa (Jeater 1993; Hughes 1999; cf. Kopytoff 1987). Unable to stay for a long time with their natal family due to disgruntlement or outright refusal by their elders, they also found it difficult, if not impossible, to acquire land as women—let alone single women, in the communal lands or resettlement farms (Goebel 2005). As single mothers, they unsettled dominant modes of belonging that operated on the scale of families and territorialized domains such as the small-scale farming areas, as well as at the scale of the nation (Kaler 1998). As a consequence, they found it difficult to access resources for their livelihood and that of their children. For example, one woman—who was a mother of five—noted in 2000 that she had arrived at Upfumi in 1997 from her parents' musha in Murewa, where she had gone after divorcing her husband, the father of her children. She left the musha, she said, "Because I did not stay well with my young sisters. They and my parents urged me to leave because I was a divorcee and they said it might cause my sisters' husbands to divorce them for as I had no husband I would burden them, asking for food from them and their husbands. Even though I was surviving by farming at my parents' musha, I decided to start my own life without their interference."

There were often limited opportunities in towns for women who wanted to start their own lives. If they lacked schooling of at least O Levels[5] as well as contacts in remunerative urban jobs, they faced a job market that was not only experiencing high levels of unemployment of more than 30 percent in the 1990s but one that was also discriminatory toward women (see, e.g., Adams 2009). The common urban jobs for such women were the often lowly remunerative, if not potentially risky ones found in what is conventionally called "the informal sector," such as street marketing and prostitution (e.g., Horn 1994; Magaisa 1999). Like many women in the colonial period, many labeled "disrespectful" for not being married ended up seeking refuge in these sectors in the postcolonial period (Schmidt 1992; Jeater 1993; Scarnecchia 1999). Others, like these women, found jobs on commercial farms, whose employers were typically willing to hire them for some type of job regardless of qualifications or contacts, particularly during times of expanding production such as during the 1990s (Amanor-Wilks 1995).

For many of these women, working on farms became a refuge, perhaps temporarily, and a place where they could earn some money for themselves and their children. They would often periodically send back part of their wages to whomever was looking after their children to help pay for their upkeep, including paying school fees, when they had extra money, and they dwelled on the nyaya of "our children which we cannot look after." But accessing resources on farms meant subjecting themselves to very different forms of gendered dependencies than those found, say, at their musha (see, e.g., Pankhurst 1991; Kesby 1999, for an analysis of gender dynamics in the communal lands).

Upfumi expanded production in the 1990s, as the owner was able to secure accreditation with the European Union to sell vegetables in the expanding and changing markets there (Gibbon and Ponte 2005). As is common in the horticultural industry in Zimbabwe as well as other parts of Africa (Barrientos, Dolan, and Tallontire 2003), the farmer hired mainly women on the belief, these women averred, that they were more pliable and quicker than men. As the vegetable production expanded, so did the workforce to a point where it stood out from those on surrounding farms that were still largely growing tobacco or maize, or raising cattle in the early 1990s, and relying largely on a permanent male workforce. There were so many women workers at Upfumi that it became marked as a place of single women (see also Rutherford 2001a, 181). Women workers told me in 2000 that the male drivers and conductors on the buses and kombis (mini-buses), plying the Harare–Mutare highway in the 1990s, nicknamed it "Upfumi Girls High School," an appellation speaking to its sexual possibilities and not any putative educational functions. Sexuality and predation were also key themes in the workers' accounts of the mode of belonging on the farm, the labor relations and living conditions.

In these accounts, the central figure in the early 1990s was the black manager, Victor, who shaped daily actions of many of the farm workers, with particular consequences for women workers. More than Mr. Botha, Victor loomed large in these histories because the farm workers said he was given great leeway and authority by the boss. A number of them even noted that Victor copied Mr. Botha's sartorial choices to stress an indexical link to the farmer's power and authority. As recollected by Maria, a woman who worked at Upfumi from 1991 to 1996, Victor "wore the same uniform, clothes, as the *murungu* [white farmer], Botha. If the boss was wearing khaki shorts, Victor would also wear that. He had the same quality as the boss's clothes because they were one." Black versus black was always understood through the racialized territorialized power of the commercial farms in which management workers were employed. Although black management workers may have been harsh, workers always understood their actions as enabled by the overarching sovereign on the farm—the murungu, the typically white farm owner.

Agricultural labor is frequently physically demanding, often monotonous, and, at the same time, potentially delicate as workers have to ensure not damaging the plant or the harvested produce or err in their tending of either of them. In my experience of conducting research on Zimbabwean commercial farms in the 1990s, a common assumption held by Zimbabwean commercial farmers was that farm workers had to be physically trained, bodily disciplined, and constantly supervised, to do the job properly (see Rutherford 2001a, inter alia; for a historical account, see Rubert 1998). As the chairman of the Agricultural Labor Bureau (ALB), the employers' association in the commercial agricultural sector, informed the Commercial Farmers Union annual congress in 1984, in light of recently introduced government legislation that made it difficult to easily dismiss farm workers, farmers were wary of employing many given the difficulties of control: farm workers "are lulled into a false sense of security believing that, irrespective of how indisciplined they are or how little they contribute to the overall productivity of the farm on which they are employed, government will ensure the preservation of their employment" (ALB 1984; see also Ladley and Lan 1985). Disciplining here was not simply inculcating a habitus for the workers to learn the appropriate bodily skills and knowledge, but also could bleed into more coercive power through the application of various forms of penalties and occasional corporal punishment as a way to try to ensure compliance. Coercion complemented disciplinary power.

I heard many tales of Victor's harshness, of how he did not respect people—"Victor mostly shouted at people, using abusive language," as

Faith disparagingly told me. He also would hit people who worked too slowly or refused to obey his commands, creating an atmosphere in which, as Efiah put it, the foremen under him employed the "same system" of abusing workers. As outlined by Faith, who had started in 1992, "Victor used to beat people. If you had a problem, you better be quiet or leave, otherwise if you complain to him he could beat you." Faith characterized the violence as a routine part of the work day: "Each morning, Victor would line up people, men and women, who had spoiled work the previous day, beating them up before we all started work for the new day." To make it plain that Victor was doing this with the blessing of the farmer, Mr. Botha, she added that "the foremen and management used to beat up people in the presence of the *baas* (boss), Botha. This made us have nowhere to report to." The microcolonialism of commercial farms sought to ensure that the rules and orders and dependencies were solely within their territorial boundaries, where power operated without rights.

Several talked about particular punishments Victor would give if a worker was late or transgressed another of the farm rules. Many recounted how he would make violators run laps around fields. Another humiliating and physically challenging punishment mentioned frequently in the accounts I heard was described by Maria: "He would tell you to lift up two bricks while standing on one leg, with the other leg being folded. If you dropped those bricks and they broke, then he would whip you." In other recollections, people had to stand on their toes with the bricks in their hands. The duration was said to be for ten to fifteen minutes. The aim was to discipline the worker through punishing his or her body. As one woman recalled, after being punished that way the worker was extremely stiff in his or her legs and humiliated for being punished as such, and many of them ended up resigning.

The on-farm authority relations on Upfumi were gendered, which also operated through a sexual economy (see Rutherford 2001a; Addison 2014). Men and women workers were vulnerable to very different forms of corporeal threats. Only men were physically beaten; women suffered other forms of bodily risks from the black management workers. Victor was most notorious for his sexual harassment. Maria succinctly summarized his particular form of predation, as well as possible rewards to those who complied:

> If he lusted after you, it was a must that you make love to him in return. If you refused, he could fire you or give you hard jobs. Every woman with whom he had an affair would be marked an extra day [of working] for that affair [in the

time books]. The beloved ones were usually called into his office and they would have sex. After that she was told to go home. You also could be promoted because of that. . . . All the men [workers] were told not to approach his girlfriends. The same applied to the other foremen, while they were also told to promote those with whom he was having an affair.

Like all forms of power where, according to Foucault, there is an inherent "'agonism' between power relations and the intransitivity of freedom" (Foucault 1982, 223), at times Victor's plans did not work. Sometimes the boundaries of the territorial sovereignties of commercial farms were not impermeable to wider authority relations, although it was not necessarily a straightforward demonstration of, say, state power. For example, when Victor gave Maria the punishment with the bricks, she told her brother, who was a policeman living in the vicinity. A few weeks later, when her brother saw Victor at what I call "Kunwa Doro"—a popular drinking spot about ten or so kilometers away—he confronted the foreman and, she flatly declared, "punched him in the face." She said the next work day, Victor glared at her but from then on he "became my best friend," and she was promoted from her field job picking vegetables to the pack-house to work as a quality checker of the vegetables being packed and shipped to Europe. According to her, she benefited from his power without subjecting herself sexually to him.

Others mentioned different forms of gendered power, attempts to mold labor relations by influencing the conjugal and reproductive possibilities of women workers. Some women noted how women workers who were married but whose husbands worked elsewhere could not visit with them in the compound. Nor could they have children in the compound. Rebecca, who started in 1992, said, "During those days, no woman was allowed to fall pregnant. Once it was obvious you were pregnant, you were fired." Others said that in the mid-1990s, older workers, above the age of forty-five or so, were let go as the farmer wanted only "young and strong workers"; moreover, in Jane's words, the older ones were suspected of "playing with witchcraft."

Victor's value to the farmer was finally reappraised—not because of his violence and intimidation of the workers, but because of his transgressions toward the farmer's own property. Workers told me that Victor had a number of scams to get extra money, including stealing goods from the farm and selling them on his own. In the mid-1990s, he was caught selling fertilizer from the farm to friends in Epworth, a high-density suburb southeast of Harare, for his own profit and was fired. The corporeal punishments stopped then but the sexual harassment continued at Upfumi, marking the mode of belonging shaping the livelihood practices for women farm workers. For example, a former irrigation worker recalled that whereas men had to buy groceries and gifts for the irrigation foreman to ensure that they maintained their job, any women had to have sex with him to secure their position, and so, he continued, "most of the women working at night on irrigation were unmarried as husbands prevented their wives from working the nightshift as that was the time of prostitution in the fields." Without too many other options, and often marginalized by the forms of territorialized modes of belonging elsewhere, these women workers endured. For those who subjected themselves to the sexualized dependency, these relations could potentially help them acquire a better job, easier working conditions, or other marginal gains within the territorialized mode of belonging. Others sought to avoid them or left for other farms or other locales looking for livelihood possibilities.

Whereas these workers subjected themselves to the conditional belonging on farms due in large part to their gender, the other significant translocal dimension that influenced people to become, or remain, farm workers was national citizenship itself. This was particularly the case for many of the male workers on Upfumi, although the coding of farm workers as foreign as a represented community in Zimbabwe also affected all farm workers, regardless of their actual citizenship claims.

Mabhurandaya: "Foreign" Farm Workers and the Zimbabwean Nation

In October 1999, I had arranged to interview five *vadhara*, old men in their fifties and sixties who were part of the Upfumi labor dispute, about changes on farms since they began working on them in the colonial period. A recurring theme in our two-hour conversation was the role of citizenship in shaping their livelihood opportunities. Four of the five men were born outside of the country—three in Malawi and one in Mozambique. The other was born on a musha in the northeastern part of Mashonaland East province.

Near the start of our interview, while they were talking about how the low wages before independence tended to buy more items than their current higher wages, Chiko segued from the example of school fees—"Long ago, one was able to pay school fees, even if one had ten kids"—into the issue of certificates: "The story of birth certificates [*nyaya yemaburti*] is causing problems these days. If you see a child growing up without a birth certificate, you then go to the government office and beg for one. But if you are alone, they [the officials] say 'you have no proof this is your child, you stole him' and they laugh. . . . When you do not have a wife, they say 'Fuck off. This person does not know what he is saying and we do not understand him.'" Such a dismissive attitude toward Chiko was a common experience of many farm workers in interactions with government officials who saw them as low-status, deficient citizens, if not aliens.

Chiko explained that his wife, whom he had met on the farms, had returned to Mozambique with her parents, leaving their three children (aged then at eighteen, fourteen, and ten) with him. They did not receive birth certificates when they were born on Zimbabwean farms. As recounted earlier, when Chiko tried to get birth certificates for his children when they were older, government officials in the district administrator's and Home Affairs offices were hostile to him as he had lacked proof they were born in Zimbabwe. As a consequence, his two older children stopped school in grade six as the headmasters started demanding birth certificates, which were required to write the grade seven exams. Chiko speculated that his youngest will stop at that grade as well if he remains without a birth certificate.

Chiko's difficulty was compounded because he himself was not a Zimbabwean citizen. He did not have any Zimbabwean identification; he said that he had thought of trying to apply for some but, given his failure in getting birth certificates for his children, he was reluctant to make numerous trips to the government's offices in town. As he put it, "I only saw that this would eat a lot of my money," by paying the transportation costs without guarantee of success. Even those who had claims to Zimbabwean citizenship were uncertain whether Zimbabwean authorities would recognize the legitimacy of their claims.

Halfway through my interview with the vadhara, one of the old men, Edgar, left for his grass and pole hut nearby and returned with a slightly crinkled piece of paper from 1985 stating it was a "Certificate of Registration as a Citizen of Zimbabwe." He and the others said that before the 1985 national elections, ZANU (PF) officials were going around the farms saying foreigners could become citizens and vote if they paid Z$1[6] for it. Yet, as some noted, the certificate had no government stamp on it, unlike almost every other government document Zimbabweans receive. Moreover, Edgar observed that his *chitupa* (the national registration card), which he received after paying for his citizenship, still had "NCR" on it, standing for "non-citizen resident." Chenjerai, the vice chairman of the workers' committee of the fired workers who had been listening to the interview, added that Edgar had been prevented from voting in elections held since 1990 because officials told him he was not a citizen. The "one-dollar citizenships" of 1985 had no legal weight but were instead, as a district administrator told me in 1992, "an electioneering gimmick by ZANU (PF) to ensure that farm workers vote for them" (Rutherford 2001a, 226). This is but one of many examples of how the ZANU (PF) government deployed state practices to amplify the insecurity of farm workers in the guise of aiding them. For even as state-authorized objects and practices can be used "as a resource for seeking certain rights," Veena Das points out, that in many postcolonial contexts it is "a resource whose use is fraught with uncertainty and danger" (Das 2004, 226) given the potential volatility of many postcolonial state's practices toward its citizens and subjects.

There is a widespread assumption held by many Zimbabweans that farm workers are *mabhurandaya*. The label refers to Blantyre, the Malawian city where foreign workers from Nyasaland, colonial Malawi, met recruiters to work on Southern Rhodesian farms or mines. Its semantic entailments are more disparaging, a term for foreigners, non-Zimbabweans, particularly farm workers (Muzondidya 2007, 334–335). The association of farm workers with mabhurandaya refers to the history of labor immigration in the colonial period, especially from after World War II to the 1950s, when as many as 60 percent of the agricultural workers in Southern Rhodesia were foreigners, particularly coming from colonial Malawi, but also colonial Mozambique and Zambia (Clarke 1977, 31). Although by the late 1990s estimates were that no more than 25 to 30 percent of the farm workers were born outside of the country (Sachikonye 2003, 66), yet even those who were born on Zimbabwean farms had great difficulty acquiring documents saying they were Zimbabwean (Muzondidya 2007, 331). Many farm workers and commentators assumed that they were eligible for citizenship based on being born in the country, although Constitutional Amendment Number 14 of 1996 actually removed the right of citizenship for children of parents who were residents of Zimbabwe but not citizens (Fisher 2010). This amendment became incorporated into the Citizenship Amendment Act of 2001 which required those Zimbabweans of foreign descent to provide documentary proof to the Ministry of Home Affairs that they renounced their claim, even if potential, to citizenship of the country of descent or lose their

Zimbabwean citizenship; a move that explicitly targeted farm workers and white Zimbabweans in view of the upcoming 2002 presidential vote as discussed more in chapter 4 (Muzondidya 2007, 335).

There were many children of foreign farm workers whose registration cards indicated that they were NCR, even though they were born in Zimbabwe. This may have been due to the 1996 constitutional amendment, although almost every farm worker and government official with whom I spoke assumed that birth in the country guaranteed citizenship. For example, Tapedza, the chairman of the workers' committee of the fired Upfumi workers, was born on a Mashonaland farm in the late 1960s. Although his parents were able to get him a birth certificate and a national registration card in 1979 which allowed him to continue with his education, his chitupa identified him as an NCR and had the Mozambican village in which his father was born before he entered into Southern Rhodesia in the 1940s as Tapedza's own place of birth. As he declared with disgust to me in August 1999, "when I register to vote I need to show them my birth certificate that demonstrates I am a citizen. It is embarrassing." When he approached the Mashonaland East Office of Home Affairs in Marondera, the provincial capital, in 1997 to change his chitupa, they initially assumed he was lying. As Tapedza bemoaned, these officials told him that "You are a farm worker, so you must be an alien." Once they were convinced by his birth certificate, he continued, they reluctantly said they could change his national registration card for a hefty fee. Because Tapedza did not have the money, he was still officially identified as an NCR.

The lack of documented citizenship helped to keep many farm workers on the farms. For some, like the children of Chiko, it limited their educational opportunities.[7] For others who did receive education like Tapedza, they experienced a range of discrimination against them, particularly when interacting with government officials. Like many of the women discussed above, they also typically did not have a network on which to draw to find a remunerative urban job, even if they had educational qualifications of, say, O Levels; many Zimbabweans perceived such networks as increasingly necessary with such high unemployment in the country. Instead, these children in the 1990s, like many children of farm workers before them (see, e.g., Grier 2006, 188ff.), tended to draw on their existing networks on commercial farms. Unlike the colonial period, however, better educated children of workers often entered into the greater number of managerial and supervisory jobs opening up (such as clerks, checkers, foremen, even managers) for black workers. These positions opened up because most farmers no longer reserved these positions exclusively for whites and, moreover, the overall expansion of production, particularly for export, on many commercial farms necessitated the creation of more management workers of various levels. Children of long-time workers or favored workers (such as domestic servants, senior foremen, gardeners) were especially selected for such positions. For some of these workers, this was frustrating as they had assumed they had qualifications to allow them to leave farm work but had to confine themselves to live within the mode of belonging, which their forebears, led much, if not all, of their working lives.

One day in September 1999, Tapedza explained that he had once hoped to enter into teacher's college after completing his O Levels, but he failed English and did not have high marks in the other school subjects. Chenjerai said, "Too bad you don't have family connections." He related that he had met a prosecutor who was boasting that he got his sister into teacher's college even though her grades were lower than required to be accepted. Tapedza sighed, noting that Upfumi was the third farm he was working as a clerk, making Z$1200 (approximately US$32 in 1998) per month, which was higher than the then minimum wage of around Z$1000 (US$27) per month. Although this was the highest he had ever earned, he gloomily noted that he had not progressed from the situation of his father: "Till death, I will work on farms."

The other main issue of citizenship that confronted the livelihood opportunities for many farm workers was the acquiring of a musha, a rural home. Before 2000, the dominant modes of acquiring access to rural land for the majority of black Zimbabweans was either to acquire a musha in the communal lands or a stand on a resettlement farm. For foreign farm workers, both options were difficult but not necessarily insurmountable.

As others have shown (e.g., Hughes 1999, 2006; Spierenburg 2004; Moore 2005; Alexander 2006), there were always competing land-giving authorities in the communal lands, both before independence and afterward. In many communal lands, preference is given to those who have patrilineal relatives already farming there. Due to various reasons[8] in some communal lands, at different points in time after 1980 those who were strangers to that land area were able to acquire a musha. "Strangers" here refers to those who either came from a different part of Zimbabwe or who were from—or descended from—outside the country itself. Chimhowu and Woodhouse (2006) call such transactions a "vernacular market."

I met many farm workers who had acquired a musha in the 1980s or 1990s through such a market, sometimes paying up to Z$500 for a small piece of land or just paying a token gift for access to one. However, as one farm worker noted in 2000, it is often "necessary to obtain citizenship when you are staying in the rural areas [communal lands] as the authorities can ask to see your chitupa and chase away those who are viewed as noncitizens." He himself was born in Mozambique but came to Zimbabwe in 1980, blending in with Zimbabwean refugees returning to their country from the camps in Mozambique after the war ended. He never attempted to get citizenship until 2000, since he acquired a musha through his Zimbabwean wife whose family gave them a small piece of their land in a communal land. Now the localized land-giving authorities were asking to see his citizenship papers.

In regards to resettlement land, farm workers found it easier to acquire a stand in this state land up to the late 1980s. As noted in the introduction, until that point the government was privileging "land-poor" candidates in its selection criteria of settlers on the farms they had purchased from white farmers, which included many farm workers, even some who were not Zimbabwean citizens (Moyo 1995; Moyo, Rutherford, and Amanor-Wilks 2000; Rutherford 2001a; Alexander 2006). However, once the government started prioritizing land reform and land-use planning over land redistribution and began selecting candidates with agricultural training and monetary resources (Moyo 1995; Goebel 2005; Alexander 2006), farm workers were viewed as unsuitable candidates for resettlement. This exclusion was based on assumptions that they were foreigners and, especially, that they lacked the proper development ethos to work for themselves because, putatively, they were accustomed to working for a (white) boss and thus lacked self-motivation (Moyo, Rutherford, and Amanor-Wilks 2000; Waeterloos and Rutherford 2004). Such sentiments drew on a wider moral economic evaluation found among those who live in the communal areas, one that scorns those who do not farm for themselves but engage in agricultural work for others; a moral appraisal that Terence Ranger celebrated as the "peasant option" in his trailblazing book (Ranger 1985). Norma Kriger (2003, 93–94) noted that this sentiment was held among many guerrilla ex-combatants after the war who resisted training to work in agricultural cooperatives as a form of compensation for their military service. Kriger quotes one staff member of an agricultural training center tasked with training ex-combatants in the early 1980s who observed that the former guerrillas "saw themselves as a kind of elite. You couldn't expect these people to accept rustication to become farm workers" (quoted in Kriger 2003, 94). Such a sentiment reemerged among many war veterans and others who led the farm occupations after February 2000.

Many farm workers had personal experience of this discrimination, if not at the hands of government officials, then in everyday life outside the farm. The negative assessment of the personhood of farm workers as a represented community on the scale of the nation also influenced assumptions about their bodily hygiene, a common form of discriminatory distinction that became consolidated during the colonial period (Burke 1996, 174ff.). As one woman farm worker said one day, "We farm workers sometimes have problems with transport as bus drivers say 'we do not carry people of the farms.'" Another woman elaborated, "People say we do not bathe; that we are dirty." And still another said, "People say farm workers have no musha... that they are half-human [*vanhu vemumapurazi hamuna kukwana*], which is the worst insult we get." The heritage of colonial represented communities continued to shape public perceptions of farm workers.

As a consequence, many older people who came to colonial Zimbabwe in the 1960s or earlier, as well as their children, if not grandchildren, remained working and living on commercial farms, subjected to this particular form of territorialized mode of belonging and its forms of dependencies that were largely circumscribed by the boundaries of the property itself. However, such a life was not necessarily disparaged by all farm workers, as some sought to deploy and work through the dependencies and inequalities for their own purposes. Chiko, one of the vadhara, put it starkly when he reminisced that in the past the farmer was someone who you approached with your problems for "your murungu [white person, boss] was your father and your mother and when you had a problem about anything, you would approach him with it." He thus drew on the racialized paternalistic inequalities of the power/sovereignty dynamic to try to acquire some assistance—although at the discretion of the farmer.

These boundaries of rule of domestic government were not simply maintained by white farmers, independent of the Zimbabwean state. Instead, state formation in independent Zimbabwe both challenged and relied upon them.

Boundaries of Rule: Domestic Government and Translocal Practices

As a form of microcolonialism, the ideal for many commercial farmers I met was to solely determine and manage the labor relations and living conditions on the farms. They assumed private property entailed the ability to strongly influence, if not direct in a paternalistic sense, the lives of farm workers. In turn, many of those men and women farm workers who spent a long time working on the farms, including many who were born on them, saw the farmer, in the words of Chiko, as "father and mother" (see also Du Toit 1993). If workers obeyed the performative practices that enabled positive recognition by the farmer, the particular requirement of the "declaration of dependence" (Ferguson 2013), then perhaps they could acquire sufficient resources for a minimal form of livelihood and satisfactory living conditions. For some of those recognized as favorites of the baas, there were also possibilities of acquiring resources for productive activities on the commercial farm, at their musha, or elsewhere. Whereas many workers who had spent decades under this territorialized rule, like Chiko and the other vadhara I interviewed, generally saw this as a regime in which they could operate, others, particularly younger, more educated ones, were not necessarily satisfied with it—particularly when talking about working conditions.

Many of the fired Upfumi workers detailed to me a long list of the violations of labor conditions before 1997, including not being given any protective clothing if working in the fields during the rain or with pesticides; no extra pay when working on a Sunday or a holiday; fired and punished at management's discretion with no administrative appeal, let alone any system of warnings; and no control over the form of contract under which they worked. Faith summed up the latter by noting, "If the farmer said I was a 'seasonal,' I was a seasonal worker. If he then said I was 'permanent,' I was a permanent worker. It did not really matter either way as my treatment was the same."

Many of the older workers tended to frame such complaints as a form of neglected obligations on the part of the farmer, as the baas not properly providing their paternalistic duties toward his workers. In contrast, younger workers often framed these recollections to me and to each other as an abuse of their rights, as a violation of farm workers more broadly.

Much of the social science literature on farm workers in Zimbabwe, little as it is, also tended to depict labor relations as an abuse of rights (e.g., Clarke

1997; Loewenson 1992; Amanor-Wilks 1995). This literature has reinforced a long-standing depiction of white farmers as abusive, racist, and exploitive; it even fueled a minority critique of European farmers in (Southern) Rhodesia by some public health and native affairs officials, urban-based industrialists and commentators, and writers such as Doris Lessing. Upon the switch from a white minority nation to a black majority nation at Independence, the heretofore minority critique became a dominant representation of white farmers in Zimbabwe in the words and policy documents and other writings of politicians, academics, and journalists, both Zimbabwean and non-Zimbabwean. White farmers became a public target of many. Along with their control of a significant amount of often good, agricultural land, their treatment of workers became iconic of their uncertain citizenship claims to the new postcolonial nation (Rutherford 2004; Fisher 2010; Hughes 2010; Kalaora 2011; Pilossof 2012). The organization of labor thus demonstrated these racialized inequities.

A common way of organizing many production tasks in the field and pack-houses was using *mugwazo*. A mugwazo is the task used in piecework regimes. The workers would be given a particular task to do, such as weeding a certain number of lines of plants or packing so many kilograms of vegetables for the day. They could leave work after finishing it, no matter how long they had spent at the task. The potential is for the worker to finish earlier than usual if he or she is able to complete it in a timely manner. Hence, farmers and labor experts sympathetic to the CFU (Commercial Farmers' Union) often portrayed it as an incentive, if not a bonus. If the workers found the set task to be too hard, which was more common, then either they would work an extra long day to complete it—or not complete it until the following day or more and resulting in a reduction in their wages for the extra time it took them. In the colonially induced idiom of farm workers, they would not be paid their "ticket" for the day if they did not finish their task.[9]

Farmers could change the mugwazo as a way to reward or punish workers and allowed foremen to have such arbitrary authority—a perfect example of the aforementioned influence afforded to the foremen by the racialized domestic government. For instance, Patience, one of the fired workers, explained that when she started in November 1996, she was working in the fields where "I encountered problems as the foremen would ask me to love them and when I refused they would say, 'I will give a painful mugwazo [task] which you will find it difficult to finish.' I was given a mugwazo which took me three days and I could not finish it. . . . When you failed to finish a mugwazo you were just marked a half day's pay."

By the 1990s, the collective bargaining agreement in agriculture prohibited piecework regimes, yet they were still widely practiced on many commercial farms (Rutherford 2001a, inter alia). In contrast, there was no legislation covering living conditions of farm workers. On Upfumi farm before 1997, living conditions were poor. There were too few houses for the hundreds of workers—five hundred or so by 1997—and many slept up to six or eight in a room. Women recalled the lack of privacy, the problem of theft, and the embarrassment when they or a roommate would bring a man into the room to spend the night. The latter was a significant concern for single women as some of them saw building a stable relationship with a man as a source of livelihood opportunities and security. Batsirai explained that not only did she have to deal with the possibility of theft of her food or money and hearing complaints from her roommates that her items were taking up too much room, but "it also was difficult to bring your boyfriend into that room. The danger was that your boyfriend could end up in love with all the women in that room! And so I looked for a place to stay alone so I can do my things without anyone interfering."

There were no separate huts or rooms for the kitchen, and, during inclement weather, the workers would cook in the room, filling it up with smoke. The drinking water came directly from a dam, with no filtration. The workers told me that the dam itself was full of chemicals from the fields and rubbish that people used to dump in the streams going into it. Diarrhea and stomach aches were a common complaint. As reported by an evaluation of Zimfarm (IFC [International Financial Corporation] 1999, 51),[10] when buying Upfumi in February 1997 the company "inherited an old, inadequate and, by objective measures, substandard housing stock."

Recalling when she started work at Upfumi in September 1995 when she was eighteen, Nyasha remarked that the head security guard allocated her "a room which already had five women, so I was the sixth person in the room. There was a problem of people stealing from one another, constant theft. Sometimes we could not get along well. Because we were too many in one room illness spread easily. Coughing was common which, if one had it, it would quickly spread to the others." One woman observed that when she began working there in 1992, "rooms were so overcrowded; tuberculosis and other transmitted diseases were common. As we drank water directly from the river many also got dysentery, made worse as we were ten people sharing a toilet. Moreover, overcrowding leads to hatred, theft, and a general untrustworthiness among each other."

If gender and citizenship helped to prefigure some to subject themselves more than others to this mode of belonging and of domestic government as a way to acquire a (portion of a) livelihood, there were also translocal practices that conditioned and at times challenged the boundaries of rule on commercial farms. Commercial farm workers were not hermetically sealed off from wider forces, despite the attempts by white farmers and management. In the following sections, I will examine three specific examples concerning Upfumi and many other commercial farms: the actions of ZANU (PF) and governance of living conditions, the actions of ZANU (PF) and trade unions in regards to labor relations, and preternatural forces and the labor regime. At times, these translocal forces threatened the established power/sovereignty dynamic within domestic government and at other times reinforced it.

Governance of Living Conditions and Outside Intervention

In the colonial period, it was common for the entire labor force to live on the farm in a compound (Rubert 1998). White farmers governed the workers living in this space by often appointing a senior worker like the "boss-boy" (head foreman) to be responsible for distributing rooms or places for new workers to build their huts, mediating petty disputes, and generally by trying to keep peace in the farm compound. Although this practice continued after 1980, this order was also challenged by the new source of power and authority in the new country: ZANU (PF).

Until 2000, the workforce on many commercial farms still lived in farm compounds or in what some nongovernmental organizations (NGOs) started to call "farm villages" (Auret 2000). Yet, depending on the location of the farm and the demand for labor, at times some or many of the farm workers lived off-farm in nearby townships, communal lands, resettlement farms, or on other farms. Upfumi was such a farm, given its location not too far from Harare and adjacent to what people called "plots." These latter pieces of land were much smaller than the average-sized commercial farms. Some were subdivided commercial farms and others were part of what are called "small-scale commercial farms," the postcolonial name for African Purchase Area Farms, the colonial land category in which a small number of Africans were allowed to lease or potentially purchase small farms on condition that they meet particular requirements set out by the colonial Native Affairs Department (Cheater 1984; Shutt 2000).

Given the rapid expansion of its workforce in the 1990s and the lack of investment in the compound, many Upfumi workers had accommodation off the farm. Some lived in the high-density suburbs of eastern Harare, like Mabvuku, or stayed with a spouse or a relative working on other farms. Upfumi routinely sent a tractor, truck, or even a bus to different locations to pick up workers. Others began to rent rooms or huts on nearby plots. These farms were typically owned by black Zimbabweans, and, as the workforces expanded on the surrounding commercial farms that had increasingly switched to horticultural production in the 1990s, many of the owners of the plots built huts to rent out or, more commonly, allowed workers from nearby farms to build mud and pole huts in their compound in exchange for a nominal rent. As explained by a farm worker renting land from one of these black farmers, once given permission to build a hut, "we get poles and thatching grass from the nearby forest and build our hut. When we leave the farm we shall sell our hut for whatever the going price is"; which in 2001, was around Z$300.[11]

These compounds could have a hundred or more people renting from them or as few as four or five families. Given the limited agricultural production occurring on many of these plots, the rents proved to be an important income stream. It also was a revaluation of an older colonial form of economic arrangements. When white farmers had such arrangements in the colonial period, it was scornfully called "kaffir farming" by white critics who were advocating for clearer racialized lines on European farms, and the elimination of African labor tenancy and similar agreements that enabled Africans and their families to live on the property without simply being full-time farm workers. Such criticisms contributed to the forced removals of hundreds of thousands of black families after World War II. In contrast, in the 1990s, nonwhite farmers who engaged in a similar practice were not publicly criticized. Rather, they and officials explained the practice as a strategy to cope with the inhospitable economic climate of structural adjustment.

A colored[12] part owner of one of the smallholder farms near Upfumi at that time, Carl, explained to me in June 2000 how demand for housing on his plot emerged:

> The women workers were complaining that they had no privacy on Upfumi. They would be packed into one room, and, as they are all looking for marriage, they found it difficult to take a [male] visitor in the room. This is how

you explain people renting places here, on my small plot, while they are from the commercial farming area. They want privacy, cooking and eating without others looking, hosting visitors—where will you put your mother if she visits you? Allowing people to put up their huts here on the farm started in 1991. . . . When I started allowing people to build here, it spread like wildfire onto Mupungu's farm.

Mupungu, a businessman based in Mutare, bought a farm that completely surrounded Carl's plot in the early 1980s. In the late 1990s, he rarely visited the farm and left the running of it up to a foreman called Antonio. In 1999–2002, Mupungu farm employed four workers and had dozens of houses on the farm, many of which were rented by former or current Upfumi farm workers. Many of these were women who could be deemed to be "looking for marriage." Though, as discussed in chapter 4, some were more comfortable being unmarried.

The rent for the huts charged by both Mupungu and Carl in 1999–2000 was Z$100 (US$2.50) per month per room—meaning, for the most part, a mud and pole hut, sometimes built by the renter himself or herself, paid to be built by the renter, or purchased from the previous occupant if he or she had built it. Farm workers sometimes received Z$50 (US$1.25) per month from their employer in lieu of having accommodation provided for them. The vast majority of the accommodations on both farms were without electricity and had only a few water taps in the compound to collect water as well as a minimal number of latrines. Most people used the "bush system" to relieve themselves. As observed by Grace, a woman participant in the Upfumi war who rented a hut from Mupungu, "every year people suffer from *manyoka* [diarrhea], perhaps because so many of us use the bush for the toilet."

During this time, Mr. Mupungu assigned an older woman to collect the rent on his farm and to deal with minor conflicts and lock the rooms of those in arrears for more than six or so months. Mai Shingi did these tasks in exchange for not paying rent for her two-room brick house. She was in her late fifties and had lived on Mupungu since the early 1980s, when it had still been owned by a white farmer. Her husband had been one of two employees of the white farmer who had been retained by Mr. Mupungu when he bought the farm, although she had been a widow since her husband passed away in 1988. Mr. Mupungu selected her for this position of authority in part because her husband had worked for him but also because she had been the village chairwoman for ZANU (PF) at the nearby Karigamombe Training

Centre before she and her husband moved to what was now Mupungu farm. Her position was a direct result of ZANU (PF) activists seeking to impose their authority on white farms in the 1980s.

The Karigamombe Training Centre refers to a nearby farm owned by the government since independence. It initially was used to train women ex-combatants. Later in the 1980s, the Karigamombe Centre became involved in training Mozambican refugees, and, by the late 1990s, it became a location to train street children picked up from Harare, sometimes identified by donors and supporters as "AIDS orphans." As Carl and others told me, it was run by members of the ZANU (PF) Women's League. It also was next to a public primary school with the same name attended by many children of Upfumi and other farms.

Mai Shingi had come to the farm on what became known as Karigamombe Training Centre in 1971. At that point, she was a single, widowed mother, and she had been living with her children at her parents' musha in the Rusape area. She had heard that the grading shed in the Berkshire area, where Upfumi is located, needed workers, so she left her children at her parents' musha and got a job working at the tobacco farm. She met her second husband at this farm. When the new postcolonial government took over the farm in 1980 and ex-combatants arrived to be trained, the new trainees also aided in the establishment and extension of ZANU (PF) structures on the farm and surrounding area (see also Kriger 2003, inter alia). Some former farm workers like her husband were initially retained, and Mai Shingi was selected to be a village chair, a position that emerged among the guerrillas during the war as a form of court for addressing marital and family disputes (Kriger 1992, 118).

ZANU (PF) cadres established village committees on many farms in the 1980s, which were more or less directly linked to party and national government efforts and acted to settle family disputes; assisted the occasional governmental programs that included farm workers such as national censuses and supplemental feeding of school kids; and worked to ensure worker support to ZANU (PF) during national elections (Rutherford 2001a).

In 1999, Mai Shingi described her role in the early 1980s: "I used to judge cases which were brought to the Karigamombe Centre and I was working under the organization of *Baba* [Father] Mugabe, ZANU (PF)." But, she noted, eventually the party cells died and if cases came to her attention, she sent them on to the police. By the latter part of the 1990s, ZANU (PF) cells were not that active in the Upfumi area. They had a much stronger presence in the 1980s and were reanimated in 2000 after the defeat of the constitutional referendum, as discussed in chapter 4.

Chenjerai informed me in October 1999 about his ties to the training center: "My uncle was an ex-combatant who was being trained at Karigamombe in the early 1980s, before he got a resettlement farm near Macheke in the mid-1980s." His uncle was also one of the ZANU (PF) leaders in the area at the time and told Chenjerai (in Chenjerai's words): "Plenty of [farm] foremen were assaulted at that time. . . . Anyone within ZANU (PF) could do what he pleased because farmers were scared. Also, at the time, the comrades could just say to a farm worker that they heard that you are in good relations with the murungu and they would say you are on his side and we farm workers would be beaten a lot."

Chenjerai was adding these comments as I was interviewing the five vadhara in late 1999. When the old men told me that they first started to see General Agriculture and Plantation Workers' Union of Zimbabwe (GAPWUZ) people in the early 1990s, I asked them what other organizations were involved in labor relations in the 1980s. Tapera, one of the vadhara, responded, "There were too many and some we did not know where they were coming from and what they were doing—it was difficult to see." It was at this point that Chenjerai interjected by explaining the role of the ruling party in solving labor disputes at that time. Everyone with some leadership role in the party—"the youth [wing] was saying we can help the workers, the women wing was saying it can help the workers"—sought to intervene in disputes on the farms at that time. The ex-combatants were the ones that the old workers feared the most, for they could discipline anyone they viewed as comporting themselves improperly. As in other Zimbabwean workplaces in the early 1980s, many ex-combatants were militant and intervened in not only personnel issues but also personal issues as well as other areas of daily comportment (Kriger 2003, 164ff.). They did this as a way to demonstrate their authority over others.

In the Upfumi area older workers recalled that just after Independence if ex-combatants had determined farm workers had a case to answer, they would be punished. Tapera and the other vadhara called it *kuporuna*, "to prune," as in trimming, cutting back, or shaping vegetation; or in this case, to be beaten to conform to the standard of behavior expected by the ex-combatants. Anyone whose behavior was deemed to be wild or wayward was pruned, so to speak. "The ex-combatants used to beat up anyone, even if you had quarrels with your friend. When the ex-combatants see you they would beat you up so much that you would fail to understand who told them about your quarrelling," recalled Tapera, shaking his head, before continuing. "Even the beating of wives was no longer done; when they heard that so and so beat up his wife, they would come to you and it's all over—they would break your ribs." These ex-combatants used violence and its threat to try to shape actions, to bring the white commercial farms—including labor relations and domestic relations—into contemporary Zimbabwe, for they often saw white farmers as anachronistic leftovers of the colonial era. Farm workers were also associated with that colonial era by virtue of working for white farmers.

Moreover, these ZANU (PF) activists sought to install themselves and the party as the sovereign arbiters of disputes and new rulers of the land of the nation. In the early 1980s, party activists associated their authority with the ZANU (PF) government and, through it, with the sovereignty of the state. Their rule and rulings in provisional courts, commonly called "kangaroo courts," were to be taken akin to those coming from state courts. As Carl, who was the political commissar for the ZANU (PF) local branch right after 1980 recalled, there "were many of these kangaroo courts formed, where people would be thrashed. Instead of going to jail, they would get so many cuts with a whip or cane. The ex-combatants used this system during the war—there were no holding cells then—and they followed the same system here." As liberators of the country from white rule, some of these ex-combatants and some members of the new black government were seeking to establish their rule over the comportment of those whose loyalties to ZANU (PF) and the new nation were unclear (Kriger 2003, 2005, 2006).

The early 1980s was a time when the ruling party was trying to establish its rule and control over the country, the administrative machinery, its former adversaries in the Rhodesian forces, and in the other major guerrilla movement turned political party, Zimbabwe African People's Union (ZAPU) (Sylvester 1991; Alexander 2006). How this played out depended in part on the type of land category in which people were residing, the forms of leadership that were preexisting, and the particular social projects that were operating in and through the territorialized space. Authority over the land in Zimbabwe, as Jocelyn Alexander (2006) has eloquently demonstrated, always has "remained in the making" (see also Moore 2005). There was great ambivalence toward white commercial farms, given that they were very much at the forefront of the Rhodesian Front hegemonic project and the battlegrounds of much of the conflict in the 1970s (Rutherford 2004), although they were as fractious as any other identified represented community (Selby 2006). Farm workers were caught up in this ambivalence, particularly given their contingent location on white farms, their uncertain loyalties toward the liberation struggle (because of their employment for white farmers, who were clearly identified with the colonial Rhodesian side), and their own origins by birth or descent outside of Zimbabwe.

When Chenjerai said that farm workers were easily intimidated because most of them were from Malawi, the old men nodded saying that many of the *vakuru* (big people) of the party would promise "If you do not support ZANU (PF) we will send you back to Malawi where you came from!" As Edgar explained, "In the early 1980s, if we had big problems we took them to the ZANU (PF) chairman on the farm or to the ex-combatants or to [the local party hierarchy based in [what I call] Oxfordshire. We had to do so as they were the new rulers."

Another farm worker ironically used "colonized" to describe the actions of the ruling party—the same process ZANU (PF) claimed to be fighting—when he said in early 2001, "You know most of the people in this country were very colonized by the ruling party in the 1980s." He added, "It was really dangerous to say anything against it back then like what the children of today were saying [in the late 1990s]. And look what has happened since 2000." The violence unleashed by the ZANU (PF)-controlled state since 2000 was viewed by most Zimbabweans as well-rehearsed practices from earlier periods. However, by the 1990s on Upfumi and many other farms I had researched (Rutherford 2001a), the presence of ZANU (PF) was often quite minimal. The person with some authority over housing and perhaps settling disputes in on the farm compound may have been there because of residual authority from the ruling party, like Mai Shingi on Upfumi in the 1990s. Most often, however, ZANU (PF) committees on commercial farms were nonexistent or dormant by the late 1990s.

Labor Relations and Competing Politics of Recognition on the National Scale

This history of ZANU (PF) involvement in judging cases in the 1980s indicates how the boundaries of rule within domestic government was challenged on many farms by extra-farm sources of authority. This included the domain of labor relations. The localized history of ruling party involvement on the commercial farms is relevant to understanding some of the dynamics of the later dispute at Upfumi and wider interventions on farms in Berkshire/Oxfordshire. It also speaks to the changing governance of labor relations on farms on the national scale.

In September 1999, Phillip Munyanyi, the then general secretary of GAPWUZ, discussed how ZANU (PF) acted as a midwife to the trade unions in the agricultural sector in the early 1980s, chuckling in light of the launch of the MDC that month and its close ties to the ZCTU: "I don't have to hide from the fact that ZCTU and unions had close ties with the party back then." He himself was a ZANU (PF) activist in 1980 and became national organizing secretary for ZAWU (Zimbabwe Agricultural Workers' Union) that emerged with ruling party support in the early 1980s. In 1982, he and others formed GAPWUZ, and he then became the deputy general secretary. He recalled this period:

> ZANU PF had a labor desk then [in the early 1980s] to solve problems with workers. Initially workers could go to either the party labor desk or to the union. I went from the party labor desk to the union ZAWU as I saw it was more secure in the union. Look today, there is no labor desk at ZANU (PF). The labor desk ran from 1980–1985. There was one in each district.
>
> The party would set up the village committee. It was very political. Most unions were not registered and the party had more influence. So ZAWU and GAPWUZ [which emerged as a breakaway union from ZAWU] would use party structures in their activities in those years. Farmers would listen to GAPWUZ out of fear [given that the ruling party supported it]. At that time, there was no distinction between party and union. Sometimes [union] officials could get papers—like [political party] ID cards—from the party to gain authority to recruit workers and deal with labor problems.

ZANU (PF) committees and individuals intervened in workplace disputes in the 1980s (Kriger 2003, 163ff.). Mai Shingi recalled that occasionally she dealt with labor disputes on commercial farms and any cases she was unable to resolve, she passed on to her seniors in ZANU (PF) based in Oxfordshire fewer than ten kilometers east of Berkshire. Overall Mai Shingi did not play an active role in labor relations in the area.

Carl, the colored plot-holder next to Upfumi, was one of the ruling party leaders in the Upfumi area who dealt with farm worker cases in the early 1980s. As political commissar for the area, one of his duties was to deal with grievances in the whole area. There was no trade union at that time and the labor department then, he claimed in 2000, was still staffed with "[Ian] Smith's people" who were not sympathetic to the new labor relations laws (see also Raftopoulos 1986; Rutherford 2001b). He and others helped to establish party committees on many of the farms, and, when farm workers had grievances they would have to get a letter from the ZANU (PF) chair on their farm saying something like, "Cde. Carl, see to this man's case." At that time, Carl continued, "workers' committees and party committees were the same thing." He would then go to speak with the farmer, and, if he could not settle the dispute, he would send it a step further to within the ZANU (PF) hierarchy. He also said that he and others within the localized party structures involved in dispute settlement would receive money from the farmer as a gift of thanks for solving labor problems. Carl reflected that he and other ZANU (PF) interveners in labor disputes faced resistance from many farm workers "Since they were fearing the boss—what will happen when the ZANU (PF) guy left? The fear with farm workers then and now is that basically they need a place to call their own, to have a musha to love. They didn't have it then and many still don't have one. Any time they can be told to move on, especially once they become elderly."

Farm workers' claims in the mode of belonging of domestic government were very conditional on the disposition of the farmer and management more broadly. The active presence of ZANU (PF) in the early 1980s amplified that ambivalence. Some farm workers took these activists as their liberators who would displace white farmers and make life better on the farms. The "politics as liberation" narrative resonated for them. As *mudhara* (old man; singular of vadhara) Edgar said sheepishly, recalling a common millennialist assumption he and many other farm workers held at the dawn of independence, "we, not the white farmers, would be the ones driving the cars and trucks around here." Others were scared of the party activists, particularly their potential for violence. The "politics as oppression" narrative and practices instilled fear in many. They were also scared of the farmers' reactions to this attempt of outside interventions into their rule and these challenges to the mode of belonging of domestic government.

Mr. Chishiri, a ZANU (PF) official who came from Ruwa to Oxfordshire, elaborated for me on the role of the party in labor relations at that time. In July 2000, he said that when he arrived in Oxfordshire in 1982 there had been little to "no politics on commercial farms, so I came and tried to educate farm workers and teach them their rights in the industry." The talk of rights thus has a history on commercial farms. However, this talk of rights was specifically tied to a project of consolidating and extending ZANU (PF) rule throughout the country. Discourses concerning rights are not independent of different social projects, which may be quite different from what one may imagine human rights sociality should look like (Englund 2006).

By 1983, Mr. Chishiri was officially working for both ZANU (PF) and GAPWUZ, establishing workers' committees, educating farm workers, and trying to solve labor problems. According to his presentation to me, his method was to first talk with the farmer and then, after getting their approval, talk to the workers. Yet, he also fondly recalled that in the early 1980s, fear also worked to his advantage: "After independence, some of the farmers were afraid of ZANU (PF) because of the war and they quickly responded. Farm workers were very much afraid because of the war and also responded very well."

Although the frontline of the 1970s war was relatively far from Oxfordshire-Ruwa, fear of ZANU (PF) was visible and visceral; a fear, as discussed in later chapters, that is very much part and parcel of *poritikisi* (party politics) in Zimbabwe (Scarnecchia 2006, 2008). For older workers and for some of the older white farmers I met, the early 1980s was characterized as a "time of poritikisi" on the farms as ZANU (PF) activists and, at times, trade unionists arrived on many farms attempting to assert authority over various aspects of life in the compounds and at the workplace. They were the new rulers, not only of the state but also the nation and the socio-political lives of many deemed to belong to it (see, e.g., Kriger 2003; McGregor and Alexander 2014).

By 1987, Mr. Chishiri left GAPWUZ. Afterward, when workers came to him with their grievances, he said he would refer them to the GAPWUZ office or the Ministry of Labor office in Marondera, although he noted that GAPWUZ was not necessarily that effective when it no longer worked closely with ZANU (PF). For many active in intervening in labor relations on the farms in the early 1980s, the sense was that *simba* (strength or power) in dealing with labor relations rested, in part, on poritikisi (see also Kriger 2003, 164). The then general secretary Munyanyi reckoned that when GAPWUZ became the only registered trade union in the agricultural industry in 1986 (since the Labor Relations Act at that time demanded one union per industry) the ties between ZANU (PF) and the union began to weaken.

This transition from trade unions involved in electoral politics to a growing cleavage between GAPWUZ and ZANU (PF) in the Berkshire area did not occur abruptly. Carl observed that farmers started reporting to the police that ZANU (PF) officials were not authorized to deal with problems on the farm, and Mr. Nhongo, the district chairman for ZANU (PF) structures in Ruwa district in the late 1980s, was "taken a number of times by the police for trying to solve cases when he was not supposed to do so." The commercial farmers also began to refuse to pay money to ZANU (PF) officials to solve labor disputes, and GAPWUZ now had full-time staff of their own. Councillor Banda told me in November 1999 that when he was youth chair for ZANU (PF) in Ruwa from 1993 to 1998 he would occasionally deal with farm worker problems since GAPWUZ was not around that much and thus, generally, did not address their grievances. Chenjerai and others also mentioned that, in the early 1990s, Banda and GAPWUZ had a large battle over solving labor problems on a Berkshire farm and "GAPWUZ had won." It is important to stress, however, that in practice by the mid-1980s the presence of both GAPWUZ and ZANU (PF) on most farms in this area was generally minimal until the late 1990s.

The iterative struggle through the 1990s over who should exercise what type of authority with respect to labor relations on commercial farms—ZANU (PF), GAPWUZ, white farmers—was, in part, about who had claims over farm workers: the ruling party with its claims to monopolize the new state; the trade union with its claims to work within an effective bureaucratic administrative system over labor relations; or the farmer with his or her system of domestic government. The division was not always that clear-cut since at times both ZANU (PF) activists and GAPWUZ officials would support farmers' claims to be ultimately in charge of the disposition of farm workers. For the most part ZANU (PF) officials played an increasingly smaller role on farms as the 1990s progressed. This left it up to GAPWUZ to try to represent farm workers, although they were relatively weak in their capacity and did not have much of a presence on many farms. But these were strong sentiments—belonging to ZANU (PF), to a bureaucratic liberal state, to the farmer—that could be mobilized within particular social projects. Yet, many commentators tended to reify these social practices into essentialized predispositions and structures.

The party officials' sympathetic recollections of the role of ZANU (PF) in labor relations and their concern that a more bureaucratic system did not serve farm workers' interests is shared by Andrew Ladley and David Lan (1985) in their analysis of this transition on a Mashonaland West farm in 1982. They thoughtfully used a case of a white farmer's decision to brave possible antiwhite sentiments of the new black civil servants as he approached the government labor officer to confirm his decision to fire some workers. In the early 1980s, the new labor relations machinery introduced by the ZANU (PF) government set up administrative checks on employers' dismissals of employees (Wood 1988), and, given the anticolonial and antiwhite rhetoric of many ZANU (PF) leaders many white farmers assumed labor officers would automatically be against white employers.

In Ladley and Lan's account, to the farmer's surprise and the workers' disgust, the labor officer approved of his decision to fire some farm workers. This decision went against the expectation of the farm's workers' committee and the farm workers who had assumed the loyalties of the new government to be with the *povo* (masses); they roundly condemned the "sellout" civil servant, a black official whom they claimed went against the interests of black Zimbabweans in the new African nation. These workers had heightened expectations because ruling party structures in the Mashonaland West district had often confronted their farmer and other employers with some success in challenging the farmer's power and authority—similar to the recollections of many of those in the ZANU (PF) structures at Karigamombe and elsewhere operating in the Berkshire area at this time. Moreover, the leaders of the workers' committee, like the others on the surrounding farms, were also the leaders of the ZANU (PF) cells on the farms. Ladley and Lan (1985, 100; italics in original) characterized the white farmer's pleasant surprise at the result in the following way:

> For the farm owner land is a way of life, as well as a commodity which can be bought and sold. The title deeds give him the right, as he put it, "to make the decisions about what happens on my property." Of course, his right has changed in the last few years. There *is* something of a new order in the land—the minimum wages, the committees, the labor officer, etc. But although this must be accommodated, his intention remains to guard the areas of authority which he holds over his land and labor force.... To his surprise, he discovered a member of government whose handling of labor matters corresponds approximately with his own and who is unequivocal about his right to own his land and determine its future use. For him perhaps the distinction between Party and Government, Labor Officers and District Party committees, has begun to come clear.

Their description of the white farmer traces the mode of rule I call domestic government—private property as a form of microcolonialism, a territorialized rule over the labor force and others living on his land. Yet, Ladley and Lan take the ruling party's claims at face value.

Accordingly, they argue that the workers were united with the party because, following Lan (1985), the war experience forged a link between ZANU (PF) and the ancestors; and thus, Zimbabweans assumed that the ruling party represented indigenous Africans like these farm workers: "To the workers and to many others in rural Zimbabwe, the establishment of the Party committees represented the most dramatic concrete manifestation of the new law of the land and of their regained autonomy. But the Government has adopted the laws of the land of their predecessors in office and put aside those observed by their ancestors perhaps forever" (Ladley and Lan 1985, 101).

As many writing on Zimbabwean land issues in the 1980s, Ladley and Lan had a relatively accepting view of ZANU (PF) and an overly simplified understanding of power and coercion (see Kriger 1992 and Worby 2001, for a broader critique). They also mistakenly assumed that most farm workers viewed themselves as "indigenous Zimbabweans" and, as importantly, the party officials and other Zimbabweans took them to be so. Their category of "Africans" ignores how territorialized power helped to condition differential representations via administrative arrangements and political practice. Their invocation of African nationalism downplayed how its proponents, during other times, distinguished farm workers from peasants in great part due to how the territorialized mode of belonging on the commercial farms and in the communal lands configured them very differently on the national scale. Nor did they foresee that ZANU (PF) officials and cadres would at times challenge the boundary between labor relations and politics that, they accurately noted, had started to firm up in the early to mid-1980s in many farming areas. What they did capture, however, was the sense held by many farm workers that the ZANU (PF) government had forgotten about them by this time. And these expectations of a state helping to improve their lives (reinforced by the African nationalist claims of ZANU (PF) leaders) are what many farm workers would stress in those few communicative contexts in which they could make claims on politicians or engage in political discussion without fear—contexts that were not too common before 1999.

GAPWUZ became the single recognized trade union for the agricultural industry in 1986, acquiring recognition by the relevant authorities after legislation forced a single union per industry. At that time, it was relatively weak in many of the farming areas with limited vibrant on-farm structures (Loewenson 1988; Rutherford 2001b; Tandon 2001; Kanyenze 2001). Simultaneously, there was a growing effort by many trade union leaders to become more independent from ZANU (PF), as there was a reorganization within ZCTU leading to Tsvangirai's election as its secretary general in 1988 (Raftopoulos and Phimister 1997; Raftopoulos and Sachikonye 2001). This was occurring around the time of the growing separation between ZANU (PF) and GAPWUZ in the Berkshire area, disparaged by Councillor Banda and other ZANU (PF) activists to me in the late 1990s. It was also at this time that there was a growing movement—among students, academics, trade unionists, lawyers, and others—against plans by ZANU (PF) to constitutionally create a one-party state around itself (Mandaza and Sachikonye 1991; Moyo 1992). The leaders of the ruling party made it known they preferred this route after it swallowed the main rival political party, ZAPU, in 1987—thanks largely to the unrelenting state terror in southwestern and central Zimbabwe known as *gukurahundi*.[13]

The debates and successful protests against implementing the one-party state in the late 1980s are often considered the start of what emerged as the broader movement for democratization in the mid-1990s. Brian Raftopoulos (2003, 226) argues "the first decade of independence ended with growing economic problems, an embryonic opposition movement, and signs of serious fractures in the notion of national unity imposed by ZANU (PF)." Yet, the violence associated with politics of the colonial era and with the ZANU (PF) postcolonial state shaped both the targets and the reception of this movement—a movement that had very limited traction initially on farms in the Upfumi area.

By the time Mr. Botha bought Upfumi in 1991, both ZANU (PF) and GAPWUZ had negligible roles or presence in labor relations on the farm. Farm workers had different recollections about whether there was a workers' committee operating on the farm before Zimfarm bought it. Some workers said that there was a workers' committee established on the farm in the early 1990s and many workers were GAPWUZ members, while others said neither was present. Those who recalled a workers' committee and a GAPWUZ presence at that time before February 1997 were so negative in their recollections, though, it is not surprising that others denied the committee's existence. "During that time, GAPWUZ only came to talk to the managers and never the workers," was a common theme. As Precious scoffed, GAP-WUZ came and sold memberships but then never came around or did anything. Others said that the GAPWUZ officials would have tea with or receive vegetables or fruit from the farmer—indicating to them whose interests they were promoting. As was common on many farms at the time, farmers appointed the workers' committees, which were often comprised of foremen, clerks, or other management workers. The main logic for such a widespread practice was that the farmer only listened to or spoke with the "big workers," such as foremen or clerks, so it made sense to have these people representing the workers. But from the perspective of others, such as those who were engaged in the Upfumi struggle, such a workers' committee, in the succinct words of Jane who arrived at Upfumi in 1994, "does nothing." As she explained, "At that time [the workers' committee on Upfumi] was selected by the management and it only looked at protecting the management, not the workers."

In 1995, Frank, the main farm clerk and personnel officer, headed the workers' committee on Upfumi. He was a person, Faith scornfully noted, "who was responsible for employing and firing people and was also involved in the payment of salaries. People would give grievances to Frank but he did not listen to them because he was management. People at that point did not know their rights and just did what management wanted them to do." A man who was a junior foreman at the time recalled that the other members of the workers' committee included the senior clerk of the pack-house, the head foremen of irrigation, and the dispatch clerk in the pack-house. All were senior members of the workforce he emphasized, so if "you had any problems and went to the workers' committee it would not solve anything because it protected the boss." Supervisors had the right to fire with no hearings, and if workers complained to the workers' committee, as everyone told me in their accounts of the history of labor relations on the farm, "nothing happened." Such negative recollections were informed in large part by the significant change in 1997 after Zimfarm bought the farm and the establishment of what these workers called a "real workers' committee."

By 1997, the politics of recognition revolved around the farmer and management with the workforce having little institutional role over their labor conditions and with limited, if any, external interest or presence interacting with the mode of belonging on the farm. The two main potential extra-local forces that had or could have influenced labor relations, ZANU (PF) and GAPWUZ, were barely visible in the lives of farm workers at that time everyone agreed. When management wanted to fire them, change their contractual arrangements, or other such interventions into labor relations, the farm workers said that they more or less complied or left the farm. The mode of belonging was extremely conditional; recall Jane's comment about the letting go of people older than forty-five whereby no one could do anything. One of the motivations of ridding the farm of older people was to address the other force that interacted with production processes at that time: a preternatural one.

Hauntings

Preternatural forces intersected in production at Upfumi in two ways. The first was the assumption held by some workers that the fields were haunted. "The farm was placed on a burial ground of the local chief's," Rita averred, referring to one of the traditional leaders of a communal area no more than twenty kilometers away, and "no spirit medium came to try to put the disturbed spirits back to ease." Looking back at all the various conflicts that had occurred on the farm, Rudo speculated in 2001 that this was because "the owners of the farm just removed the graves without telling the chief." I heard the occasional stories about irrigation workers seeing spectral presences when working at night: "Sometimes, when changing the irrigation pipes at night, you could meet a person who was very bright, and, if you try to talk to that person, it would not answer you," recalled one man. Others told me about tractor drivers unable to plough certain sections of fields as some force prevented their tractors entering into those lands. Maria observed that "The fields were full of graves, and when we had to cut down trees sometimes you would see corpses." But these were passing concerns and did not seem to constitute a significant presence in the farm workers' lives or situation. In contrast, witchcraft was a much more palpable and constant concern and it intersected directly with the labor regime.

Many workers talked about how the foremen occasionally used *mishonga* (medicine) and herbs to ensure their position, but they mainly used it against competitors including rival foremen or others who may be aiming to take their jobs. This was typical on many farms (Rutherford 1999; Rutherford and Nyamuda 1999). For example a farm worker on a neighboring farm told the story about a feared foreman from Oxfordshire who would travel to Marondera by foot, more than forty kilometers away, and reach there in ten minutes thanks to magical means of transportation. Or he would travel to Malawi by night to visit relatives and return the next morning with fish and rice from the country where he was born. "He could tell you that you will be dead the next day, which would happen unless you go and talk with him about whatever problem there was between you and him. This old man was much feared on the farm and in the Oxfordshire area." Whereas witchcraft could enforce the dependencies of the farm, it did not always do so as it could also be used by workers against other workers independent of managerial workers. However, when addressing witchcraft concerns the power relations of the modes of belonging typically were involved.

On Upfumi, this was very clear in the mid-1990s when many farm workers began to suffer from varied illnesses, which did not cease after they received treatment at the health clinic. Gutu observed that "Workers were often beaten in the fields by what is called *zvishiri* [preternatural creatures sent by witches]." Workers began suspecting witchcraft and some started thinking of leaving work at Upfumi if it was not addressed. Carrying these complaints and their own concerns about witchcraft, foremen convinced the farmer to find a way to minimize, if not neutralize, the threat. The farmer complied and management hired a *n'anga* (healer) who performed a witch-finding ceremony.

Such ceremonies in the region follow certain performative practices to justify the authority and ability of the n'anga to identify and isolate witches (e.g., Auslander 1993). In addition, the relevant authorities for the territory often compelled the residents to participate, regardless of individual belief in the actual divining ability of the witch-finder. As Precious recalled, management forced every worker to comply with the n'anga's demand to drink a potion under threat of being fired. The territorialized mode of belonging supported the position of the witch-finder. If a worker vomited, Precious said that the n'anga determined the person to be "clean" and not a witch. Those who did not vomit were said to be witches and were then put into a circle. Precious continued, many of "those in the circle began to behave like hyenas and practice what they did when they moved around at night as witches. I myself saw some moving like hyenas and heard some say 'my [spiritual] airplane is taking me to Malawi. I want to get there before the plane gets burned by the mishonga.' Another said they ate a child who had recently died." The witch-finder warned the discovered witches that if any of them returned to their nefarious ways the potion inside of them would kill them.

Management took a different tactic, as Precious observed, "Those who acted that way got fired." Those fired were mainly older women and a few men.

Management thus used the preternatural forces to consolidate their authority. The translocal force of witchcraft and the witch-finding authority bolstered management, for it was they who arranged for the witch-finding n'anga to come to the farm, compelling the workforce to be tested, and then firing workers deemed to be witches. Its support of management was not uncontested, at least in its recounting.

Chenjerai, who had been listening in on our conversation, scoffed. "Where, Precious, did the people who were getting sick work?" he demanded. She replied they were mainly picking raspberries. She said that by midmorning a preternatural wind, *mamhepo*, would come and affect them. Chenjerai started lecturing, saying there is a scientific explanation for the illness. "The employer was not providing protective clothing, were they not?" he asked Precious. She concurred. "So the chemicals which they were spraying would stick to the berries when it was very hot and it was these people who got sick. It was chemical poisoning." Precious did note that at that time the system was that pickers followed those who sprayed chemicals, and, often when picking, they would also eat a few. And it was, she continued, the raspberry field foremen who talked to the management about the sickness and the mamhepo and asked for a witch-finder; and that management agreed to hire one, with every worker paying Z$5 for the "test." Chenjerai looked victorious, saying "this is where your witchcraft is." Precious did not look quite convinced, but did not continue on the topic. Chenjerai then added "as a black person, I do not deny witchcraft. But, in this case, it was from chemicals and not witchcraft."

As I shall discuss in chapter 4, Chenjerai definitely was not indifferent to, or viewed as innocent, when it came to using witchcraft. He also was very effective in putting himself into a position where he was able to express judgement and to arbitrate, if not rule, over deliberations on disputes and actions occurring among farm workers in the area.

Conclusion: Shifting Grounds

In early 1997, farm workers at Upfumi farm were largely ensconced in the dominant mode of belonging of domestic government. The majority of the five-hundred-plus workers were single mothers subjecting themselves to the hard labor and possible sexual harassment and assault as they sought out a place to stay and wages to pay for some of their own and their children's sustenance. Many of the men were of foreign descent—with a few, largely vadhara, who were born in Malawi, Mozambique or Zambia. They were ensnared by both the wider way in which farm workers were represented on the scale of the Zimbabwean nation as foreigners and by the limited livelihood opportunities that existed for them outside commercial farming; although the feeling of entrapment was more intense among the younger men and women than the older ones, who had become inured to the dependencies and conditionalities of domestic government. Those living off-farm, the somewhat distant history of ZANU (PF) interventions and the rare GAPWUZ ones, and preternatural forces show that the commercial farms were not immune to translocal, national scale, or otherworldly actors. Although there was a brief period when demands for rights for farm workers were heard, these calls were closely tied to the attempts by ZANU (PF) activists to extend their authority over white farmers and—more importantly—black workers. By 1997, however, rights did not have much, if any, purchase within the on-farm landscape as other modes of recognition, dependencies, and their performative audiences were more dominant at that time.

Into this social landscape, Zimfarm stepped. This change of ownership facilitated changes in the government of labor, as I will discuss in chapter 2. At this time, Zimfarm itself was changing its economic activities as the company was taking advantage of another landscape; one in which its scale of production was intersecting with assistance and encouragement on the national and international scales, creating a "scale-making project" (Tsing 2005) that investors were endorsing.

In 1997, Zimfarm was in the midst of expanding its horticultural processing and marketing. It had been a successful, relatively small fruit and vegetable wholesale business for many decades. The company started to respond to the liberalization of export and import regulations and growing domestic and international fruit and vegetable markets at the start of the 1990s; expanding its warehouse and distribution capacity, and diversifying its products and corporate structure. It also became listed on the Zimbabwe Stock Exchange. Until 1997, all of Zimfarm's fruits and vegetables had been produced by others under contract, when its purchase of Upfumi opened new productive possibilities: "Upfumi's farms comprise some 460 acres, two dams, a pack-house, and, most important, accreditation from the European Union (EU)" (IFC 1999, 47).

Zimfarm's expansion in the 1990s was enabled by the Zimbabwean government's structural adjustment policies and a number of wider-scale actors: securing access to the International Financial Corporation (IFC) of the World Bank in 1993 for an initial low-interest US$4.8 million loan and then subsequent investment into its shares; partnering with a Dutch firm in establishing an export-oriented vegetable dehydration facility; and going public on the Zimbabwe Stock Exchange to purchase Upfumi. The IFC documents all this in its review (IFC 1999), providing insight into the company's productive processes and the cultural assumptions shaping some of its investors. The IFC (1999, 48) viewed its own role as crucial, both enabled by the government's neoliberal policies and, without irony, offering a route for Zimfarm to avoid some of the negative consequences of structural adjustment; for ESAP (Economic Structural Adjustment Programme) was one that the World Bank and the IMF largely responsible for designing (Bond 1998):

> Though the government supported Zimfarm's expansion efforts, it was IFC's loan—by providing the necessary foreign exchange—that enabled the company to import essential cold storage and refrigeration equipment. Toward the end of 1994, the need to obtain import licenses was removed, and exporters are now allowed to retain foreign exchange earnings.
>
> Another crucial element in IFC's first investment was the provision of financing at terms and maturities unavailable in Zimbabwe. Controls on interest rates, which had kept nominal rates low, were relaxed starting in 1991. The government's tight monetary policy—part of its structural adjustment program—led to a sharp increase in commercial bank lending rates, with the result that real interest rates were driven to very high levels.
>
> In addition to providing needed financing, IFC's subsequent equity investment played an important role in the success of the company's private placement. This initial placement helped transform Zimfarm from a family-owned and -managed business to a transparent and publicly held company that is accountable to outside shareholders.

In the period it reviews, the IFC notes that the operation profitability of the company increased dramatically from 1993 to 1998, with profits going from 1 percent to 7 percent of fiscal turnover. Zimfarm also enjoyed a number of tax breaks, given that some of its facilities were in export-processing zones and other areas that enjoyed reduced taxation. By 1998, Zimfarm controlled about 45 percent of the formal market distribution of fruits and vegetables in Zimbabwe, while the exports, predominantly to the EU, went from 22 percent to 40 percent of its total sales between 1994 and 1998.

As the agency that promotes private sector investment in developing countries in the World Bank group, the IFC has a broad development mandate that requires it to document its development impacts. In terms of its investment in Zimfarm, its report (IFC 1999) observes that Zimfarm's number of employees went from 503 in its two branches in 1993 to more than 2,760 employed in its five branches, two farms, and two joint ventures in mid-1998. Of those, 1,560 were classified as farm workers employed mostly on a contract basis compared to the 250 salaried staff members, most of whom were permanent. The report (IFC 1999, 50) did claim, however, that "[c]ontract workers who have remained in continuous employment with the company for more than one year are granted permanent status"; a claim, as will be clear in the following chapters, that did not necessarily hold true for Upfumi.

The report also discusses a number of benefits Zimfarm offered to salaried workers. For farm workers and other contract workers, it lists AIDS education, occupational health and safety standards, improved housing stock, transportation, a rent subsidy, and the distribution of annual salary increases before the annual collective bargaining agreements on the national level. Given these development impacts on the labor front, the report positively claims (1999, 51), "This, along with the benefits described below, may explain why there have been no work stoppages at Zimfarm."

As with much of World Bank literature, even according to an evaluation of its economic research that it had commissioned (Bannerjee, Deaton, Lustig, and Rogoff 2006), this report tends toward "proselytization and not taking a balanced view of the evidence." The very first day that Zimfarm bought Upfumi there was a work stoppage—the first of many labor actions at that farm during the next eighteen months. This labor action greeting Zimfarm's acquisition of the farm may have been another reason why Zimfarm's then human relations manager, Mr. Nyikayapera, had encouraged the learning of labor law among supervisors, the workers' committee, and the workers. Yet, as with many Zimbabweans at that time, the learning of rights went in many directions on Upfumi and other commercial farms as the wider movement for democracy and the donor-funded support for good governance became entangled in the mode of belonging of domestic government and varied social projects of different farm workers, farmers, and other interested parties. Into this ground of racialized and gendered hierarchies of commercial farm livelihoods and the growing resonance of rights entered some of the networks and power, or simba, of electoral politics.

CHAPTER 2

THE TRACTION OF RIGHTS, THE ART OF POLITICS: THE LABOR "WAR" AT UPFUMI

October 27, 1999
Downtown Harare
Office of the International Socialists Organization (ISO) of Zimbabwe

"*PASI NAMUGABE!*" ("DOWN with Mugabe!"). The loud words hung in the air, silencing the murmurs and whispering that had been growing in the packed office; a room that had been heating up in temperature and in temperament. Crowded around me, a few of the fired Upfumi workers audibly drew in their breaths. Many looked furtively around, checking the reactions of others and, more importantly, to see if there were any strangers in the room. A General Agriculture and Plantation Workers' Union of Zimbabwe (GAPWUZ) official seated next to me laughed nervously. And Chenjerai, the person who cried out the slogan, while bringing his right arm down, fist clenched, then asked Munyaradzi Gwisai about the different consequences for whatever legal options they pursued next.

Gwisai, who has had an occasional presence on the national scale in Zimbabwe since the late 1980s, initially made his mark while a University of Zimbabwe student leader involved in the protests against an attempt by ZANU (PF) to institute one-party rule. In the latter half of the 1990s, while a University of Zimbabwe faculty of law lecturer, he was in the media as an activist and sometime spokesperson for ISO when they were involved in workers' disputes and protests against economic inequality and political repression (e.g., Gwisai 2000). As part of a loose coalition organizing for the Movement for Democratic Change (MDC), which many initially took to be a workers' party, he successfully ran as their candidate in the June 2000 parliamentary election for the Harare constituency of Highfield.[1] Gwisai was also a lawyer for the Zimbabwe Labour Centre (ZLC), a small nongovernmental organization (NGO) he formed that did legal work for GAPWUZ and other trade unions. It was through this affiliation that he had been providing legal representation to the fired Upfumi workers.

Gwisai had just returned from the Labor Tribunal, the highest arbitrator of labor disputes in Zimbabwe, and was explaining to the fired Upfumi workers why their case was postponed and why the judge was encouraging the workers and Zimfarm to settle the dispute themselves. Nearly two hundred former Upfumi workers, from the *musososo* (temporary farm worker camp), neighbouring plots, Harare townships, and elsewhere, initially gathered at a downtown park before 8:00 a.m. They had expected to make their way to the tribunal, but before they did one of the ISO comrades diverted them to the ISO office. They were not expecting this news from Gwisai, and many were becoming disgruntled by their lawyer's explanations when Chenjerai made his pronouncement that momentarily shocked the room into silence.

"*Pasi na,*" chiShona for "down with," is the second half of the call-and-response couplet that ZANU (PF) had monopolized in its political mobilization since 1980.[2] Chenjerai and the others had been using this couplet at the Upfumi rallies, signaling that their struggle was entangled in party politics. But he had never used this slogan to publicly declare "*Pasi naMugabe.*" This was a public condemnation that was still quite rare in Zimbabwe at that time—at least on the farms in Mashonaland East province.

On this morning it elicited silence, nervousness and some fear among the assembled workers. The resulting silence, the lack of the conventional "*Pasi navo!*" signaled the uncertainty among the assembled about potential repercussions from the Central Intelligence Organization (CIO) (the state security agents) or ZANU (PF) activists who may have been present or could hear about it later. Before 1999, particularly during the time of the *gukurahundi*, such a public condemnation of Robert Mugabe could have led to violent repercussions and by 2002 such a statement could have led—and has for some—to criminal prosecution.[3] That no harm came to Chenjerai for making such a public statement, let alone his daring to make it, signifies that 1999 was a time when political change, democracy, and rights seemed possible in Zimbabwe. "Pasi naMugabe" in that context signaled the support for this wider struggle. It also demonstrates how Chenjerai asserted himself as someone brave or reckless enough to make such a statement; a bravery or recklessness that was buttressed by being involved in *poritikisi* (party politics) himself. The excitement of political change combined with the wider push for democracy and rights on the national scale intermeshed with the labor struggle on Upfumi largely through Chenjerai's efforts. But this entanglement was very much shaped by the specific social environment of Upfumi itself.

Like many forms of social mobilization, the struggle on Upfumi was the object of conscious attempts at bringing people together for change. In this case, the executive of the workers' committee of the fired workers, particularly the vice-chairman Chenjerai, had an explicit agenda, a pedagogical project, in mind. Chenjerai aimed to shape the actions of other farm workers in the name of mobilizing them to demand their labor rights. He drew on a variety of techniques and, especially, extra-local networks and ties to achieve his goal. The key source of these extra-local ties lay in poritikisi.

There have been a number of careful studies of democracy in Zimbabwe, historicizing its development, contests, barriers, and challenges (e.g., Moyo 1992; Ranger and Bhebhe 2001; Sachinkonye 2011, 2012). There have also been a wide range of NGO reports, particularly since 2000, on the ZANU (PF) regime's attacks on democracy, which have been published by international and national human rights NGOs, such as Amnesty International, International Crisis Group, Human Rights Watch, Zimbabwe Human Rights Forum, International Bar Association, and so forth. For this period, there have also been astute analyses produced that have provided substantial insight into the national-scale economic conditions and political stakes that led to the militarized responses by the ZANU (PF) regime and the expanding economic and political crisis in the country (e.g., Bond and Manyana 2002; Raftopoulos 2001, 2003, 2006; Dorman 2003; Moore 2004; LeBas 2011). But these analyses of national-scale processes tend to assume politics operates in the same manner throughout the nation, untouched by differing, and at times competing, territorialized projects; let alone how it can be intertwined with territorializing projects of various, potentially competing, scales. That is, there is not always a focus on how the practice of politics articulates with other projects that may be geared toward asserting control over territories and the people who live on them at more localized scales.

A similar analysis can be made about the thrust of the projects of these commentators and analysts as well, since most of these studies are self-consciously political, seeking to engage in the political processes within or about Zimbabwe. Indeed, critical social scientists, or those of us who characterize ourselves as such, often imagine contributing to progressive change, or at least aspire to it, and often deploy politics as an analytic and ethical form for doing so. Yet, it is also important to recognize how such alignments and imaginations, including those of the social scientists, are situated through "friction" (Tsing 2005) and "entanglements" (Moore 2005) in particular locations, with inherited and changing institutionalized forms of representation, interpellation, and intersecting social projects that do not necessarily mesh easily or in a straight-forward manner with those about whom one is writing.

As a number of scholars have shown, examining "political imagination" is a productive way of analysing how politics is a species of cultural assumptions, social practices, and historical circumstances (Comaroff and Comaroff 1999). Yet there seems to be little sustained ethnographic examination of the power-laced receptions of politics *qua* party politics in particular places and for particular represented communities, like farm workers, including: the assumptions that politics invoke; how politics differentially interpellates people in particular ways; the power dynamics involved; their intersection with other social practices and agendas; and the resulting struggles and forms of contestations, inclusions, and exclusions. How does politics involve national level institutions and considerations in varied locales, constituting or unsettling spatial boundaries and differentiated senses of belonging and routes of social agency, as well as contributing to configurations and capillaries of power associated with the state and/or society? In other words, what are the cultural politics of politics?

It is important to recognize how politics as a discourse configures audiences and public responses in particular and potentially limiting, if not visceral, ways. For the mobilizing and immobilizing effects of politics depends on how particular publics and dispositions are interpellated by these activities; forms of interpellation that need to be analytically understood, and not assumed—for audiences only become so "through the circulation of discourse as people hear, see, or read it and then engage it in some sort of way" (Briggs 2004, 177). The reception depends on how people are grounded in particular places with specific subject positions—what I am calling a mode of belonging—and the dynamics of the specific struggles or social projects. The narratives of "politics of liberation" and "politics as oppression" resonate with many observers within and of Zimbabwe. But both of these narratives are also deployed within specific instances of electoral politics, resulting in varied consequences as they become articulated with specific places and projects, such as those who were part of the Upfumi struggle.

My analysis of the cultural politics of electoral politics views them as scale-making projects (Tsing 2005). These projects traffic in signs of routinized and novel represented communities, intersecting with the political economy of place and the social and cultural dynamics of those implicated as their bearers or their targets at particular historical conjunctures. As in all political imaginations, party politics are engaged with constituting scales, of locating actions at the scale of particular locales, be they the nation, municipality, the globe or a combination of them (Tsing 2005, 58–60; see also Moore 2005). Party politics also are vehicles of represented communities (as noted in the introduction), "'communities' renewed in their existence not only by representations in the semiotic sense, but also by representations in the political, institutional sense" (Kelly and Kaplan 2001, 22), via deployment of preexisting communities, helping them to take form in people's lives and understandings, or by seeking to forge new ones. Such actions take—or fail to take—traction and are entangled differently in particular places, depending on the wider political economy, varied social projects, and forms of mobilization and immobilization operating in such locations. In short, party politics are part of the social landscape of the state and its constituted subjects. Its resonance depends on the particular receptions and interpellations of the discursively constituted semantic domain of politics, with its possible visceral social memories, and their articulations with localized or wider-scale social projects, meaningful practices, and struggles at that historical moment (see Moore 2005).

My ethnographic examination of the intersection of party politics with the Upfumi labor struggle focuses on how poritikisi informs a particular political imagination that motivated struggles and social mobilization, as well as immobilization, on Upfumi and surrounding commercial farms. It examines what it meant to align politically on the farms. What actions, in other words, did politics enable and disable for different Upfumi farm workers from 1999 to 2003? Critical social scientists and humanities scholars may see politics everywhere in the constitution of social life, but others can reserve the term for very particular sets of actions with very different expectations and responses toward it. By focusing on the translation of "politics" for these farm workers in the late 1990s, I suggest one gains a rich understanding of this important dimension of their mobilization and how it connected with wider events and actions on a national scale.

This chapter begins a fuller examination of the traction of rights. In this case, labor rights on Upfumi up to the end of 1999 was part and parcel of the wider push for democratization in Zimbabwe; a push more broadly and a traction more particularly intertwined with poritikisi. I give a more sanguine view of electoral politics in this chapter, trying to capture my own optimism at the time. Like many other Zimbabweans, and observers of this southern African country, by 1999 I was starting to think that party politics held great promise in terms of challenging entrenched class interests on Upfumi and, by extension, the inequalities promoted and relied upon by the ZANU (PF) regime. By the late 1990s, ZANU (PF) increasingly appeared to many, including many farm workers, to be a ruling regime that enabled and profited from national and regional configurations of social and economic inequalities; a viewpoint articulated by a growing number of Zimbabweans in country-wide protests, strikes, and emergent civic movements that had been mobilizing increasingly around labor, constitutional, and livelihood issues as the 1990s progressed (Raftopoulos and Sachikonye 2001; Bond and Manyanya 2002).

This national-scale ferment of democratic demands for better livelihoods intersected with the unfolding labor struggle at Upfumi in 1999; as its leaders were widely perceived to be connected to the mobilization of the MDC (the opposition party launched in September of that year), Zimfarm appeared to be getting support of some of the key ZANU (PF) leaders in the district, including Mr. Livingstone Manhombo the then member of parliament. I did recognize then that it was not completely clear-cut, and that the sides of the struggle did not neatly correspond with the emerging electoral contest, especially since Councillor Banda was a key supporter of the fired workers and yet was within ZANU (PF). But "workers" was an ardent and powerful cry and electoral politics definitely brought a source of *simba* (power), which seemed necessary in order for the farm workers to try to amend arrangements within their mode of belonging.

The "art of poritikisi," however, also had a more violent side, which became more obvious in 2000 to many observers including myself. The violent aspect of this source of simba and the fear of it were never far from the assumptions of many of the farm workers involved in the struggle, as exemplified by the silence that greeted Chenjerai's *"Pasi naMugabe!"* that warm October morning in the ISO office in downtown Harare.

The Discontent of Labor

To reach this point in 1999, let me start with the recollections of workers concerning how the change of ownership of Upfumi shaped their sense of the possible. Precious, the secretary of the workers' committee of the fired Upfumi farm workers, recalled in late 1999 how they greeted their new owners: "We heard on February 16, 1997, that Mr. Botha was selling Upfumi and the new company [Zimfarm] was taking it over the next day. So we talked amongst ourselves that since no one had formally told us, we decided not to go to work on February 17 until someone formally told us what was happening. Perhaps Mr. Botha was trying to avoid paying money owed to us workers for leave, holidays, etc. Zimfarm came and [seeing that none of us were working] learned they had to speak to us."

According to a few of the workers, Mr. Botha, the previous owner of Upfumi who was initially kept on by Zimfarm, addressed the protesting workers and assuaged any concerns they had about the new owners and they returned to work. The protest signaled a tendency toward militancy on the part of Upfumi workers, in advance of Zimfarm's purchase of the farm.

Shortly after Zimfarm bought the farm on February 17, 1997, and, perhaps in response to this labor action that greeted the new owners, a new workers' committee was established. As many recalled, company officials told workers that this should improve communication channels and minimizing the kinds of miscommunication that had occurred when Zimfarm bought the farm. But such assumptions ran aground on the mode of belonging of domestic government and a social project of mobilization interlaced with poritikisi.

On May 15, 1997, Mr. Nzou, the senior labor relations officer for the Department of Labor, Marondera (the capital of Mashonaland East province), arrived at the farm to allow the workers to elect a new workers' committee. He went to each of the farm's departments—fields, irrigation, spraying, and pack-shed—to elect representatives to the committee. According to several of the workers, Mr. Nzou told them that the executive should come from the pack-shed since they have much easier access to the phones than the fieldworkers in case they needed to communicate with senior management at the farm and in the Harare offices. The workers selected Moses as chairman, Tapedza as vice-chairman, and Precious as secretary. All three were relatively well-educated, finishing at least form 3, if not their O levels, and held supervisory jobs. Tapedza was a receiving clerk, Moses was the senior clerk of the pack-shed, and Precious was a checker of the graded vegetables. The workers said that Zimfarm brought Labor Officer Nzou to conduct the elections, rather than merely appointing workers' committees as it had been "done under Boss Botha."

However, there were continuities between the ownership regimes. Moses had been a member of the previous workers' committee under Mr. Botha and workers told me in 1999 that they had elected him, since Moses had a close relationship with Botha, whom Zimfarm had kept on in a management role. Keeping Moses on the committee, these workers reasoned, helped to ensure that they could maintain those ties of dependency to the new company; others, in light of the labor dispute unfolding in 1999, were dismissive of Moses in their recollections, seeing him "as a tool of management."

The workers associated this Zimfarm policy of having workers elect their own committee to the motivation of the then Group Human Resources manager for Zimfarm based in Harare, Mr. Nyikayapera. In my interviews with the fired workers in 1999, Mr. Nyikayapera came across as someone who wanted proper labor relations. He opened up a canteen on the farm similar to that found in Zimfarm's packaging operations in Harare. He ensured the field workers received protective clothing. Chenjerai observed that when Nyikayapera asked for some water in the field, he was told that he had to get it from the irrigation pipe, proving that the drinking water for fieldworkers came directly from the dam "contaminated with pesticides and other chemicals" that was used on the fields. In response, a few other workers informed me, Nyikayapera "was so furious" that he ordered water bowsers (water tanks) to be brought to the field containing clean drinking water. He also ensured fieldworkers got *maheu* (a nonalcoholic drink made from maize), like the pack-shed workers received, when he realized the former were discriminated against. He organized training sessions for supervisors and the workers' committee in labor relations, saying that this should make his job easier. He supported the workers' committee organizing lessons to educate the workers about labor relations and their rights. As Chenjerai succinctly stated, "He treated us with dignity, as partners in the productive enterprise."

However, this did not mean labor peace emerged. Rather, the farm workers said that they became emboldened to start demanding their rights. "If Tsvangirai and the workers in the cities can do stay-aways and protests for their rights, we can do the same here," Jane stated matter-of-factly, referring to the largely urban protests that increasingly took place starting in the mid-1990s. I will briefly illustrate the labor strife on Upfumi after Zimfarm purchased it.

There were at least three work stoppages after February 1997 and before the major labor strife in October 1998. In talking with me, workers portrayed the first strike as an illustration of their growing recognition of their rights as workers. Shortly after acquiring the farm, the Zimfarm management at Upfumi had a meeting informing the workers that they were now going to use a piecework system (*mugwazo*) in the pack-shed, paying them per kilogram of vegetables packed, the price depending on the type of produce. This ranged, for example, from Z26¢ per kilogram for runner beans, which are easy to work with, to Z82¢ per kilogram for mange-tout, which need their tops and tails clipped off. Previously, workers in the pack-shed did not use a mugwazo system and were paid per order, working about eight and a half hours per day unless there was a large order, and, in those cases, they received time off in lieu of extra wages. Although a bit wary of the new "kg [kilogram] system," the workers initially complied with it. The system appeared to be transparent, since the recorders who noted the kilograms each day would feed the information into computers that printed out the information, documenting how much each person had packed that day. Yet, on the October payday in 1997, these workers told me in 1999, that many of the women workers in the pack-shed received less than expected, based on the information on the printouts. They even received less than the minimum wage. At one of the lunch breaks following the payday, the pack-shed workers refused to take lunch and demanded to speak to management about their concern over the disparity of pay. Instead, the management workers decided to take their lunch and leave the workers inside. Tapedza recalled that the workers declared: "'Fine, we will take our lunch too but won't return to work.' Instead we stood outside the pack-shed demanding to talk to Nyikayapera."

The pack-shed manager for Zimfarm at that time phoned Nyikayapera and arranged for him to come from Harare the next day. The pack-shed workers went home and came the next morning for their meeting with

Nyikayapera. After hearing their grievances, he scrapped the kilogram system and everyone went back to work. As Chenjerai noted, Nyikayapera was attentive to workers' concerns if they made valid points. Moreover, the personnel assistant at Upfumi who introduced the system was fired shortly afterward and replaced by a man who had been the workers' committee chairman at the Zimfarm processing plant in Harare.

The pack-shed workers went back to working per order. Moreover, they started to be paid overtime in cash if they wished, for this was "our right, according to the regulations," Tapedza declared. This, Precious said, was something that Chenjerai informed workers about. In a positive tone, which matched the optimism of the workers fighting for their rights by September 1999, one of the pack-shed workers remarked, "Working conditions were perfect in the pack-shed by this time since we had selected a strong workers' committee." Indeed, the pushing against the limits of domestic government came from a strong workers' committee, which became particularly emboldened once Chenjerai joined it in 1997 (as discussed below).

The workers characterized labor disputes in June and July 1998 as examples of how workers were becoming more forceful, by proactively supporting their representatives who had been increasingly harassed once Nyikayapera left the company near the end of 1997. In August 1999, for instance, shortly after I met him, Chenjerai dug out the minutes of a December 31, 1997, Upfumi meeting between management, the workers' committee and field supervisors. Rummaging through a pile of documents he had sent a young woman to retrieve from his place at the musososo, Chenjerai pulled the minutes from a manila envelope. In the document, management admitted that recent industrial action had occurred because some supervisors saw the workers' committee as a threat, so they had influenced a worker to make a false report to the police; a report, Chenjerai added, that led him to being arrested for a brief period.

According to Chenjerai and other workers involved in the labor struggle, the situation became worse when Mr. Brown arrived as a new farm manager in July 1998. The workers alleged he did not like the fact that the workers' committee had been educating and mobilizing workers and, they claimed, he tried to undermine it. For them, Brown was your "typical farming *murungu*" (white person). He embodied the racialized sense and sensibilities of the mode of belonging of domestic government through which workers had limited, or no, claims in shaping labor relations. Their claims to the farm were contingent on the wishes of management. His attempt to reassert management prerogatives over labor relations, combined with a human relations officer who supported him and a simmering dispute over Zimfarm's proposed contract, eventually led to the major labor dispute, the war (labor dispute) that ultimately lasted twenty months. For the workers I was talking with in late 1999, this labor action spoke to what they saw as the main reasons for the October labor strife that followed three months later.

In July 1998, the workers went on strike again to protest attempts by the company to force those on eight-month contracts to sign three-month contracts. The company and the workers' committee called in outside mediators—namely representatives from the National Employment Council for the agricultural industry (NEC), GAPWUZ and Mr. Nzou, the senior labor relations officer. Some sort of resolution seemed to have been agreed to until, the workers' narrative went, management attempted to bolster their ability to impose their wishes, regardless of the workers' interests, let alone "our rights." From the evidence of the workers, one could say that management wished to reassert the dominant mode of belonging, domestic government, by conspiring with compliant outsider officials.

After the GAPWUZ officials and Mr. Nzou left the farm in July 1998, assuming a deal was reached, the NEC representative remained. The fired workers informed me in 1999 that, in coordination with Mr. Schultz, the production manager at Upfumi, this NEC official tried to force them to sign three-month contracts. As recounted by Hope, a former healthcare worker who was staying at the musososo in the latter half of 1999, "We were told to sign the three-month forms and the murungu [Schultz] said 'If you do not sign, you will be fired.'" Yet the workers continued to refuse and remained on strike. For, as Hope plainly put it, "the workers' committee knew the law and was working with the labor officer to say if you worked for more than eight months you became a permanent worker. The workers knew they had the law behind them." Soon after, Mr. Nzou returned and, according to the workers, when he realized what had happened he said they should remain on their eight-month contracts. Nzou said that their contracts could not be annulled that way. The company "reluctantly agreed," in Hope's words, and the workers returned to work. It became clear that the workers had allies in their growing demands for rights; at least intermittent ones like Nzou and GAPWUZ.

Yet Chenjerai and others said that the company was unhappy with this intervention not only because of the result, but also because management wanted the workers to abide by the same company code of conduct in effect at their commercial plants in Harare since early 1997 and certified by the Department of Labor in March 1998. The man who signed it, Mr. Choto, as chairman of the workers' committee of Zimfarm's Harare plants, was the same person who was promoted to human relations officer for Upfumi farm later in 1997. The company code sought to minimize outside intervention by government labor officials. In contrast, the Upfumi workers' committee wanted to abide by the industry-wide collective bargaining agreement for the agricultural industry. They said that the company code of conduct allowed for long suspensions and, moreover, they had no role in drafting it; if they abided by the company code, then the labor relations officers and the NEC officials would have no role to play in labor disputes. By mid-July 1998, management and the workers' committee had failed to come to an agreement on this issue.

The account of this labor action raises three issues that are very pertinent for understanding the extended labor war that soon broke out at Upfumi. First, management was keen on signing people for three-month contracts, rather than the previous norm on the farm of eight-month contracts. The workers not only wanted the greater security of the eight-month contracts, but they also argued that the Labor Relations Act declared them permanent workers once they worked continuously for more than eight months, regardless of any additional contract they sign. As Chenjerai informed me, "The signing of the three-month contracts which Zimfarm wanted is the point on which the argument began. The company used to do eight-month contracts, asking workers to re-sign them after eight months. But we argued that workers who re-signed an eight-month contract, immediately after finishing the last one, are permanent workers." By keeping them as seasonal workers, there would be no legal requirement for the company to provide certain benefits (e.g., maternity leave, vacation, etc.) to the majority of their workers. This lack of benefits stood in stark contrast to the additional benefits the company provided to their managers, the few permanent staff Zimfarm employs, who, according to the World Bank report (IFC 1999), gained much from their company (as discussed in chapter 1).

Secondly, the NEC official who was supporting management's attempt to impose three-month contracts was none other than Mr. Chapunga. Once Mr. Choto, the man who had been the human relations manager at the time, passed away in August 1998, Zimfarm East hired Mr. Chapunga. This followed a common practice in Zimbabwe of hiring labor officials away from the government, Agricultural Labor Bureau (ALB), or even GAPWUZ. Workers assumed Chapunga was hired, in part, to subdue the workers' committee. It is unclear how far astray from domestic government and toward a more bureaucratically administered labor relations machinery Nyikayapera and others were taking Upfumi. Nonetheless, for the workers who spoke with me, it was clear that in 1998 the new managers were trying to reassert the more familiar hierarchical mode of belonging on the farm, which the workers' committee objected. This is the final relevant issue. The workers' committee was strong. It was not only occupied with educating workers about rights, sitting with management to discuss labor issues (and retaining copies of minutes), but also connected to outside authorities (e.g., working with the labor officer) to help them in their pedagogical project. Such activities, let alone a somewhat functioning workers' committee, were quite rare on commercial farms in the 1990s (Rutherford 2001b, Tandon 2001). This Upfumi workers' committee was somewhat exceptional. The key ingredient to its success, its ability to give some social traction to its project of supporting workers' rights, was in large part due to the involvement of Chenjerai with electoral politics, who himself also had a particular pedagogical project in relation to farm workers.

Pedagogical Projects in a Time of Political Ferment

The 1998 Upfumi workers' committee was quite exceptional compared to others I had encountered, let alone heard about, on more than twenty commercial farms in the Mashonaland provinces. The desire to better understand this phenomenon led me to research how it emerged and what differentiated it from the previous ones on Upfumi. I became especially interested in the actions of its executive, particularly its vice chairman, Mr. Chenjerai, who articulated a very explicit project of educating and conscientizing farm workers. His words and deeds appealed to my sympathies toward changing the situation of farm workers through actions of farm workers themselves while, more importantly, strongly resonating with the wider mobilization in the name of rights and workers unfolding on the national scale at that time. I will briefly describe the characteristics of the three leaders of this workers' committee, before analysing Chenjerai in more detail. I will also examine his particular pedagogical project and his ability to draw on wider networks, including those that were linked to poritikisi.

Every worker to whom I spoke agreed that the workers' committee was strong in 1997 and 1998. Even when divisions among the fired workers expanded by the end of 1999, including those who had visceral disagreements with members of the executive—particularly Chenjerai—they all concurred that it had been a strong committee. This was expressed by saying it had simba. In mid-1999, everyone underscored that they finally had an effective workers' committee, one that "was chosen by us." When I asked them how they decided for whom to vote as their representatives, they said that the candidates must be good speakers, willing to listen to workers, to tell management the truth, and, especially, "not to be afraid." The latter trait was crucial. As Ambuya Grace, one of the older women living in the musososo from 1999 to May 2000, summed up the traits of this committee: "If we sent other people to management, those workers would be afraid or simply agree with management on every point. But these ones, they are not afraid. If management does something wrong or if workers do something wrong, this committee will tell you. They are not scared."

Tapedza and Precious were on the first workers' committee elected under Mr. Nzou's supervision in May 1997. They were selected, many told me, because they were educated and respected other workers. Precious stood out, in part, for being a woman in the executive position. Even though the workforce was predominantly female, both men and women workers suggested that women were "too timid" and "too scared" to take a leadership position and be subject to the demands of being on the committee. Moreover, they reasoned they would have a hard time gaining the respect of other workers and management. Diana, Tapedza's wife, explained, "If we women want to make a protest we tell the workers' committee, who are men who will then lead, and the women will follow singing and chanting and telling the men what they want and let them go and fight. Women and men work together. There are more men than women on the committee because they have more power than women—power to talk and to fight. Although men have this power and strength, at times they still cannot do anything."

As will be noted, timidity was not necessarily a trait of all of the women farm workers. The issue of respect was key, however, since both management and the workers tended to view younger women, particularly single mothers, as sexualized beings—not as leaders. This was not always the case, as in the situation with Precious. She was there, a few suggested, because she was a businesswoman; she knew a lot of people, having travelled to many Zimbabwean cities, and having dealt with the Upfumi workforce and those on surrounding farms, as a salesperson. She also was successful in her business pursuits. When combined with money from her boyfriends, some workers privately suggested to me that she was making close to Z$5000.00[4] or more per month in 1998; five times more than the minimum wage for most farm workers at that time. Once she became a member of the workers' committee, she gained even more respect and power. One woman recalled that, "When Precious told you something to do in the grading shed, you better do it, as, otherwise, she could cause problems for you through the workers' committee."

Tapedza was initially elected vice chairman in May 1997. He called himself a "soft leader" and tried to facilitate participation by others. He rarely became angry or harsh with others, which, he commented, always marked him as an "unusual leader." He noted that he was elected prefect when he was doing Forms I to III and was deputy head boy at his government secondary school in Form IV; others thought he should have been head boy, since he had been given an award for being one of the best prefects. But, as Tapedza recalled, the headmaster of the school said "Tapedza was too soft to be head boy." This association of public intensity and masculine leadership, of being able to command respect through one's ability to wield words and possibly intimidation, as will be clear further on, is widely held by Zimbabweans.

Even after Chenjerai joined the workers' committee, most workers continued to be sceptical of it. Tapedza explained plainly that, "They were accustomed to the [passive] attitude of the previous workers' committee." Everyone agreed, however, that once they saw the committee start to help workers the perception of many at the farm began to change.

The change in attitude toward the workers' committee, as it became more effective in assisting the farm workers, occurred when more workers expressed dissatisfaction with Moses as chair, which eventually prompted Mr. Nzou to come out to supervise another election. The membership remained more or less the same, save that Tapedza was now chairman and Chenjerai became vice-chairman. This dissatisfaction with Moses was fanned by Chenjerai himself, and, once he took an executive position, the workers' committee became stronger through its linkages to external groups. Chenjerai definitely was not a soft leader.

During the labor struggle, Chenjerai liked to present himself to others as someone who came to farm work with a project in mind: the project of educating farm workers of their rights. He thought of himself as having a mission, typified by the story he told about how and why he ended up working at Upfumi. He had been working in the small town of Ruwa, east of Harare and west of Berkshire, and had a friend who was working at Up-fumi. Often over beers, they would talk about working conditions on the farm, and Chenjerai would despair at his friend's inability, or anyone else's, to improve their conditions. Later, when Chenjerai was looking for work, his friend challenged him to get hired at Upfumi to see if he could make a difference. As he put it, "I accepted the challenge." In June 1997, he was hired to work in the irrigation department at Upfumi. He told me in August 1999 that even though he had not foreseen himself being a farm worker for a long time, but given the war he was leading by then, "I cannot leave farm work now."

Leading is the appropriate verb here, for everyone acknowledged Chenjerai as the main person who gave strength, simba to the workers' committee. Tapedza even would say he learned the rules about labor relations from Chenjerai: "He taught me to read documents before signing, whereas in the past I would just sign them. He taught me about overtime payment. Chenjerai gave me books on the Labor Act, the ALB, and how to handle the disciplinary hearing. I did not get this information from GAPWUZ." In terms of why he was only vice chairman and not chairman, Chenjerai would reply that Tapedza had received more respect from farm workers than himself since he had grown up on farms and was a Christian, whereas, "I am a stranger and some people don't like me."

Chenjerai said that, shortly after he was hired, he convinced a representative from irrigation to resign from the workers' committee so he could replace him. Then he and others started advocating for change. At that time, the disciplinary committee was comprised solely of management workers. When management then dismissed a woman worker, he contacted Justice Watchi, the GAPWUZ representative in Marondera (the capital of Mashonaland East province), whom he knew from when he had been living there. Justice wrote to management to demand a proper hearing. Management acquiesced, set up a disciplinary committee with equal worker and management representatives, and, with Chenjerai acting as the woman worker's advocate, her firing was revoked. Instead, she was given a written warning. He had shown his knowledge of the rules and his ability to access extra-local networks. So when he started to face resistance from Moses, the chairman

of the committee who was feeling undermined by Chenjerai's rising domi-
nance, he was able to engineer a wider vote of no confidence in Moses and to
get Mr. Nzou, whom he also knew from his days in Marondera, to return and
supervise a vote for establishing another workers' committee. It was then
obvious that Chenjerai would replace Moses on the executive, because farm
workers said that he had simba and would clearly use it for "us workers."

Chenjerai brought with him experience in labor organizing, which,
in my experience, at least, was relatively rare for farm workers. Earlier in
the 1990s he had worked at the Cold Storage Commission (CSC) in Marondera where he had helped to organize a strike—a strike that eventually
led to his dismissal. The Marondera-based senior labor relations officer, Mr.
Nzou, knew Chenjerai when he was at CSC and recalled, "He is quite armed
with organizational ammunition and eloquent speaking. This young man
grew up in labor issues and knows the labor law." This sentiment was also
expressed by Carl, the then coowner of the plot near Upfumi, who told me
in November 1999, "Chenjerai is a big brother to the workers. He knows the
law and tells them their rights. There are some workers who say Chenjerai
spoiled things as 'we had been working nicely' with the murungu. But you
need to tell them that he is trying to make it better for everyone and if they
win their labor war, there will be relief on other neighbouring farms. They
will say 'We now have a chance!'" Chenjerai's project was not simply confined to Upfumi's farm workers but was also directed toward other farm
workers in the Berkshire area, if not, in his more expansive thoughts, in the
national agricultural sector.

After being fired from CSC, Chenjerai went to Ruwa and started making contacts with GAPWUZ and assisting them in organizing on some of
the farms; a task he took up more actively once he began working at Upfumi.
Nonetheless, he recognized that he was a bit of an outsider, someone who
was foreign to life as a farm worker. As an activist who was keen to challenge
the dominant forms of governance on the farms, he recognized that his style
of leadership (drawing on ties to poritikisi) marked him as relatively distinct
among farm workers—although this form of political leadership actually
has a long history in Zimbabwe (Scarnecchia 2006, 2008).

Conventionally, leadership for farm workers in Zimbabwe is equated
with being a *munhu mukuru* (a big person). It is closely wrapped into the fibre
of belonging on the farms and its dominant authority relations. A somewhat
lengthy quotation from Chenjerai, reflecting in 2002 on leadership and farm

workers, is insightful. This excerpt comes from an interview I had with him after the ambivalent ending of the long labor war, concluding with much animosity between the fired workers and their workers' committee and during the uncertain time of *jambanja* (the politicized violence associated with land occupations and evictions). He started by agreeing with Chapunga, the acting group human resources manager of Zimfarm East, who often told him "You are the most militant of them all."

> Yes, I am a militant; a militant who is on the wrong front, among people [farm workers] who will never understand me and who I don't fully understand. Until 1997, I had never eaten anything in my life like these *mandere* [flying insects with hard shells found in trees in November-December], but I began eating them to be part and parcel of them. Until 1997, I had never drank *chikokiyana* [a home-brewed, one-day fermented beer], but I drank this with them. I did all what I could their way. I have taught most of these people something and they have taught me something. I now know what it means to be a farm worker, how to talk to them and how to approach them. The first and foremost thing I have learnt from these people is that farm workers accept all what they are told by their employers; not because they want to, but because they say to themselves, "Who are we to refuse? We are only farm workers and no one can help us." GAPWUZ does not help us. The government tried to help us farm workers but in the end did nothing. Farm workers have a mentality of despising themselves. My own evaluation of farm workers is that they want a confidence booster. I want to educate them but not using seminars held in Jameson Hotels [in Harare] but where farm workers are, here in the farms. Neither GAPWUZ, nor NEC, nor Farm Community Trust [a Zimbabwean NGO that works with farm workers], understand farm workers. . . . ZIMTA [Zimbabwe Teachers' Association] is being led by teachers, CFU [Commercial Farmers' Union] is led by commercial farmers. But it is only domestic workers and farm workers who are being represented by outsiders. Unions like GAPWUZ do not know or understand their constituencies. . . . Farm workers need someone to lead them as they do not know where they are going. Farm workers need someone to help them respect themselves. . . . You know, in the farms the *vanhu vakuru* [literally, big people; leaders] are big and respected because they are witches; big and respected because they are foremen. . . . You need to be a bit fearless to go against them.

In his candor, Chenjerai laid out an explicit pedagogical project of engaging with and changing farm workers—people who he clearly saw as belonging to a different class than himself. In his pedagogical project at Upfumi, Chenjerai drew on extra-local connections and outsiders—his existing and expanding network—to bolster his leadership credentials and to show that he is not another farm worker confined by the dependencies of domestic government. Those workers, in his characterization, do not respect themselves but only follow those they fear such as witches, management workers like foremen, or both. He thus saw most farm workers as people who were of different traditions and economic class than himself, and in need of being educated. For him, the older ones, in particular, were inured to being subservient to the murungu. They were, what some of them called without irony, accustomed to *upenyu hwemabhoyi* (life of boys), of being treated like "boys" in the discriminatory racialized practices and arrangements of commercial farms. From this perspective, farm workers were inscribed within the lineaments of conditional belonging. He viewed them as wary about advocating, or pursuing, their rights; instead they had a "mentality of despising themselves."

Chenjerai's pedagogical methods drew on those being disseminated in GAPWUZ's increasing, donor-supported activities at that time, as well as those with a longer pedigree of performativity of political leadership. He told me that in July 1998, he heard from Watchi, the main GAPWUZ official in Marondera, that the trade union was organizing study circles. Chenjerai then helped to organize a meeting at Karigamombe School for about forty to fifty farm workers from Upfumi and surrounding farms, where GAPWUZ officials came with books about agricultural labor relations on the farms and tried to increase their membership. Chenjerai took those books and arranged meetings with Upfumi workers after work and, on occasion, during work hours in different areas with the support of management.

As Nyasha recalled, this committee was effective and helpful. For example, she explained, Chenjerai and Precious occasionally taught people in the grading shed during work hours about the purpose of contracts. They would explain, for instance, that if workers signed a three-month contract, "it means that you are not a permanent worker." More typically, Chenjerai and Tapedza, she pointed out, would have meetings in the evening in the compound just after work. During these meetings, they "would tell us that 'if you have a problem you have to report to us and GAPWUZ. Do not be afraid to tell us or GAPWUZ since it is an organization that judges whether the management is right or wrong.' Ahh, the workers' committee of Chenjerai was there for challenging management when they have wronged us."

Another woman worker in the struggle, Agatha, had a similar portrayal, telling me in October 1999 that many people would attend those meetings where the executive would "read to us from the code of conduct." She recalled such laws as, "'We should not leave work without telling the management that we are not at work.' Another law was, 'Do not sign the three-month contract after you had worked for a number of months.' We were told that, 'If a person has worked for more than eight months, that person becomes a permanent worker.' At one of the meetings," she continued, "Chenjerai and Tapedza told us that the 'signing of a three-month contract made workers useless, as people who could be fired any time.'"

Other workers told me about how Chenjerai provided information on working conditions. One sprayer noted that Chenjerai educated those who worked on the pesticide spray team: "He taught us that overalls should be washed every week after spraying and to clean our hands with soap after work and before going home. Chenjerai also taught us that as soon as the gumboots or overalls were torn or had a hole we were to request for new ones. We also learned that we were not to work in the spray section without gloves or masks. Chenjerai told us that if the murungu does not buy these things for us then the labor laws said we were not supposed to work." Some women gave the example that Chenjerai told workers at a meeting that they should not bring their own tools, that the company should supply them. Soon afterward, the women refused to bring their hoes to work, and the supervisors told them to go home. The workers' committee contacted Mr. Nyikayapera, who came out and confirmed that it was the duty of the farm to supply farm tools; the women were then paid for the day, and management told them to go home.

This was the key difference that workers noticed between the workers' committee with Chenjerai and the previous ones: it had some success. The workers' committee was active, often effective, and largely helpful to workers. Nyasha gave a few other examples. She noted that when workers changed jobs from a higher-paying position to a lower-paying one—for instance from sealing or weighing where they earned Z$30 per day down to general grading, earning Z$25 per day—"Chenjerai and Tapedza would fight it out with the management so that the person maintained their higher wage, regardless of their being changed to another grade. When workers saw that they [Chenjerai and Tapedza] were able to convince management to keep workers at a higher salary, they started to see them as people who were able to represent them."

Another fired worker, Hope concurred, said with force, "They solved problems, even for me. I was underpaid as the farm health worker and I went to the committee and they forwarded my complaint to the murungu [farm owner; in this case Zimfarm management] and I became better paid." Such testaments of the strength of the new workers' committee were common, especially in 1999 when the struggle seemed to be heading to a successful conclusion and most people involved were still openly supporting the committee and the labor war.

Chenjerai said that Nyikayapera gave the workers' committee a meeting room on Mondays to discuss both potential grievances as well as ways to improve production for the company. Occasionally, they met with farm management and supervisors and kept minutes of those meetings. They would meet with workers about every two weeks in the compound to address any issues people wanted to raise.

The committee also began to access outside organizations that could bring their knowledge of laws and rights to bear on the farm; the term "to bear" is deliberately chosen here, for it was not a neutral act and suggests going beyond the frontiers of the farm or company and drawing on those who operated on the scale of the nation. This workers' committee "soon forged ties with GAPWUZ and the Department of Labor," Hope recalled as we sat down in the musososo in December 1999, as she caught her breath after walking about five kilometers back from the closest health clinic where she had been for a maternity checkup. At that time she was six months pregnant. When officials from these outside groups came, she continued, "It was a problem for management to say, for example, they did not want a workers' committee, as it was a law. The foremen, supervisors, and management as a whole were against the workers' committee. They hated it and oppressed the committee. They made the members work hard and told other workers that this committee cannot help you." Archie, who was whittling wood listening to our conversation, added, "Management did not like this [workers'] committee because they knew if they did anything wrong, they would be judged."

Chenjerai ensured that these outside organizations would come to the farm to listen to, if not act upon, farm workers' grievances. GAPWUZ is a good example. Previously on Upfumi, and in their experience on most other farms where they worked or lived, the fired farm workers said that GAPWUZ was rarely present. They would sell membership cards and then never come to visit. Or, when they did, they never talked to the workers but only to management who, they alleged, would give the union representatives gifts—fruit, meat, money—to keep them quiet. But with a strong workers' committee, they said it not only helped GAPWUZ by representing farm workers in their grievances but it also helped to ensure that GAPWUZ came more often than they did previously to provide assistance to its members. As Patience stressed, "When the workers' committee of Tapedza was elected they started phoning the GAPWUZ office and got them to come out more often. And when they came, they would talk to the workers' committee, which was chosen by the people; they were not simply management people."

Chenjerai had other networks that drew on forms of authority and power that were not focused on (labor) law, but rather came from electoral politics (poritikisi). Before coming to Upfumi, he also had been mobilizing for ZANU (PF) in both Ruwa and Marondera. The ability to forge a connection, to have the simba to pursue and, at times, acquire these external, extra-farm linkages, was greatly facilitated by his involvement in electoral politics. In 1999, he tried to square his long activities within political parties with his declared project of educating farm workers by asserting that his goal, and the goal of the workers in the Upfumi war, was to ensure workers' rights became established and not to help a political party win office. This sentiment came through most eloquently at a rally for their struggle on August 22, 1999, when he was talking to Mr. Manomano, the representative of the Zimbabwe Federation of Trade Unions (ZFTU), the newly created national trade union association supported by ZANU (PF) to try to undermine the strength of the ZCTU. Chenjerai declared that he did not care whether ZFTU was "ZANU or MDC or whatever." He emphasized that Mr. Manomano should not view Upfumi's workers "simply as peasants who want land," as one of the ZANU (PF) narratives had characterized them given the sporadic land occupations during the previous year.

> Mr Manomano, we are not land hungry. We are here for our rights as workers only. Politicians came here. We tend to say "yes" to what they want us to do, for if you say "no" it tends to be a problem. But we know who we are. If the [Labor] Tribunal says "no" to us on October 27, we will accept that. We actually want that decision around sometime yesterday. The rains are coming and our shelter is poor. We have no political interest. We don't need to be heard by everyone. We are just asking for a small democracy. It's being denied to us. The right to represent and talk about our working conditions are being denied to us.

At this time Chenjerai and others were very clear that they were not affiliated with a political party, that their goals were procedural. They only wanted a small democracy, without the need to convince every one of their agenda. Indeed, his success depended on antagonizing those who were satisfied with the previous regime, the dominant form of domestic government. A junior foreman at Upfumi at the time said that in 2001 Chenjerai's committee "was very rude. He did not want the foremen [to have any authority] and caused many to leave their jobs at Upfumi. He also influenced other workers to be rude to us." The workers' committee's success depended on challenging the dominant hierarchies. But to do so, Chenjerai had to ensure he became a *munhu mukuru*, a big person, by drawing on the networks of *poritikisi* and some of the characteristics of their activists, rather than through those authorized under domestic government.

In order to demonstrate that he could assist farm workers with labor grievances, Chenjerai had to earn respect and create dependencies by showing he was connected to outsiders. For connecting to such social forces could assist one's social struggles. For Chenjerai, GAPWUZ and the formal labor relations machinery (such as the labor relations officer and the NEC) formed one such outside source and political parties formed the other. As Diana said, politics is power and provides the strength "to talk and to fight." Although by late 1999 Chenjerai was no longer obviously supporting ZANU (PF), he had already clearly demonstrated his strength through his work in helping to elect Banda the ZANU (PF) councillor in their ward.

Chenjerai had known Banda in Ruwa. Banda had been the youth chair for the ZANU (PF) branch in Ruwa from 1993 to 1998, and they befriended each other through ruling party activities at that time. In turn, Chenjerai said that Banda was someone who could help farm workers, since he himself grew up on a farm. His father was from Malawi and had worked on white farms in Mashonaland East.

Chenjerai assisted both GAPWUZ and Banda, and they, in turn, assisted him. For GAPWUZ, Chenjerai helped to mobilize some farm workers during the September–October 1997 strikes that occurred in Mashonaland East province and other parts of Zimbabwe (as discussed in the introduction). Before this strike, he had visited many farms during his off days to encourage farm workers to put pressure on the farmers. He said that GAPWUZ was doing this behind the scenes, as they did not want to be responsible for organizing an illegal strike. And then, some farm workers jumped the gun. Chenjerai said that the "Hortco guys" in Shamva, referring to farm workers on a large agribusiness farm in Mashonaland Central province, had "disagreements with workers on neighboring farms so they went on strike early to put pressure on them." And then it gathered its own momentum, and "unfortunately some workers got carried away and assaulted people and burned things." Yet the workers at Upfumi did not join the work stoppages because, Chenjerai argued, Nyikayapera had good labor relations and Zimfarm offered a 40 percent salary increase in July 1997, before the collective bargaining was concluded in October, ensuring that no one wanted to join the protest.

Yet the Upfumi workers did play a significant role in the election of Banda. When Chenjerai arrived on Upfumi, there were no existing ZANU (PF) structures. The political roles of Carl, Mai Shingi, and the ZANU (PF) structures based at Oxfordshire had faded from these Berkshire farms long before 1997. Chenjerai said that the Oxfordshire ZANU (PF) leaders asked him to set up a party branch in the winter months of 1997. The workers' committee became the ZANU (PF) branch, as they often did in the early 1980s when ZANU (PF) cadres established cells and trade union structures on many farms (see chapter 1). Many workers told me that this branch did not do much until the following winter months, around August 1998, when Chenjerai started using it to campaign for Banda. It was an electoral contest between two ZANU (PF) candidates; a contest that became quite bitter and whose result rested, in part, on the constituency of farm workers and the work of Chenjerai.

Until 1998, local government elections did not include farm workers. Since they were neither property- nor lease-holders in the commercial farming wards, they had no vote in these elections for almost twenty years after independence. Even after gaining the electoral franchise for these elections in 1997, most farm workers saw these elections as nonevents. In 1998 and 1999, when I asked farm workers on various Mashonaland East farms about their relationship with the Rural District Council (RDC), or whether they ever saw their councillor, most would look at me blankly. If they had a musha or a stand, they may have known the councillor in the communal area or resettlement scheme, but not the councillor representing their place of employment. At best, they would say that during the local government elections in 1998 they had heard of a rally or two but that was the extent of it.

There were only two groups of farm workers whom I met who knew the name of the councillor or even met him (or more rarely, her). There were those who were active in the Farm Community Trust of Zimbabwe

(FCTZ), which established committees and projects; through this involvement had attended various workshops and adult literacy school openings where the councillor was present (see Rutherford 2004). The other group were workers involved in the Upfumi labor dispute.

Both friends and foes of Banda argued that he won the 1998 election mainly because of the Upfumi workers, in general, and Chenjerai, in particular. As Tapedza reflected on Councillor Banda's support for their war against Zimfarm, "Chenjerai was a major campaigner for Banda during the council elections in 1998 and thus Banda cannot do anything against us but needs to help us, for it was Chenjerai's campaigning that won him his seat." Banda was indebted to Chenjerai, since he was the outside ZANU (PF) candidate running against a candidate selected by the Oxfordshire ZANU (PF) structures. Many of those still firmly ensconced in ZANU (PF) positions in 1999 said the reason there were two ZANU (PF) candidates for that ward election was that just before the election ZANU (PF) decided to return Berkshire to Mashonaland East province. From the late 1980s until 1998 it was part of Harare province and fell under Ruwa's administration in terms of party structures. But a decision was made by ZANU (PF) leaders that it better fit Mashonaland East. Banda, based in Ruwa, a town in Harare province, had been preparing to run in the Berkshire area for the upcoming election, until it went to Mashonaland East and its ZANU (PF) structures had by then selected Mr. Chishiri to run in the same ward. The previous white farm owner who had been councillor (and chair of the Goromonzi RDC) before the enfranchisement of farm workers declined to run in the new RDC elections, recognizing, as she told me in an interview in October 1999, that "ZANU [people] had already picked the seats." But it was not quite that straightforward in her old ward.

When Banda decided to run in the ward against Chishiri anyway, even though he had been selected through Harare province, the leaders in the ZANU (PF) structures in Oxfordshire-Berkshire were not pleased. Banda informed me in November 1999 that the national political commissar for ZANU (PF), Moven Mahachi, who at that time was also minister of defense in the Zimbabwean government, had told him he should withdraw, as it was not appropriate to have "ZANU versus ZANU." Banda ignored the advice, recognizing that he had a good chance of winning in the area given the support he was receiving from some groups of farm workers.

Banda began to spend much of his time on farms, seeking to meet with farm workers; although some farmers or farm managers (like Mr. Brown at Upfumi) tried to prevent him from campaigning on their property, even after working hours. Although Banda claimed that, unlike himself, Chishiri was someone who "failed to serve the people" and was uncaring about farm worker issues, the farm workers I talked to on Upfumi did not know much about Chishiri or any differences or similarities between the two candidates. Rather, they knew that Chenjerai, who was leading them in labor issues, was mobilizing for Banda. In turn, Banda appeared to be interested in farm worker issues, whereas Chishiri never appeared at Upfumi. Chenjerai sold membership cards for ZANU (PF) and organized rallies for Banda on Upfumi and neighbouring farms. "If our leader tells us to vote for Banda," said Patience, "we are going to vote for him." In his pedagogical project of promoting rights, Chenjerai was also establishing ties of dependencies with workers.

It also helped that Banda was an outsider, although still within ZANU (PF). Workers said with all the protests and demands for democracy occurring in Harare and other Zimbabwean cities in the late 1990s, that they too wanted to support a candidate who challenged the localized authority-holders, including leaders from the local ZANU (PF) structures. The only barrier to voting was that many did not register for voting, assuming that they would just need to show their national identity card to vote. This did not work, and the voter's roll had not been renewed for some time, so many Upfumi workers failed to vote. Nonetheless, Banda won the election in the ward in October 1998.[5]

The successful election of Banda augmented Chenjerai's reputation as an organizer and a mobilizer, someone with solid connections to translocal authorities and to electoral politics. Moreover, the successful election in October 1998 gave them momentum for what became the most significant labor strife of them all at the end of the month.

The Upfumi War: Unlawful Strike or Unfair Dismissal?

From what the fired workers told me, the main impetus for the labor war was the attempt of the new management of Upfumi to roll back gains their workers' committee had recently made. Before the start of the Upfumi war, the workers' committee, and Chenjerai in particular, expanded their challenge to what they saw as arbitrary powers of management. Chenjerai and the committee moved to bring workers a small democracy that clashed with the management's attempts to keep, if not to gain back, what they took to be their normal decision-making powers and forms of authority. Chenjerai noted how everyday spatial practices that had emerged under Nyikayapera were subverted under Brown.

For example, Nyikayapera had instituted a works council with semi-regular, minuted meetings with the workers' committee held in the boardroom, where there was a fridge containing, among other things, containers of drinking water. When the works council had its first meeting with Brown, Chenjerai told me the farm manager tensed up when Chenjerai stood up and opened the fridge door to get a glass of water. In the next meeting there were no more glasses in the room. Shortly after that Brown converted the boardroom into his own office and held meetings with the workers' committee and disciplinary committee outside.

Brown also increased the demands on workers. For example, Pedzi recalled that Brown would not pay a worker if she did not complete her designated task in the day, and forced the worker to "complete the task the following day to make it a ticket [to be paid for the previous day's work] and then start a new task that day. Also, there was no overtime paid and often no lunch given." Practices of the previous labor regimes (see chapter 1) were reemerging. When combined with Chapunga's apparent hostility toward them being recognized as permanent workers, discontent among workers and the workers' committee increased. Moreover, given the relative past successes of the workers' committee in their labor actions and the immediate success of Chenjerai in helping to engineer Banda's victory in the local government elections, many workers were confident in what they saw as their growing strength. The groundwork for a war was well-prepared. But who actually fired the proverbial first shot on October 29, 1998, became a source of debate with legal ramifications.

In 1999 and 2000, the workers in the labor dispute argued they were set up. The point of contention was the date they received their monthly pay. Ostensibly, it was a small point, but in the heightened stakes and emotions of labor relations on the farm it became the breaking point. The practice, under the previous farm manager, was that they were paid on the twenty-eighth day of the month. In July 1998, Mr. Brown paid them on the thirtieth, in August on the thirty-first, and on the thirtieth in September. They tried to meet about this issue, but management, according to Chenjerai and Tapedza, were not interested in negotiating. In its defense, in October, management noted in one of its reports to the workers' committee that they were obliged to pay within four days after "closing of the time books" (this occurred on the twenty-fifth day of each month), thus admitting they were at fault those previous times. When management failed to pay the workers by the twenty-eighth of the next month, October, the field workers met their supervisors to start the work day at 6:30 a.m., complaining about the lack of pay and their hunger.

The account I heard from the fired workers in the last half of 1999 was that the supervisors said that the workers should bring their complaints to the management block and then provided them with transport there. Management told them to sit outside the building. When the pack-house workers arrived at 8:00 a.m., they, too, declined to work and sat next to the field workers. Management next called in the workers' representatives and informed them that the workforce was engaging in an unconstitutional labor action—a strike that did not go through the various steps of mediation required by legislation. Using the Zimfarm code of conduct as justification, management then took steps to investigate the alleged unconstitutional action, which resulted in the dismissal of all 879 field and pack-house workers.

The workers alleged they were "set up." But management claimed the workers refused to obey a lawful command to start work. And, since they did not provide a fourteen-day notice of the work action, they violated the rules and were held responsible for their actions. This distinction had legal consequences and, as I later discovered, the account workers had given me during the actual labor dispute was misleading. As Chenjerai simply said in July 2002, as we were sitting outside a bottle store, "We went on strike." Until that point, he had reiterated the claim that they had been willing to return to work if management had agreed to talk with them that morning in October 1998. I realized then how I was as much a public audience for their labor dispute as others. During the actual dispute, he and the workers who he represented had to ensure that they presented the claim they were fired to relevant interlocutors in the struggle such as the Labor Tribunal, the media, and myself. This not only required consistency in presentation to the diverse audiences but also when discussed among the workers themselves, which, as elaborated in the next chapter, required various disciplinary interventions. Since the workers insisted they were not on strike, the dispute then followed administrative processes with their particular documentary requirements, which, as I discuss in the next sections, were soon intermingled with the processes of poritikisi. It is the focus of the latter, I shall argue, that enabled these farm workers to continue in their struggle, despite losing the initial administrative decisions.

As recorded in the ZimfarmEast documents as well as in the recollections of workers, the immediate steps taken by the company were breathtaking in their velocity. By 9:55 a.m. on October 29, 1997, the production manager, Mr. Schultz, passed a typed letter to the workers, via the workers' committee, asking them to explain in writing why they refused to work. The deadline for the workers' response was 10:30 a.m., so the farm could resume normal business, including distributing the pay—which had arrived by armed security courier that morning at 9:00 a.m. If no response was forthcoming by that time, the letter warned, Schultz "will be left with no option but to follow the course of action dictated by law." Such an invocation of law disregarded the dispute over which labor relations machinery actually governed Upfumi—those of the Zimfarm in-house agreement or the national collective bargaining agreement.

In response, the workers wrote a letter claiming that the workers "didn't refuse to work. But we cannot work on empty stomachs. We want money." After closing the note by writing "Workers' committee (Peoples' representatives)," the letter apologized for not including a signature, noting they feared personal repercussions if they did so. By 11:00 a.m., Schultz sent another typed letter noting that those who were not back at work were on suspension without pay. And, the letter notified them that the disciplinary hearing will occur in his office at 2:00 p.m., with four people from the workers' committee and four other workers as witnesses.

The minutes of the disciplinary committee meeting show it started at 3:52 p.m. and ended at 6:18 p.m. The minutes suggest that all the workers agreed they had engaged in an "unconstitutional industrial action." Although the minutes note that workers queried why management was not more forthcoming about when they would receive their pay, it declares that the consensus opinion of the disciplinary committee was that the workers were on an unconstitutional industrial action, with the required punishment being dismissal. Management amended the Termination of Contract of Employment Form ("HR10" being its number) to make it applicable to a number of offenders instead of one. The form initially read: "All employees at Upfumi farm and pack-house who were expected at work but refused to work on 29/10/98 at 6:30 a.m. (field) and 8:00 a.m. (pack-house)." On the amended form, instead of the name of each individual worker being listed under "Employee's Name," it had the signature of Precious, on behalf of all the workers, as secretary of the workers' committee. This suggested to management that she accepted the mass termination.

The internal company appeal processes were actuated within a few days. By October 30, the workers' committee appealed the decision to the "stage one" process. Later that day, the acting group human resources manager, Chapunga, ruled in favour of the disciplinary committee's decision. On October 31, the workers' committee lodged a "stage two appeal" and on November 2, the managing director of ZimfarmEast, Mr. Schultz upheld the decision. He dismissed the request from the workers' committee for leniency given previous unconstitutional industrial actions by the workers at Upfumi. He also gave the reason that the majority of the dismissed workers refused the offer of leniency made by Upfumi's management on October 30 "in the form of an offer to enter new contracts of employment."

For the workers involved in the labor strife, it is this very putative offer of leniency that suggested to them that their mass firing was disingenuous. Rather, for them, it was really about rolling back gains in labor relations on the farm. On October 30, Chapunga went around the Upfumi compound offering dismissed workers the chance to continue working at Upfumi. The workers would receive a small retrenchment package of two-weeks' salary in return for signing an agreement saying they have terminated their employment and have assumed a new three-month contract with Zimfarm.

The space of the compound was not under total management control and thus not impervious to counteractions taken by the leaders of the workers. The workers' committee and others circulated in the living spaces of the workers, telling people not to sign, because they would lose what gains had been made. One older woman agreed with them, indignantly recalling the following year that "I had been working on the farm since 1991 so I refused to sign the contract form. Signing the contract form meant that I was going to start working as a contract worker, so I did not want to do so as I had worked there for a long time!" Shortly afterward, management declared that 286 of the 879 workers fired on October 29, 1998, were coerced into joining the unlawful industrial action and thus were not fired.

A further 107 employees were deemed to have never participated in the job action. These numbers refer to many who returned to work, after signing

a three-month contract, as well as some who left work after signing a termination contract and receiving two weeks' retrenchment packages. The latter
group who signed termination contracts, did so on the basis that they were
"seasonal workers" even if they had been working for several years. Some of
these people told me later that they did so because they were afraid of not
being able to find work on other farms in the area. They feared being black-
listed, which Chapunga threatened to do. Among those who the company
said did not participate in job action were workers who remained involved
in the labor struggle at Upfumi, including the three executive members of
the workers' committee, who management later declared were never fired.
This distinction came back to haunt the workers' struggle once a settlement
was achieved a year and a half later. After these weeks of lobbying and pressure, there were 417 workers legally involved in this labor dispute.

The leaders of the fired workers quickly sought to marshal some political support to aid them in their labor dispute. Shortly after the mass firing,
Councillor Banda arranged financing from a ZANU (PF) businessman to
send a delegation to Marondera to seek the assistance of Mr. Nzou in resolv-
ing the issue. Councillor Banda accompanied the executive of the workers'
committee to see Mr. Nzou. Yet, Banda told me in October 1999, Zimfarm
objected to any intervention by the government labor relations machinery.
The company maintained that by submitting to the disciplinary committee
and its appeal structure, the workers had shown to be abiding by the company's code of conduct and, thus, the Department of Labor had no jurisdiction
in the dispute. Moreover, Banda surmised to me that Zimfarm saw Nzou as
biased against them. The lawyers for Zimfarm, from the prestigious Harare
firm Atherstone & Cook, legally blocked involvement of the labor department bureaucrats.

Instead, the next appeal was to the Labor Tribunal; a court, according
to Chenjerai and others, which at that point had a backlog of more than
two years. To the workers, it seemed that management were assuming they
could easily outwait the workers, expecting that the lack of jobs or income
would drive them to abandon the case. In the meantime, Zimfarm had hired
hundreds of other workers, and even sent Chapunga to see a chief in the
nearby communal land about hiring workers from there.

In turn, the fired workers managed to get GAPWUZ to speed up the
appeal to the Labor Tribunal, and they received a hearing date for March
15, 1999. But given that their application was not complete, the company

successfully argued for the case not to be heard then, and the workers were given an extension to "regularize their notice of appeal." The hearing was postponed until October 27, 1999. The fact that they were able to receive a hearing relatively quickly speaks directly to the role of poritikisi, the domain of electoral politics, the translocal forms of power the fired workers were able to bear on their struggle; forms that were soon not confined to a single political party as the political landscape on the national scale changed significantly in 1999.

"Be Brave, Workers, Be Brave": The Emergent Simba of Labor

Once I learned about their labor struggle in August 1999, I started to visit and, over the next four months, spend more time with them at their musososo and the surrounding areas. During this period, a question I continually sought to answer in my research was what made them united (*kubatanana*)? Their endurance was both inspirational and puzzling. By August 1999, they had already been involved in the dispute for ten months; a lengthy period of time to go without steady income, even if it is the often meager wages of farm work. From my research on other commercial farms, particularly in Hurungwe district[6] where I carried out research in 1992–93 (Rutherford 2001a), I recognized the strength of the interpellation of the power relations of domestic government and the fear of going against management and senior workers: the farm *vanhu vakuuru* that Chenjerai mentioned earlier. These workers participating in the labor dispute could have taken the short contract offered to them by the Upfumi management or looked for work elsewhere, giving up the struggle, like many of the other fired farm workers did. But they stayed. For me, the endurance and solidarity of these Upfumi workers was extraordinary. As someone who had become cautious about being carried away by dreams of radical change, I was impressed with their organization and solidarity. I felt the pull of their cause as they explained it to me, particularly through the often eloquent words of Chenjerai.

There are a number of contextual issues that help explain the workers' solidarity. The majority of the workforce was quite young, and many who I met were relatively well-educated compared to those on farms further from Harare. As noted in chapter 1, before Zimfarm bought the farm many older workers were let go. Aside from a few *vadhara* (old men), the vast majority of the workers I met were in their twenties or thirties, with some in their late teens. Among the men who grew up on farms, many had attended secondary school and, like Tapedza, had achieved their O Levels. And many of the young women who came to commercial farms in their adulthood had gone to secondary school, since they grew up in the communal areas or in towns. This gave them an expectation of a better life than that of their parents. And for many, it meant a disdain, dislike, or suspicion of older workers who were accustomed to life on the farm, *upenyu hwemabhoyi* (the life of boys).

Single women, who formed the majority, were definitely more vulnerable than many of the men. They felt their options were few if they lost their job. But aside from the few women who were in lower management positions, many did not feel any strong attachment to the farm. I have argued that the allure of domestic government is generally strongest for men, who usually receive more resources, positions of authority, and privilege than women (Rutherford 2001a: 154ff.). Once mobilized, the women, particularly single women, were often more willing than the men to challenge authority or public decorum (see, e.g., Hodgson and McCurdy 2001). For example, when Mr. Choto, the human resources manager (who was then replaced by Chapunga) died in August 1998, women farm workers broke out in song celebrating his death. Workers recalled this event for me, noting that this reportedly infuriated Mr. Brown and other managers. But Chenjerai explained it through the context of labor relations, that these women were simply expressing their frustration with management. Thus, the young, relatively educated workforce, comprised largely of single women, was willing to challenge and stand up for themselves, if wider conditions were supportive of such actions.

Another facilitating condition was its location close to Harare and the main highway linking it with Marondera, the provincial capital of Mashonaland East. Unlike many farm workers, who lived on farms far from a main highway and with limited or nonexistent public transportation, the Upfumi workers lived within fifty kilometers of Harare and next to a route well-plied by private transport. This greatly facilitated the travel of their leaders to Harare- and Marondera-based organizations, and vice versa.

These factors were not solely found on Upfumi farm; there were other farms that had similar conditions. A further distinction during this period at Upfumi was the emergence of a management under Zimfarm that supported, at first at least, more bureaucratic labor relations arrangements. This helped build the workers' committee, and some of the workers' sense of a stake in the farm; a sense of belonging to its labor relations machinery at least. However, those expectations started to be undermined when new managers drew on more familiar routines of domestic government. The leadership of the committee amplified this concern into militancy. This is the last key factor—the pedagogical project of the leadership of the workers' committee. This leadership took the space offered by the company to become active in labor relations and used it for a wider project of social mobilization of farm workers; a project assisted by translocal networks, particularly those intertwined with electoral politics.

Such mobilization was greatly buoyed by the changes and currents occurring on the national and transnational scales. These scales helped to provide a structure for the struggle for rights and democracy and provided support to Zimbabwean organizations and individuals keen on "doing good" (Fisher 1997; Bornstein 2005). Zimbabwean and foreign NGOs, international donors, and national and international church groups increasingly played a role in the daily life and public discussion of the state and economy in the structural adjustment era of the 1990s (Bornstein 2005: 16; Moyo, Makumbe, and Raftopoulos 1999; Rutherford 2004). They provided material support and ideational forms and content circulating through the mass media, workshops, and projects. Many Zimbabweans viewed such organizations as potential, if capricious, sources of support, if not simba.

For example, in the last half of 1999, Chenjerai was in iterative contact with ZimRights, then a prominent Zimbabwean human rights NGO, trying to gain legal or material assistance from them.[7] Although nothing substantive came from it,[8] the odd contact and discussions Chenjerai had with it and its leader, David Chimhini, who was then a public figure in Zimbabwe, gave a sense to the workers in the struggle of being connected to wider supporters. It gave a sensibility of a belonging outside of the farm—a tie to the wider national scale—as well as to social networks to apply such a sentiment of national belonging to their struggle to gain their rights.

In his discussion of their labor war, Archie, one of the few male workers staying at the musososo in 1999, associated their struggle against Zimfarm with the launch of the MDC in September that year: "We would not hear the speeches of Tsvangirai or see the strength of farm workers like us in the early 1980s. Then in the 1990s it changed. It is like telling the child to say 'Mother' but then the child learns the mother's other name. The mother and the other adults then ask, how did the child learn to know this? ZimRights and other human rights groups have taught us that those who we have taken to be our parents are just adults like us."

The metaphor he uses of children becoming adults is cogent given the strength of paternalism within domestic government. But it was not simply the MDC that facilitated such a sentiment, for ZANU (PF) individuals and structures assisted in, as well as hindered, the struggle. For both political parties, Chenjerai was the lynchpin.

In 1999, it was becoming more common on Mashonaland East commercial farms, similar to other places in Zimbabwe, to hear workers openly criticize ZANU (PF); although, *"Pasi naMugabe!"* was not commonly declared in public gatherings, at least in my experience. In fact, many involved in the Upfumi dispute had ambivalence about which political party to support through 2000 and into 2001. What mattered during their labor strife was access to electoral politics in order to put pressure on management, to embolden the workers' committee and, through them, many of the workers. Poritikisi was a simba, a form of power that could attract national-scale players and actions to localized disputes—for better or for worse.

Most of the remainder of this section provides various examples of the fired workers drawing on individuals, practices, and organizations associated with electoral politics as a way to assist their struggle. I then return to the October 1999 Labor Tribunal hearing, with which this chapter started.

In November 1999, Tapedza and Tawonga had a discussion about the relative merits of ZANU (PF) and MDC for their case, while I was walking with them by the musososo. Tapedza said, "No one here will openly buy MDC cards. Not out of fear but out of respect as ZANU (PF) protected us when we set up our musososo here. The company and others in ZANU wanted to remove us because Upfumi people supported Banda over their candidate [Chishiri] and Chenjerai was no longer attending ZANU meetings. Chenjerai is a very strong politician and they thought he was avoiding ZANU and now was with MDC, adding salt to their injury. But Banda and the ZANU (PF) chairman of the Goromonzi [Rural District] council protected us."

He then started discussing other instances when ZANU officials helped or hindered their struggle. "But," Tawonga interjected, "those individuals who helped us in ZANU are equivalent to those against us in ZANU. But in the end, they will be together. It no longer seems any ZANU is good." Tapedza nodded, saying "If one is a sinner, they all are sinners. . . . But we won't tell them that to their face, but accept their membership cards and join their structures."

Poritikisi was a route through which expectations of power and liberation for the oppressed could be generated and articulated. It also was a medium through which violence could be waged. Both of these traits were commonly present in Zimbabwe, in particular within ZANU (PF) that had dominated and saturated the domain of politics since 1980. For example, President Mugabe publicly boasted of his party having "degrees in violence" during an election rally in 2000 (Blair 2002; see also Kriger 2006). Since the Unity Accord in 1987, when ZANU (PF) swallowed ZAPU after unleashing the state terror in southern and western Zimbabwe (as mentioned earlier), it had become common for Zimbabweans publicly demonstrating support for, if not fealty toward, ZANU (PF); even if through dissimulation or due to fear in light of potential violent consequences when one does not exhibit behaviour deemed appropriate by politicians and party officials. Regardless of whether genuine or feigned, such fealty could lead to material support (as discussed in chapter 4), and forms of pressure, for particular struggles and projects.

Chenjerai resurrected ZANU (PF) structures on Upfumi. In particular, he mobilized workers at Upfumi, and surrounding farms, for the RDC elections in 1998. This helped to bring political party support to the labor struggle, particularly from Councillor Banda. However, this ward election was divisive within the ruling party, and the cracks of dissension immediately translated into diverse ZANU (PF) responses to their labor struggle. What had been an internal ZANU (PF) division in the localized area bled into the war on Upfumi.

Councillor Banda recalled that on the Saturday after the firing of the workers on Thursday, October 29, 1998, he arrived and tried to speak with the farm manager, Mr. Brown, who refused to meet him. Instead, Brown called the Zimbabwe Republic Police (ZRP) and said that Banda was causing problems. The police came and took him to the station in Goromonzi before letting him go. Banda then phoned the member of parliament (MP) for the constituency, Livingstone Manhombo, to inform him about the strife at Upfumi to see if he could intervene. Like 98 percent of the elected 120 ministers of parliament at that time, Mr. Manhombo belonged to ZANU (PF).

The narrative trope given to me by Councillor Banda and the workers involved in the struggle to explain the MP's visit was that of betrayal, of the ruling party foregoing what was assumed to be not only their councillor's allegiances but also that of the poor black workers. When MP Manhombo arrived at the farm on November 2, 1998, Banda was waiting for him, along with other fired workers outside the main gate. But Banda and others said that the MP refused to stop and discuss the labor strife with them, saying he wanted to talk only to the managing director, Mr. Schultz. Awhile later, MP Manhombo returned, but did not explain what he had discussed with the director. Rather, according to Banda and others present, he offered the workers a deal: everyone would be rehired, save for a half dozen or so members of the workers' committee. As Mr. Nzou, the senior labor relations officer from Marondera, succinctly characterized the MP to me in a conversation on November 30, 1999, "he gave an attitude that was pro-employer."

The response of the assembled fired workers was vitriolic—the MP was hounded away from the farm, protected by ZRP officers, and the workers started assuming he was "bought" by the company. He was a sellout to the ruling party, the fired Upfumi workers expressing the same opinion uttered by the farm workers Ladley and Lan (1985) wrote about (as discussed in chapter 1). Contrary to their analysis, however, these workers did not think that they were betrayed by ZANU (PF) on the assumption it should be representing indigenous peoples, but because they considered electoral politics a power to be used against management—not the workers' committees. Electoral politics, for these workers, should be directed to help the exploited and not the exploiters. This also confirmed for the workers that Zimfarm was more interested in "killing our leaders," as Mercy put it (in the sense of having Banda temporarily arrested), rather than following labor law and ensuring that they respected "our rights."

A similar experience happened on December 19, 1998, when a senior ZANU (PF) politician in Mashonaland East province, Jerry Gotora, addressed the workers. At that time, Gotora was the provincial party commissar (as well as chairman of the Mutoko RDC).[9] According to many of the workers present, Gotora assured them that he would speak with the managing director of Zimfarm and "the workers will be back at work in early January 1999." Several of the workers involved in the labor struggle told me, later in 1999, that they knew Gotora met with the managing director, but he avoided addressing the workers again. This left them uncertain of what transpired and increasingly frustrated with the ruling party. Many of the fired workers in late 1999 assumed Gotora, like their MP, had sided with management.

By the time I first met the workers in August 1999, the general consensus in the musososo was that ZANU (PF) had abandoned them and taken the side of the bosses. Mercy put it simplest: "I don't like ZANU (PF) because when it came and addressed us, it promised it was going to help us; everyone will be back at work on January 1, 1999. Then that day came and we went to the bosses and they said there is no work for us. We were so angry. Instead of helping us they were being given bribes by our bosses. ZANU did nothing for us."

Others tried to work through different channels in the ruling party, in the hopes of bringing its simba, its strength, onto the management of Upfumi. Agatha worked with a ZANU (PF) Women's League leader based at the Goromonzi turnoff, whom she knew from the NGO, Kunzwana. The ZANU (PF) leader worked with Kunzwana to establish and support women's clubs on Upfumi and other farms in the area. Agatha knew her, since she had been involved in the women's club at Upfumi before she was fired. She said, "When we were evicted [from the farm compound] in 1999, I then went with the Women's League leader to see Mr. Nhongo and others at the [ruling party's] Fourth Street offices in Harare. I also went on my own to the ZANU (PF) people in Harare but nothing was done to help us. Comrade Nhongo simply said, 'We will bring you food and blankets,' but nothing ever happened."

But political parties were not homogeneous entities. Councillor Banda consistently advocated for them. Initially, he worked through labor relations channels, and then through political channels, as he aimed to find support among his seniors in the ruling party. As noted earlier, he attempted to involve Mr. Nzou in the dispute. Banda then arranged meetings with various leaders of ZANU (PF), including senior leaders from the province who had influence on the national scale, like Solomon Mujuru and Sydney Sekeremayi[10] and the then minister of public service, labor and social welfare, Florence Chitauro. He also contacted senior ZANU (PF) leaders and wrote letters to various officials, including the president's office on December 10, 1998. The campaigning succeeded in getting a letter from the president's office to Minister Chitauro on February 3, 1999, that asked her to ensure an urgent hearing before the Labor Tribunal and to brief the president himself about the matter, which Chenjerai showed me.[11] These tactics thus ensured that they did not need to wait a long time to receive a hearing at the Labor Tribunal. Moreover, the fact that these meetings occurred, with documentary evidence such as this letter, became potential currency in the hands of Chenjerai, Banda, and others. It showed that their case was being heard by vanhu vakuru on the national scale. It also illustrates scale-making at work as this labor dispute on a Berkshire farm was getting attention by national leaders.

Councillor Banda assisted in finding funds to help transport workers to various hearings in Marondera, and to meetings in Harare in the first few months of the struggle. He also helped organize a Christmas party for the dismissed workers. As a way to counter the 10 percent bonus and the Christmas party Zimfarm threw for its current workers, which many of the fired workers who remained living in the compound (as they waited for their case to be heard) at the time found to be humiliating, Banda sourced money from a war veteran on the Harare provincial committee of ZANU (PF), and Mr. Mhanya, a businessman and a member of the Mashonaland East provincial committee, to fund a Christmas party in 1998 only for those fired workers.

In the last half of 1999, the other key reason the fired Upfumi workers supported Banda was because he had helped fight the eviction of those who had remained in the farm compound awaiting the result of the Labor Tribunal. These workers who had refused to leave their accommodations were constantly quarrelling with women who were hired after they were fired. Some of them even lived in the same dorm rooms, resulting in an underlying tension because, as a few women told me simply, "we did not trust each other." Atherstone and Cook, the law firm representing Zimfarm, filed an application in the Marondera magistrate's court in early July 1999 for the eviction of 138 fired workers still living in the compound. The workers' lawyer, Gwisai, was not available to make the hearing and the eviction was granted. Each of the 138 workers individually received an eviction notice.

Chenjerai and ISO organized a small march of some of the women in Marondera to protest their looming eviction. They went outside the provincial administrator's office and he told them to get in touch with the ZANU (PF) political commissar, Jerry Gotora; the one who had promised them before the previous Christmas that they would be back at work in the new year. They then went to the office of the ZANU (PF) governor of Mashonaland East province, David Karimanzira, and his assistant sent them to see Mr. Nzou. Mr. Nzou informed them that his office cannot deal with it since the company was following their own code of conduct. With mounting pressure from others within the ruling party, Karimanzira finally granted an audience to the delegates of the fired workers. When he had heard that their lawyer was unable to make the hearing, he asked who the lawyer was. Then, Chenjerai told me in October 1999 with a smile, when he had heard it was Gwisai, Karimanzira exclaimed, "Why him?" They eventually found a private lawyer, who filed an urgent review of the order on July 22. "Yet," Chenjerai sighed, "we never found out the result of that motion, for then came the truck."

On July 26, 1999, the sheriff arrived to evict them. With support of the Upfumi security guards, the sheriff threw everything identified by management as the property of the 138 workers into a lorry supplied by the farm. Workers alleged this eviction left some of their more valuable property in the compound, while breaking others into pieces. The sheriff had the property dumped in front of the district administrator's (DA) office in Goromonzi, tens of kilometers away. The DA represents the central government in each district (and is the inheritor of the colonial native commissioner's office). By being the recipient of the belongings of the evicted workers, it signaled that the evictees were viewed as a national-scale concern by the sheriff's office, if not by the company. Whereas Zimfarm mobilized the courts and through them the sheriff's office, the workers' committee drew on political connections to assist them.

As their belongings rumbled out of Upfumi's gate, most of the evicted workers went to a highway rest area a few kilometers past Upfumi. Four of the evicted workers then made their way to the DA's office and found that some of the property had been stolen, since it had been sitting unprotected. They remained overnight guarding their beds, clothes, and other personal items. The next day Tapedza went to Goromonzi and Councillor Banda brought him to meet the then DA, Mrs. Musabayana, to explain the situation. Tapedza told me that she replied that it was beyond her control and offered no help.

In the meantime, Chenjerai was collecting donations and loans from farm workers on neighbouring farms and from the affected workers to hire trucks to bring their possessions back to the rest area. On July 28, Banda took him to Ruwa to see the chair of the Goromonzi Rural District Council, who was also a ZANU (PF) leader in Goromonzi. The three of them came to the rest area. In Tapedza's recollections, after the chair received confirmation from Chenjerai that all the evicted fired farm workers were ZANU (PF) supporters he said that the rest area was not an appropriate place for them to stay as it was principally for highway travellers. More importantly, they were too far from the farm to put pressure on the company. Tapedza and Tawonga informed me that the chair of the Goromonzi council suggested they occupy Upfumi. "He told us, 'people are now entering the farms [elsewhere in Zimbabwe] and no one has been shot. If you enter Upfumi, your case will be solved quickly!'"[12] Instead, they decided to set up a camp, a musososo, near the highway next to the driveway going to Upfumi. As Chenjerai declared later that year, "Our case is a labor, not a land, issue"—a distinction that began to dissolve by 2000.

On July 29, the day after their belongings were trucked to the site near Upfumi, Chenjerai said that the human resources manager, Chapunga, phoned the police, a private security company, and the farm guards to evict them from this private property. The workers challenged that claim, and a few of them, and some managers of Upfumi, went to the Goromonzi RDC office in Ruwa to check the official property maps. The maps held at this office showed that the property of the farm did not go all the way to the highway. Supposedly angered by this development, Chenjerai recalled, Chapunga drove away, putatively to the ALB offices, and came back with a map that showed Upfumi's boundaries extended to the highway. But the ZRP and the RDC officials did not agree with Chapunga's map, and they said that the workers could camp there until the dispute was over.

On December 3, 1999, Mrs. Musabayana, the DA, told me that after the evicted workers established their camp, Banda came to ask her office to provide a borehole or a tent. But, she sighed, that "would mean our office is blessing their squatting. We are in solidarity with them but they are squatters and we cannot legalize it. Besides, they are on state land which is mostly administered by the Goromonzi RDC [Rural District Council]." At this time, senior government officials were still officially upholding the sanctity of existing territorialized property regimes; if and when administrators tried to do that a few months later, after the emergence of the violent land occupations, they risked being attacked for being sellouts and having their offices occupied by war veterans and their supporters (see, e.g., McGregor 2002).

Preparing for Change

Councillor Banda sought to drum up ZANU (PF) and government support for the fired Upfumi workers, but he was not the most successful. There were, however, alternative networks involved in electoral politics that were emerging at that time. August 22, 1999, was not only the date of the rally at the musososo with Councillor Banda, ISO and ZFTU representatives from Harare, and workers' committees from neighbouring farms (as discussed in chapter 1). At the same time the ZANU (PF) Harare and Mashonaland East branches were having a picnic at the ZANU (PF) office at the Goromonzi turnoff. When Banda arrived at the musososo for the rally, he offered the use of the RDC truck for those who wanted to join the ruling party's party. Chenjerai called on some men and women to "crash" the party, shouting, "We can steal the tents they are using to protect the *chefs* [leaders] from the sun as we need them to protect us from the coming rains!" He then wrote a poster for them, saying, "ZANU (PF), we are starving." And, as the truck readied to leave with its back full of people, Chenjerai called on Tapedza, who was standing next to me, to join them since he was "one of our leaders"; so Tapedza squeezed himself into the back as the truck rumbled away.

The following week, the workers who crashed the picnic told me they were frostily received. They said that Mr. Nhongo, a ZANU (PF) leader in the Harare branch but who operated in the area and who was a rival to Banda, said that Upfumi workers were "dissidents"; this term is resonant in Zimbabwe with deadly treason because this was the label used to justify the gukurahundi attacks and massacres in southern and central Zimbabwe in the mid-1980s against ZAPU members and supporters—and SiNdebele speakers more broadly. The ZANU (PF) celebrants told Tapedza and others from Upfumi that Chenjerai was the main instigator, as problems only emerged since he had arrived in the Berkshire-Oxfordshire area. Tapedza recalled that Nhongo suggested Chenjerai was "working for Tsvangirai," who was at that time organizing for the imminent launch of his new political party, the MDC. The next day people from Goromonzi RDC came to try to evict the Upfumi protestors from the musososo. The workers assumed this was due to the role played by another provincial member of the party, Mherera who lived in Oxfordshire and worked for the RDC as a driver. Several of the workers went to Ruwa with the RDC officials and talked to the chair of the Goromonzi council who confirmed that they should stay. According to Tapedza, the chair confided in them that party leaders in the area wanted to evict them but he had resisted because, like Banda, "we are also ZANU (PF)." Yet, increasing doubts of political loyalties and intentions began to be amplified in the Upfumi case, as well as within Zimbabwe on a wider scale, in the last third of 1999.

The doubts of Chenjerai's political loyalties reportedly raised by Nhongo were being fanned by Chenjerai's actions. Chenjerai had dissolved the ZANU (PF) committee in the Upfumi area once they were betrayed by their MP and by Gotoro. Moreover, he, like many of the farm workers and so many other Zimbabweans, sensed a change in the air. He increasingly looked to organizations not tied to ZANU (PF), many of whom were consolidating in support behind the new MDC party, as potential sources of power to assist in their struggle.

Banda told me in November 1999 that he had received instructions from people in the Mashonaland East provincial ZANU (PF) hierarchy not to assist the Upfumi farm workers. But he said, "I have been managing to resist them." Banda firmly located himself within ZANU (PF), but within an informal movement of the "youngsters in the party" that, he averred, were pushing for internal change. With the increasing competition from opposition parties, he opined, it is important that ZANU (PF) change from the "old ways" in which people in top posts only tell its members what to do instead of listening to them. He listed for me a loose manifesto for internal democracy within ZANU (PF), akin to what then was being spoken about for the newly proposed constitution and by the opposition parties.

> Instead of imposing programs on the people, they should come from the people. For example, a few years ago we [in the party] were not supposed to vote for members of [ZANU (PF)'s] central committee. The province chose them and informed the districts. This year is the first time this has been done away with and now the provinces are simply endorsing or not the choices made at the district level. We also think it is high time for some of the old people to retire and let the youngsters become elected in senior posts so Zimbabweans know the party is changing. We also need to ensure that the party chefs are not taking all the farms that are designated in the land resettlement program but to leave them for the people. We are pushing for this, but the old people are resisting.

While engaged in the internal debate, Councillor Banda and other ZANU (PF) officials admitted that it was difficult now to work with farm workers and on labor issues. As the Mashonaland East provincial committee member, Mr. Mhanya, noted in November 1999, "Today the party is not actively involved in labor issues, the link is no longer active between ZANU (PF) and unions. GAPWUZ was once getting a lot of support from ZANU (PF) and at times we still work with them. But since the launch of the MDC, I'm not sure how we will live together. There is a bit of confusion."

The fired Upfumi workers exploited this confusion, although at times they were not sure where it was leading them. After they were fired, Chenjerai first went to his ZANU (PF) contacts. When Banda was initially unable to get them reinstated, they started to look for legal representation. Some of their ZANU (PF) contacts then directed them to a ZANU (PF) lawyer whose brother was a government minister. They had initial discussions with him, yet Chenjerai said that it had gone nowhere. At the same time, Chenjerai had been approaching GAPWUZ for help—reminding them how much he had helped them in the past and that he had facilitated the signing up of hundreds of new members. As GAPWUZ had been doing some work with Gwisai through his Zimbabwe Labor Centre, they facilitated his representation of their case. Chenjerai said that he knew of ISO's work from his days in both Marondera and Ruwa and was happy with the arrangement. The ZANU (PF) people were not pleased with Gwisai becoming their lawyer, for he was publicly critical of the ZANU (PF) government (hence, Provincial Administrator Karimanzira's concern when he heard that Gwisai was the lawyer for the Upfumi workers).

Gwisai did not just provide legal advice. Through him, ISO activists also visited the farm and a few of the fired workers, like Chenjerai, would visit the ISO office in downtown Harare. By mid-1999, both ISO and GAPWUZ were involved in the preparation for the launch of the MDC. The ISO cadres, in particular, were keen about the possibility and pushed for the creation of a workers' party by organizing within the MDC and setting up structures in the townships and farms. Whereas ISO cadres were animated by the writings and debates of Trotsky, Lenin, and Bukharin, Chenjerai admitted that their debates and dreams of socialism did not inspire him. Yet, he continued, he liked that they supported workers by "helping us be treated with dignity, with rights, as people. For that, we thank them." Between the Upfumi farm workers engaged in a labor struggle, and the ISO activists seeking to help workers, there was a convergence in this instance of social projects and a struggle for a political dispensation that favoured the working class.

ISO was one more organization with national, indeed international, reach that also had ties, although strained at times, to the new political party, MDC. Although the ZLC was independent of ISO—through Gwisai's leading involvement in both organizations—ISO cadres became involved in the Upfumi struggle. In turn, the farm workers involved in the struggle adopted

the ISO slogans on their own posters that they had strung around their musososo. These were clearly visible to the adjacent highway through posters
hanging near the musososo and facing the traffic—such as *"Shinga vashandi,
shinga! Qina msebenzi qina"* ("Be Brave Workers, Be Brave!" in ChiShona
and SiNdebele), "Zimfarm is big because they exploit their workers," and
"Zimfarm we are prepared. We have nothing to Loose [*sic*] but the chains"
(see figure 2.1). They also participated in various activities with ISO—from
going with ISO to the ZCTU-organized May Day rally at Rufaro stadium in
Harare in 1999 to attending their "Marxism 99" conference in October 1999.
ISO and GAPWUZ found funds to facilitate the transportation of some of
the workers from Upfumi, which helped to bolster their claims of having
grassroots ties to farm workers in their varied projects. And Gwisai directly
helped the fired workers by legally representing them in their labor dispute
with Zimfarm. Nevertheless, these linkages did not always mesh well. Although the wider "rights talk" and ferment occurring in Zimbabwe found
traction in the lives of many farm workers in Mashonaland East province
in the late 1990s, as I learned from talking to farm workers on more than
a dozen farms, the linkages between the translators and interlocutors and
between themselves were not always firm or without contradictions and
uncertainties. This can be seen in the case of the MDC and the Upfumi
struggle.

Between August 1999 and the end of 2000, Chenjerai and many of the
workers at the musososo were very excited about the emergence of the
MDC, the new political party led by Morgan Tsvangirai, the former head
of the ZCTU. In late August and early September, Chenjerai was busy talking to ISO, GAPWUZ, and ZCTU officials about arranging transportation
for many of the workers to attend the September 11, 1999, launch of the new
political party. But he faced some difficulty. There was tension between the
ZCTU officials, many of whom were transferring to the fledgling MDC
structures, and the ISO cadres.[13]

Chenjerai often talked about different national-scale organizations and
individuals and even met with some of them. He beseeched them to provide support to the Upfumi workers and, at the same time, increased his
own authority and reputation. Chenjerai was keen for the MDC, or even the
ZCTU, to come and speak to the fired workers, to recruit them, and to show
their support of the workers. But none came. This lack of support from the
extra-local institutions frustrated Chenjerai, who had tirelessly supported

Fig. 2.1. Signs Lining the Highway Next to the Musososo

the farm workers in their struggle to establish a fair labor relations machinery on farms and then ably represent themselves within it.

Even GAPWUZ officials rarely came. Chenjerai spent much time with Precious or Tapedza sitting in the GAPWUZ main office in Harare trying to get responses or assistance. He found the office very hierarchical, with officials immobilized until they received approval from their leaders, who often were out of the office. Chenjerai urged both GAPWUZ and the MDC to improve organizing efforts on the farms, in order that people would know who they were. "The people here want to be organized, they want change, but if no one comes here to organize, to make sure they are registered to vote properly, make sure they know the labor law, how can it happen?" In short, Chenjerai was calling for an idealized form of democratic representation, where "we make demands on the leaders who are supposed to be selected by us, and not to sit waiting for them to show and then they never come." To this end, he listed a number of meetings he had organized for the main GAPWUZ organizer in Marondera. And, Chenjerai claimed, either the GAPWUZ official would not show, or he would bristle when workers asked him tough questions and then refused to engage in dialogue with them.

He gave the example of himself. "I am now well-known on these farms—some don't like me, but they recognize that I am able to represent workers." After noting that he had set up a branch for GAPWUZ on Upfumi, he talked about his other successes, such as helping the occasional worker from nearby farms to be reinstated. On Berkshire farm he also had overseen the election of a workers' committee. Yet, Chenjerai complained, "within three weeks they all resigned as they did not know their duties and were easily intimidated by management workers." Chenjerai sighed. "The problem with us farm workers is we don't know our jobs and rights." For Chenjerai, who did not always view himself as part of the "we" of the "us farm workers," farm workers were too inured to the mode of belonging of domestic government. And for that, he lamented the lack of support from GAPWUZ. The branches, he used as an example, "are not being used at all by GAPWUZ." In explaining his argument, he outlined the possibilities of what could be:

> If GAPWUZ is having problems with transport they can use branch chairmen. They are supposed to be organizing members for unions. If I go to the farm [down the road], I could organize the workers. Yet once employers ask for my union rep card and when they see that I do not have one, they can kick me off the farm. Branch members are not paid anything—no salaries or travel fees. So we can organize for free and do it better as we know the workers. We don't need to collect cards but just need to have workers sign stop-order forms to give to the employers [which would divert a monthly fee from the worker's wages to the union].

He used a similar logic for the MDC, expressing the need to use people, like himself, on the farms, to organize in the countryside and not simply to organize in the cities. When I visited on September 12, 1999, he and many of the workers were excited after attending the MDC launch in Harare the day before. The MDC had come through with a bus to take people from Upfumi, surrounding farms, and the RDC houses across the highway (where some employees of the Goromonzi rural district council rented out their lodging to farm workers and others). They brought more than a hundred people from the locality to the launch in Rufaro Stadium in Mbare, Harare. This helped confirm to Chenjerai, and the others who went, that their struggle was active on the national stage. Attending the launch gave them succour in their struggle and, for the moment, helped to gloss over the difficulties in receiving constant support from GAPWUZ, the MDC, and ISO.

Over the next few months, Chenjerai and others on Upfumi sought MDC information through ISO, for MDC never established a structure in the Upfumi area in 1999. In so doing, Chenjerai gained more enmity from the Oxfordshire ZANU (PF) branch. Banda, who was viewed as Chenjerai's patron, received similar hostility, compounded by the resentment he faced from key members in this branch for winning the RDC election against their candidate. In the meantime, the farm workers were preparing for their October 1999 Labor Tribunal hearing. By August, the workers' committee was gathering money to pay for transportation, estimating they would need more than Z$2,000 to rent a truck large enough to bring several hundred of them to the hearing. They financed part of the trip themselves, while Chenjerai solicited help from GAPWUZ for additional funding. In addition, they had to prepare for the tribunal performance itself.

Tribunal Preparations

With excitement and nervousness, the musososo was a hive of activity in the week before the tribunal hearing on October 27, 1999. There were discussions and musings about what would happen upon reinstatement at Upfumi: for instance, they imagined how they would interact with the workers hired to replace them and with the new workers' committee that was set up by management. Some speculated on how news of their success would send a positive message to other farm workers about the need to stand up for their rights. They believed their action was having a demonstrated effect on the translocal scale, because their struggle received occasional media coverage and was widely known on the farms in the Berkshire-Oxfordshire area. On October 23, they had a *pungwe*, an all-night meeting with prayers, drinking, and a coming together of people from different areas to the camp. The next day, another meeting was held with people who were still around from the pungwe; although some, like Chenjerai, could not attend as they were incapacitated from the previous night's revelling; however, I attended this meeting.

Tapedza's voice was raw from a night of singing Christian songs. The meeting itself was opened with a hymn and a prayer. Then Tapedza explained to those present the practicalities of the transportation for the day: what time it would leave, where it would stop to pick up workers, and where it would drop them off in Harare. And he explained the great uncertainty about what would happen that day. "We do not know whether we will hear the result on the twenty-seventh, so maybe we shall keep staying here afterward. We all wish that the decision could come sooner than later as we are now entering the rainy season and those of us here do not have much protection at the musososo. But one never knows. God is for everyone. We can lose or we can win."

He then took a series of questions. Some asked if they win, would they have to return to Upfumi if they already had a good job? Tapedza said that he did not think anyone would be forced to go back. Another man said that if they went back to work at Upfumi, "The murungu will be looking out for any small mistake you do so he can fire you as the varungu [whites] oppress us." Tapedza responded, "In 1980 when this country was won, not many people thought it would be good. People did not understand what it meant to reconcile, that it brought advantages to Zimbabwe. In Mozambique, where FRELIMO [the ruling party of Mozambique since independence in 1975] chased the whites, the departing whites destroyed buildings, putting cement in toilets to block the water from running. Now, Harare and Mozambique are very different. Mugabe saw the mistake done in Mozambique, so he decided to keep the whites together with blacks." Little did he, his audience, or anyone else know what was going to commence a few months later along this much racialized political fault line.

On October 26, 1999, I stopped at the musososo on the return from visiting another farm near Marondera. The workers were sitting around a fire, taking turns posing potential questions to Tapedza, Chenjerai, and Marion, a woman supervisor. Chenjerai told her that Gwisai thought it would be in their interest if they had a supervisor take the stand. All she needed to do was "speak the truth. Do not worry, just say what you know." The questions Tapedza, Chenjerai, and Tawonga posed to her centered around what the supervisors knew and what they were doing on the morning of October 29, 1998. For example, Tapedza asked her what happened when she arrived from Oxfordshire on the farm truck to start work that morning. She replied, "I saw people not working but just standing around. Then the senior supervisors were called by the managers to a meeting. Only male supervisors went as they were the seniors. This is part of the conditions of oppression. I am a woman who worked longer than the male supervisors but they are more senior than me."

Tawonga jumped in, and asked what happened on the day after. Marion responded, "I went back to work, but I was then asked to sign the three-month contract form. I refused." Chenjerai interjected, "So you agree that you and the others took an unconstitutional industrial action?!" Marion stuttered, blushed slightly, and mumbled, "It is difficult . . ." before her voice trailed off. Chenjerai responded, "Just say you were following instructions. Could you refuse to go to the administration block on the twenty-ninth, no? "No," Marion stated, "as the order came from seniors [management]." Her bodily unease over Chenjerai's question should have alerted me to the ruse that was being performed and her attempt to agree with the narrative that the male leaders of the fired workers were putting forward. But I missed it, because I was caught up in my sense of solidarity with their struggle.

Despite all the preparation and excitement, October 27, 1999, turned out to be anticlimactic. As noted at the start of this chapter, the Labor Tribunal did not discuss their case. Instead, they postponed the hearing *sine die*, without scheduling a date to enable the parties to settle the matter amicably. The reason for the postponement seemed to be that the Zimfarm lawyers did not get their argument to Gwisai in time.

There was a fair bit of despondency and uncertainty at that meeting in the ISO office on October 27, 1999. In the discussion at the meeting, some attempted to bolster the confidence of the assembled and urged them to continue to be united. As one man forcefully stated, during the time of questions to Gwisai, "The workers showed bravery and I was very happy because our message was listened to. We could have been throwing accusations against each other but we showed bravery, a bravery we can show one more time." Yet, Gwisai also noted how the law was going to strain that unity. He explained that workers will be treated differently depending on the type of contract they had signed before or after being fired and how long they had been working there. He initially differentiated between those on eight-month contracts who had been working less than eight months and those on eight-month contracts who had worked longer than eight months. He speculated that he would have a chance of getting those working longer than 8 months to be reinstated. Then, he differentiated between those who had signed three-month contracts, before or immediately after being fired, and those who signed them after their case was brought to the Labor Tribunal in November 1998; the latter, he said, were not going to be covered by the settlement. Since they had signed a limited term contract after Gwisai had become their lawyer, Zimfarm lawyers could say they received legal advice before signing and they had signed anyway.

Gwisai continued with his analysis of their legal options. He noted that the fired workers would also likely receive different compensation depending on the type of contract they were under. In the spirit of worker solidarity, he proposed levying some compensation money from those on longer contracts to give to those on shorter contracts who were also part of the struggle. He emphasized that this was particularly important, given that many who had been residing in the musososo had been on three-month contracts, and they "publicly symbolized their collective war against Zimfarm." After a bit of a discussion, punctuated by *"Shinga mushandi, shinga!"* ("Be brave, worker, be brave!") and *"Pasi neudzvanyiriri; pasi nahwo!"* ("Down with oppression; down with it!"), there was agreement by those who spoke that this was a fair arrangement.

Gwisai stressed that they had won a victory, for the opposing lawyer, Mr. Chagonda, had admitted that Zimfarm has a case to answer—"The big war was in getting them to acknowledge they have a case to answer." Although he told them the negotiations over compensation would commence the next day, he also warned them to not "start planning to spend the money for you have not yet won the case. Which means we must do what? To continue being united, being brave. The war is still there, this is what we tell you." This is when Chenjerai uttered his "Pasi naMugabe!" slogan, leading to the nervous silences and awkward shifting in seats.

Soon afterward, Gwisai reminded the assembled workers about the ISO conference, "Marxism 99," in a few days' time. During Saturday's conference there would be discussion with the trade unions, he told them, about "the workers' party of MDC. A party can be launched and say it is a workers' party, but then it can be taken over and you end up seeing yourselves being ruled by others who are not behind the workers. So we need to see to it that it continues to remain a party of the workers." He added, "Because in your case you have suffered, you do not need to suffer again. And if you go back to Upfumi, or another farm, you need to know your rights." Gwisai clearly saw the Upfumi case as part of the wider struggle to make the MDC a workers' party. Consequently, his legal representation went hand-in-hand with trying to enlist Chenjerai and other fired Upfumi workers in this wider project of promoting workers' rights on the national scale.

However, on this day in late October 1999, the fired Upfumi workers were not enthusiastic about any wider projects—at least those with whom I was talking as we walked back to the Harare Gardens for a meeting. Many were talking about the need for compensation for their lost property when they were evicted.[14] Others were saying "the law is unfair" and did not understand why, if they had won, it was still unclear how much they would be reimbursed. Many were also talking about reinstatement. Those who had been working for more than eight months were anxious to be back at Upfumi, while some of those on different contracts were anxious about the likelihood of their reinstatement. Other divisions became more apparent to me. At that point, Chenjerai confided in me that Precious had "led a rebellion against me" the previous week, with the support of some older women, saying they wanted to get some money from Zimfarm and return to work. He said that he had challenged her then and did an impromptu vote on his leadership: forty-seven of the forty-eight people at the musososo supported him. But, he ruefully remarked, "the challenge hurt me a lot."

When we returned to the public park, all the workers were told to assemble themselves for a picture by a photographer from *The Herald*, the government-aligned daily. Phillip Munyanyi, the then secretary general of GAPWUZ, other officials from the union, and the workers crowded together for the picture. Afterward, a security guard came and said that no meetings were allowed in the park. The crowd dispersed, but a few, like Chenjerai, went to the nearby GAPWUZ office to discuss the next possible steps in their labor struggle.

Conclusion

The proclamations of unity and bravery were urgent that day in October 1999, even as the workers were already sensing that their struggle, which had stretched out over a year almost to the day, may not end victoriously; although I did not learn about how widespread that sentiment was felt among those involved in the labor struggle until the following year. At that time, I was still excited, perhaps a bit enthralled, about their longevity and all the varying ties to the momentous wider-scale party politics present in that period that seemed to portend so many promising possibilities.

For many of the workers, and those involved in ZANU (PF) in the Upfumi area, it was difficult to ascertain the political direction that Chenjerai and, partially through him, many of the workers were heading toward. Chenjerai was talking to me and many of the workers about the MDC. Yet, for other audiences, Chenjerai and others maintained that they were fully behind ZANU (PF); particularly since the ruling party had attracted other forms of support to their struggle, including media coverage in the state-operated press, television, and radio. On August 29, 1999, for example, as I returned to Harare after a day at the musososo, I heard (and jotted down) the following item from the 6:00 p.m. news on Radio 3, ZBC; this radio station, like the others on the airwaves at that point, was government-controlled. The report came from the ZFTU.

> One hundred and forty-six workers from Upfumi farm in Berkshire still live outside after being evicted from the farm last October by management, as told to ZIANA [the state-run news agency]. They are without water and sanitation conditions are poor. They are still staying on the farm on the Mutare highway. Chenjerai from the workers' committee said they were not fired but on suspension. They were illegally evicted from the compound when they went on strike.
>
> The farm spokesman said that the workers refused to renew contracts even with Z$1000–Z$2,500 retrenchment packages, with the option to return to work. The Zimbabwe Federation of Trade Unions' Alfred Makwarimba said in a press release that government should acquire the farm and hand it back to farm workers, alleging that the workers have been treated in an inhuman way.

These representations nurtured the sense held by many involved in the struggle against Zimfarm that their case was having national impact. Such sympathetic, translocal representations of their struggle were important for the workers involved, while causing headaches for the management—as Chapunga and Brian Kagoro, the lawyer who took over the Zimfarm file from Mr. Chagonda, informed me after the court case finished. I had a very small role in such representations in late August 1999. I was sitting with the workers from the musososo in a nearby field while they were having a meeting, when we saw a white couple and a teenage boy park their car near the camp and approach us. They said that they were a family from Belgium and were in Zimbabwe on holiday when they saw the posters from the highway, and they wanted more information on the nature of the dispute. Chenjerai explained their version of the story and, because the Belgian family had trouble understanding English, I helped translate into French—their second language—as best as I could. The next month, on September 17, 1999, the Belgian woman, who was a lawyer, wrote a letter to the managing director of Zimfarm—cc'ing GAPWUZ, the ALB, and myself—deploring the situation of these workers and noting that European consumers of their vegetables may not be aware of such a situation.

The workers had heard about this letter before I received a copy, since Chapunga angrily informed them about it. They said, with mirth, he had been called back from holiday to address the issue. Tapedza often referred to the letter at meetings at the musososo during the next few months, remarking that "people in Europe" were supportive of their struggle. It also may have motivated Mr. Chapunga's allusion to the "two English sayings" concerning the issue of belonging and implication I was meddling where I should not be (as discussed at the beginning of chapter 1).

It was not only the Zimbabwean media, political parties, European tourists, or Canadian anthropologists who became interested in the struggle at Upfumi and the representations of it. On October 15, 1999, Tapedza, Tawonga, and Mercy said that they were nervous about MDC people coming to the musososo because a few days earlier the CIO (the secret police that reported directly to the president's office) visited them. The CIO agent asked if any political party had paid them a visit and to inform them of any such visitors, ensuring to record vehicle registration numbers as well as types of questions asked. He also asked for information about who was driving my car as he had seen it outside the camp on a number of occasions. The people at the musososo told me that they replied "It belonged to researchers from the University of Zimbabwe," and, Chenjerai smiled, "The CIO agent seemed to be satisfied with that answer."

These workers recalled that a CIO agent based in Marondera began making visits to the farm with Mr. Nzou in 1997 during the labor disputes in July and October, although they did not know he was from the president's office at that time. Only when they had a subsequent confrontation with the MP on November 2, 1998, was he identified as a CIO member. This agent appeared several other times—when Chapunga offered a payout to the dismissed workers later that month and when they were evicted in July 1999. He had also arranged for them to meet with Governor Karimanzira when they were marching in Marondera in November 1998 and was present at that meeting. According to Chenjerai in October 1999, the CIO official told them "Don't worry, we won't interfere. We are just coming to look around and see what is happening." Mr. Nzou echoed that sentiment in an interview on November 30, 1999, when responding to my question on the issue by explaining that "the duty of the CIO is to monitor such things. It is normal practice, when the situation is like it is at Upfumi, that the arms of government, particularly those responsible for security . . . ensure that there is no destabilization of the law machinery. By that, they frequent such places." Such visits increased dramatically during the next few years, since most commercial farms became identified as "such places" during the time of jambanja.

There were many more people interested in the place of Upfumi farm after October 27, 1999, as the art of poritikisi took on the other trait associated with its practice in Zimbabwe. In addition to potentially bringing support for various struggles through accessing simba, party politics was equally involved in making threats and creating violence. In early December 1999, Diana, Tapedza's wife, who was seven months pregnant at the time, captured this feature well when she declared during a discussion we were having about political parties at the musososo, "Many people are scared of poritikisi. They fear victimization if they talk too much about poritikisi. Others understand [the issues] but don't say too much for they are scared."

CHAPTER 3

THE DRAMA OF POLITICS: DISSENSION, SUFFERING, AND VIOLENCE

October 31, 1999
Musososo, Berkshire

A FEW DAYS after the Labor Tribunal hearing of October 27, 1999, I stopped by the *musososo* in the late afternoon. When I went to park the car by the side of the Upfumi driveway next to the thatch and pole shelters, there already were two other vehicles parked on the edge: a Mercedes Benz and a Goromonzi Rural District Council (RDC) truck. There were only a few women sitting at the camp. They told me that everyone else was at a meeting, pointing to the grassy field on the other side of the road leading to Upfumi. As I walked toward the msasa tree a hundred or so meters on the other side of the field, I saw two groups—one of about twenty people comprised largely of young men and women and a larger one comprised of older men and women seated around two men sitting on chairs. As I approached, I recognized one of the seated men as Councillor Banda. When I saw the leaders of the Upfumi workers in this group, I went to join them; after greetings, they introduced me to the other seated man as Mr. Mhanya, a Harare businessman and member of the ZANU (PF) Mashonaland East provincial committee.

After introductions and small talk with Mr. Mhanya about the situation of farm workers within land resettlement and the debates within ZANU (PF) concerning this, I sat down on the ground, politely refusing the offer of the chair next to Councillor Banda, and listened to the meeting as it resumed.

Mr. Mhanya was talking about the need to stay united because their labor struggle was almost over. But his words were occasionally drowned out by songs sung by the men and women sitting in front of him. A theme of all the songs was that the government had abandoned the Upfumi farm workers during their struggle. This critique then was made in spoken words after Mr. Mhanya finished his speech and Banda indicated that "our leader" could now answer questions. There ensued a series of questions about what ZANU (PF) and the government will do given that "we won our case in the tribunal." Chenjerai led the questioning. He stood up and stated that the provincial chairman of the ruling party for Mashonaland East had simply yelled at him for contacting him a few days previously, so "what, Comrade, will you do to help us?" Then some women began singing a ZANU (PF) song whose theme was that Zimbabwe is now a country ruled by *vanhu vatema* (black people). The implication was that the government has not helped this group of vanhu vatema in their struggle against a company of whites. Mr. Mhanya calmly said, "Do not be violent. I will continue to push for your case, and it should be resolved soon."

After about ten minutes of such questioning, those from the other group moved toward us. After greetings, a young man whom I did not recognize began introducing the secretaries and deputy secretaries of the ZANU (PF) youth group for their new branch, including for the positions of information and publicity, transport and social welfare, economic affairs, legal affairs, production and labor, security, secondary education, and child health and welfare. It was a list of titles seemingly unconnected to their struggle or how they organized their lives. Later, when I queried people at the musososo about these new positions, no one really knew the actual content of their specific portfolios but recognized that bearing the title was the significant aspect of this exercise.

Mercy was introduced as one of the secretaries, although she and many of the others did not enthusiastically give their "*pamberi*" and "*pasi na*" slogans. She also was wearing a ZCTU T-shirt, the trade union congress that was strongly associated with the MDC. Mr. Mhanya and Banda then passed on information about the next ZANU (PF) meetings and said that if the assembled people wanted to do projects, the political party would support them, although since "you do not have any land here it may be difficult." The possible development enterprises the party envisioned for ZANU (PF) branches required some territorialization through which people had access to land to invest time and energy. ZANU (PF) had generally been wary of carrying out development projects for farm workers given their lack of access to land to use. For example, Banda mentioned a ZANU (PF)-organized sports tournament at the Goromonzi turnoff for netball and soccer. Mercy tartly asked, "Where shall we practice netball as there is no ground nearby?" to which Banda testily responded, "You and other women should learn to play soccer, as one can play in any empty ground." Councillor Banda clearly saw his erstwhile supporters as potentially wavering in their loyalty to ZANU (PF).

Another woman in the labor struggle then complained, "We are suffering. We are dying of hunger and you have forgotten us. We have no tent, no soap, no food." Several other women echoed her thoughts. Mr. Mhanya said, "We will look after you"; a response that left many of the women quietly complaining. Then Mr. Mhanya rose from his chair, thereby ending the meeting.

As many in the meeting walked the *vakuru*—the big people—back to their vehicles, someone started singing a song popularized by University of Zimbabwe students during their recent protests in Harare, "Care-care, I don't care about . . ." and started naming management officials at Upfumi such as "Chapunga" and "Brown" as well as ZANU (PF) leaders such as "MP Manhombo," "Jerry Gotoro," and "Mr. Nhongo," ending off with a *"Pamberi neVashandi!"* ("Forward with workers!") and *"Pasi nevanokunyeperai"* ("Down with those who lie to you!"). These critical songs did not elicit a verbal response from the grim-faced ZANU (PF) leaders. After the Mercedes-Benz and the truck drove off onto the highway, Chenjerai began to address the fifty or so remaining people from the previous meeting lingering at the musososo. He gave a speech that focused on *poritikisi*, even though it was aimed at denouncing politicians and the practice of party politics.

Chenjerai began by tracing a conspiracy between politicians and the bosses. He observed that "When we asked the councillor why they don't expropriate Upfumi for us, Banda's response was 'There are no schools on the farm so it is not appropriate for people to live here.' But with so many farm workers already here, why is it appropriate for us to live here now with no school?" Besides, he added, "we read in the newspaper ZANU (PF) officials saying 'Nyasalanders [Malawians, foreign workers] should go back home'" when people raise the issue about farm workers getting land. Chenjerai continued, "You have been told next week to do sports—but where, in the bush? Comrade Mhanya said we have no land for gardens or projects—but we have bush around us which we can use, no?"

As a leader of this struggle, Chenjerai clearly laid out some of the demands of the farm workers as he saw them—the need for social services, access to land—while targeting the government as the authority responsible for providing this support. Yet, he argued, the government has been unwilling to provide it. Moreover, when a woman interjected his speech by saying that the "party is promising us food, which is good," Chenjerai began to question the revolutionary claims of ZANU (PF) itself, echoing the more public critiques coming from the MDC and those in the self-defined civil society movement by that time.

He launched a short tirade against what he called a "divide-and-rule" policy, stating, "If you really want to be part of ZANU, then why are you sitting here? Why do you think they set up their branch amongst us and did not invite the people still working at Upfumi? It pains me seeing them take advantage of a desperate people," adding, "where were they when we were suffering? They only came here when we won." Despite the despondency after the Labor Tribunal hearing that occurred a few days earlier, Chenjerai and others were now emphasizing that the Tribunal's ruling showed that Zimfarm was in the wrong.

Picking up on his cynical appraisal of the ruling party, he recalled that "In the meetings of the 1980s, we all heard and repeated 'revolution' and 'liberation'; did we ever see those things happen? Instead food prices are so high and we are starving. But we never said no to what a comrade told us. Now it is different." After a slight pause, Chenjerai moved to critically reflect on political mobilization. He suggested that the ZANU (PF) leaders came to the camp because they knew the MDC would soon be establishing structures for them, although he added that the MDC, which had been officially launched a month earlier, could also be thieves: "If MDC thinks they have an open check for our support, they are mistaken. We workers will not be misled by intellectuals again." He then stopped abruptly and asked for a cigarette.

People dispersed, some going back to homes they were renting at Mupungu, others to the musososo, where the women began frying up some *mandere*—locusts they had gathered from the msasa trees. Chenjerai approached me and confided that he was not sure if everyone was prepared to wait another two to three weeks. "We are glad that Zimfarm pleaded guilty, but they say 'I wronged you but since I have money let's negotiate.' The bosses have courts, newspapers, the media on their side. We only have numbers and sweat. It is nothing versus everything." He then paused, surveying the camp around him, which was looking quite disheveled after several months of people living in it and after the start of the rains that had left dents in some of the grass roofs. He sighed, saying, "Everyone is tired and hungry. We wanted a decision yesterday. Can we force them to give us a decision? No? The scales of justice are not balanced. Either we smash the system or we force the system to accept us."

As I write this more than ten years later, the contradictions seem clearer to me—Chenjerai, a "strong politician," as Tapedza had called him, denouncing politics while using revolutionary political discourse; here was a man who prided himself on his analysis of events and activities, his ability to intellectualize while being critical of the intellectuals in both ZANU (PF) and MDC. However, these words appeared less contradictory to me then as I, like so many Zimbabweans and observers of Zimbabwe at that time, was swept up in what appeared to be an alternative version and practice of politics.

Chenjerai compellingly laid out the problems of different groups of people and a vision about what steps could be taken to enable more rights and better conditions. His skillful articulation of demands for farm workers more broadly and those in the Upfumi labor struggle more particularly helped to marshal wider support from political parties and others; thus, they were able to find the skills and resources to legally challenge their dismissal and, simultaneously, put pressure on the company and others to try to ensure that they succeeded. The strategy appeared straightforward: use party politics to try to ensure victory when the odds were stacked against "us." The efforts by Chenjerai and others in the leadership showed how poritikisi could provide support and bolster the demands and struggle for rights of a group very much on the margins of the body politic. Yet, party politics was not an unproblematic tool because it also often entailed practices of coercion as a means of persuasion, as will be discussed later in this chapter.

Before examining the dramatic turns this engagement with politics actually entailed as the tempo of the challenges to the ZANU (PF) government increased on the national scale—as did the intensity and viciousness of its response to this threat to its electoral stranglehold—let me turn to examine some of the livelihood practices, living arrangements, and the interlaced power/sovereignty dimensions of belonging for these farm workers. This sociopolitical ground informed the striking workers' strategies of survival while marking their sources of anxiety and social distinctions, both of which became more pronounced as the labor struggle continued for another eight months. The suffering was not mere words; it was deeply etched into many of their lives.

This examination of livelihoods, power relations, and the gendered relations of dependency shows the grounding of this labor struggle in the daily lives of those who waged it. It also illuminates some of the perspectives and reflections of these fired farm workers on the demands animating their struggle for rights and on the more national-scale political contests. As farm workers, the vast majority were accustomed to having limited resources and arduous livelihood practices. Nonetheless, being involved in this labor dispute put many of them into an even more precarious, conditional situation that was a hardship to endure. This tenuous condition was one that the vast majority of all farm workers, as well as other Zimbabweans, would soon experience even more intensely as national-scale politics erupted into the *hondo* (war) with which its rhetoric was often associated.

Livelihoods through Hardships

The musososo was an anchoring point of the dispute, the *mongo*, the "bone marrow," of the struggle, as Gwisai put it in one of his talks with the fired workers. The shelters and its posters facing the nearby highway visibly announced their presence and their war (labor dispute) with Zimfarm (see figure 2.1). It also underscored that the people living there were waiting for a resolution and not ensconced in a mode of belonging elsewhere—in a farm compound, in a communal land *musha* (rural home), resettlement farm stand, or in an urban or mining area residential zone—and its particular livelihood possibilities. Territorialized modes of belonging do not determine economic activities; much research on Zimbabwe and southern Africa has emphasized the translocal characteristics of the livelihoods of many, be they the "worker-peasants" in some depictions or "multiple livelihoods" in others (e.g., Andersson 2001; Potts 2010). Rather, the power relations involved in territorialized modes of belonging interact with social relations and hierarchies within kinship and families and along gendered, generational, classed, or racialized lines (among others) to shape economic possibilities and limits. Living at the musososo meant that these former farm workers were outside firmly settled territorialized entities. This placed them in the interstitial space, a "shadow" space (Ferguson 2006) that interacts with entities more visible to territorialized social and economic landscapes.[1] Although policy-makers may characterize them as "informal economy" activities, the varied labor, trading, and service activities these fired workers carried out cut across sites like commercial farms, which were viewed as being more a part of the "formal economy" (see also Bolt 2015). I will begin, though, by sketching out the musososo itself.

When I first visited the displaced fired Upfumi workers' temporary camp on August 11, 1999, about a month after it was established, I was surprised by its semblance of hygienic organization that seemed better than many of the farm compounds I had previously visited. The camp was situated on the east side of the road leading to Upfumi, about thirty meters from the Harare–Mutare highway. The structures next to the road were two small pole and grass huts overlain with plastic sheeting, with reed mats covering most of the ground inside. The men staying at the musososo, who rarely numbered more than ten, slept there. Next to these huts, further away from the road to Upfumi, were two longer pole and grass shelters. Both also had some plastic sheeting on top. They also had pots and pans hanging from the low rafters above the reed mats (see figure 3.1). The women and children slept here. In September 1999, there were about thirty women staying in these shelters.

Fig. 3.1. The Musososo in September 1999

Between the two women's shelters were cooking fires—each one shared by several women. Initially, the women said that they had designated a few among them to do the cooking for everyone living at the camp; this arrangement led to quarrels, though, because of differing tastes and resentment of a few women, who had the "honour of being the main cooks," as Faith put it. From mid-August 1999 onward, three to five women shared a fire, but each cooked separately. Single men would ask a particular woman to cook for them. Everyone would be responsible for collecting their own firewood, but they would share water and take turns collecting it from wherever they could. Men were responsible for constructing and maintaining the shelters.

Behind the shelters, toward the farm, were two small, roofless grass structures with empty fertilizer bags as doors. These were the bathing facilities, as signaled by the small wooden signs, one for women and one for men. Outside the women's structure was a small table made of branches with a shallow pail full of water nearby (see figure 3.2). Accessing that water, however, was a constant challenge.

On the morning when I first arrived in August 1999, Upfumi farm guards had chased musososo women away from the stagnant pools of river water located on Upfumi property where they were trying to gather water

Fig. 3.2. Women's Washing Structure at Musososo

FARM LABOR STRUGGLES IN ZIMBABWE

to boil. For the drinking water, the women often relied on the goodwill of some of the farms around them, including Mupungu farm. But this help was inconsistent, fluctuating with the level of water on these farms and the relationships between the leaders of the fired workers and those who controlled water on the neighboring farms.

There was a core of about twenty women, six men, and three children living there for the first six months. People constantly dropped by and occasionally stayed at the musososo. Some left and returned to the camp if they could not find work, they had lost their jobs, or they were returning from their musha and were using the musososo as a staging point to look for new jobs. Some of the people staying there included those who had taken the small package offered by Zimfarm and formally left their jobs at Upfumi. Others living elsewhere (e.g., renting dwellings on neighboring farms or from RDC employees who were subleasing their houses at the council camp) would occasionally spend some nights at the musososo to show solidarity. It took me more than a month after my first visit to realize that Chenjerai did not stay at the camp on a permanent basis. He had been renting a house on Mupungu—one of the brick houses that had been built by the previous white farmer, which also was one of only three habitable structures with electricity on the small farm. Although he would be there on almost every day that I arrived at the musososo, Chenjerai had access to much nicer accommodations on Mupungu farm: a house that Antonio, the Mupungu manager, called "staff" housing in contrast to the pole and mud huts rented by the *povo* (masses). Chenjerai's housing clearly signified that he was of a different social class from those who he helped to lead. "He lives like a manager," Tapedza said, "but he is our leader and deserves it."

Keeping that social distinction, however, was a source of anxiety for Chenjerai, as was acquiring a general livelihood for everyone else at the musososo. Chenjerai had been renting a staff house since he began work at Upfumi in 1997, initially for Z$200 (US$8) per month. By 1999, it cost him Z$300 (US$7.80) per month. Starting in June 1999, he wrote a series of letters to Mr. Mupungu, the owner who lived in Mutare, asking for a delay in paying rent, including the rent he owed as of April. In some of the letters I saw, he pleaded with the farm owner, saying that once their case was heard at the tribunal, all money owed would be paid. By September, he had given Antonio, Mapungu's manager, a series of belongings as security, starting with his television, his kitchen unit, and then his living room furniture. In the meantime, the rent climbed to Z$600 (US$8.60) per month in January 2000 as the Zimbabwean dollar continued to depreciate. He occasionally borrowed money or acquired funds through friends to pay some rent, but he was constantly in debt and had continuous friction with Antonio over this money owed.

Antonio also made labor tenancy arrangements for others involved in the case, those in "Chenjerai's gang" as he put it, who could not afford the rents for their huts in the povo section of the farm. If they could not pay the Z$100 rent, they worked for free on Antonio's fields to cover it. Four days of work per month was equivalent to the rent, although Antonio said that some worked more so they could also get some money to buy food.

The latter arrangement was a common labor form practiced by people involved in the case. It is called *maricho*, doing piece-work for someone in exchange for money or food, a labor form more commonly found in the communal lands (Worby 1994). These workers entered into a maricho relationship with those who had permanent jobs, such as employees at the council houses, teachers at Karigamombe School, or other workers on small-scale commercial farms. Tasks ranged from weeding and harvesting, to making bricks for new houses or other structures being built. Such jobs were few and often depended on the person having a relationship with the employer beforehand—that they were recognized by them or by someone they already knew.

Others sought and found work on other commercial farms, working as casual or seasonal workers. These jobs often did not require a previous connection to the employer or foreman, although at times it helped. A few mornings when I was sitting at the musososo in 1999, a farm truck would pull up next to the camp calling for volunteers staying there to pick fruit. Many men and women would drop what they were doing and clamber aboard the truck. Often they received less than minimum wage. At one point there were so many workers coming from this area, both those who were locked out and others living at Mupungu and Carl farms, to work at Irontree farm near Oxfordshire that the farmer would send a tractor. As Chenjerai observed in February 2000, "Our survival here has been difficult. We have had to cheat, steal, and do all sorts of things. . . . Our stay here has also benefited other farms because they managed to get a cheap pool of labor for weeding. We allowed ourselves to be underpaid to survive."

In late 1999, Mercy, Gutu, and others worked on Chibhoyi farm near Kunwa Doro. It was owned by a black Zimbabwean. They complained of being underpaid—instead of paying the required Z$38 a day, the farmer initially paid workers Z$32 and then, later, Z$29 a day, "taking advantage of our desperation," as Tapedza observed. He continued by noting that "Contracts are not really entered into. One just gets paid daily. We Upfumi people know our rights but our hunger makes us do it." The potential mobilizing force of rights was tempered by the political economy of livelihood possibilities. When a few workers complained to their employer about their low payment, they told me that the farmer threatened to pull his gun on them. They ended up leaving the job after three weeks.

A similar event happened on Nyoka farm in November 1999. On the second day of working there, a foreman was yelling at women from the musososo, saying they should not rest. As some of these women later staying at the musososo told me, the women talked back, and the foreman fired them on the spot. The next day, these women continued; they returned to the farm and confronted the white farmer, demanding to be paid for two days. According to Rebecca, one of these women, the farmer declined; when they refused to leave the office, he phoned the police. When the police came and discovered that they had signed no contracts, they advised the women that they had no case and told them to leave. When the women still refused and the police officer then discovered that they were from the Upfumi musososo, Rebecca said with a smile, "The police then left with the farmer and talked with him and the farmer returned and said he will give us our money. The police had told him, 'If you don't give them their money, you will be in trouble.'" Warming up to her account, Rebecca added, "We told the farmer that he is employing child labor, and you don't pay overtime. Then we told the foreman [who had scolded them], 'If we see you in the Berkshire area, we will beat you.'"

The farm workers involved in the war at Upfumi prided themselves in knowing their rights and in having a reputation of being bold. The labor struggle had energized and emboldened these women workers to make demands, which they told me they would not have done in the past. However, this did not necessarily translate into actually ensuring their rights were respected or acknowledged.

In the last half of 1999, Tapedza, the chairman of the workers committee when the labor dispute began, was working as a night guard at a farm abattoir fifteen or so kilometers away. He got the job because a woman who was part of their struggle was living on this same farm with her husband. Tapedza had asked her if she knew of any jobs, since he needed to get some money because he and his wife were expecting their first child; the woman told him of this guard position. He lived at this farm Sunday to Friday nights, returning to his wife at the musososo one night each week. He informed me that the workers there "are exploited," with herdsmen working for thirty days straight, with no days off, and workers receiving their monthly pay whenever the farmer wanted to give it to them, "regardless of what the Collective Bargaining Agreement for the farms states. There is no such thing as a workers committee, GAPWUZ (General Agriculture and Plantation Workers' Union of Zimbabwe) or NSSA (National Social Security Authority)," he fulminated. Yet, "No one says anything. They are afraid. They depend on the boss for maize-meal, gardens, etc. 'If I am chased away, where would I go?' they ask themselves."

No one had signed a contract, and, Tapedza claimed, people were afraid that the white farmer could physically assault them, although, he added, he never saw such an act. However, he did observe the fear during the evening when they were paid for the month: "The farmer was drunk and the workers who had been on the farm longer [than me] asked me and other new employees to enter into the kitchen to receive their pay first, as they were afraid the boss may be in a bad mood." He also noted that since he was already involved in the case with Upfumi and did not want to get involved in another one, he also kept quiet and accepted the conditions. Struggling to enable farm workers to have a say or a better hold in their conditional belonging was hard to pursue, with a high possibility of detrimental effects on one's livelihoods and emotions, as Tapedza knew well by then.

Whereas subjecting themselves to different aspects of territorialized forms of power on commercial farms was common, there were many other livelihood practices the people of the musososo pursued. Some collected grass for thatching or wild fruits during the winter season and then (along with many others living alongside the Harare–Marondera corridor) sat next to the highway advertising their wares to passing vehicles. Other income-generating activities pursued by those living at the camp or renting accommodation from Mupungu, Carl, and other nearby locations included mending and selling knitted wear to teachers and other salaried people in the area, growing and selling marijuana, repairing bicycles and radios, cabinet-making, brewing and selling beer or home-made liquor, buying and reselling different items, and sex-work. The latter was said to be a common practice among some of the women renting accommodations on the small farms (as will be discussed in chapter 4). But this was just one of many liveli-hood activities carried out by women involved in the labor struggle. All were precarious in terms of the amount of income generated and consistency of pay. Many of the fired workers engaged in some of these economic practices.

For example, one woman did hairdressing—charging between Z$25 to Z$200, depending on the service (e.g., setting hair, perming, or giving a "dread"). Another woman, Maria, pulled her children from school be-cause she could no longer afford to pay their school fees. She did maricho of weeding or selling cigarettes, and at times she worked as a bartender, al-though noting that "It was not always easy as drunk men can abuse you." Jane, Nyasha, and another woman at times went together to buy and then sell beer, sharing the profits among the three of them. Mary was working at Antonio's bar on Mupungu farm but was let go and was only paid Z$700 for three months of work, much to her disgust. She then moved across the high-way to the council houses and began buying from the Chibuku (a national brand of sorghum beer) delivery truck. She explained that "I buy five crates of scuds[2] on Mondays and Thursdays. They cost Z$450 and I get Z$600 from the sales, giving me Z$300 as a weekly profit." She said two others were also selling beer at the council houses. They went together to pay the Z$200 monthly rent for the house, which also served as the place where they sold their scuds.

Those already with some money often bought items for resale—low-grade meat from nearby butcheries; vegetables from farms or greens from people's gardens; or clothes, shoes, or other items from stores in Harare, fac-tories in Gweru, warehouses in Bulawayo, and so forth. They tended to sell these items to people who had permanent jobs, often selling the merchan-dise on credit and collecting payment at the end of the month on payday. For example, Rebecca explained that her mother, who was a "house-girl" (domestic worker) in Goromonzi, helped her by giving her some money so she could buy vegetables for resale.

None of these activities was necessarily new for these farm workers—many had engaged in such activities to diversify their livelihoods while working full-time on Upfumi or on other farms. But during their war, such activities took on greater importance. The mass firing and the struggle heightened both the sense of livelihood insecurity and the conditionality of belonging. One woman said that her survival depended on borrowed money, doing the occasional maricho for teachers and others, and selling thatching grass during the winter. She owed so much money to St. Vincent School where her daughter was in grade 7 that they forced her daughter to quit. Her daughter volunteered to go visit her mother's sister at a nearby farm to look for work to get money to buy food and pay for school fees. "Life is too difficult now," she complained. "We are suffering while waiting for the law to take its course."

Starting work in October 1998, one male worker had counted on sending his wages from Upfumi to his wife staying at his musha in Masvingo province to pay for school fees for their children. That plan ended a month later when he was fired because of "the war." As he put it, "The case of Upfumi has pained me very much as it destroyed my life because I could not send money home. My children sold eight cows so they could buy food and pay for school fees for the two sons doing O Levels." In the meantime, he made and sold reed mats on the surrounding farms, making about Z$800 every two months.

Despite the translocal characteristics of their livelihoods, which ranged across farms or involved buying and selling activities that reached across Zimbabwe, the one place that was specifically excluded from them was Upfumi itself, a mere several hundred meters from the musososo. Once the musososo was established, Zimfarm forbade its employees having contact with the people living there or staying at Mupungu and other farms. The farm guards sought to prevent those involved in the labor struggle from entering into the workplace and the compound, thus fraying, if not breaking, some preexisting economic and familial relationships. Management exerted pressure through their workers, seeking to deploy domestic government as a way to discipline some of those who were involved in the struggle against Zimfarm. Upfumi's management mobilized the power/sovereignty nexus of belonging in this struggle.

Ruth provides a good example of this. In July 2000, she explained that she ended up "quitting the war" in September 1999 because she was pregnant and was quite ill. "I thought maybe I will die before I tasted my money." Her husband who worked at Karigamombe Training Centre also counseled her to collect the payout from Upfumi. At that time, Chapunga was offering permanent workers Z$2500. She took the money, signed a three-month contract, and worked until she gave birth in January. When she went back to Zimfarm, Ruth recalled that "management told us not to talk to them [the people of the musososo] for they feared we [current Upfumi workers] may become more demanding."

In August 1999, while sitting at the musososo, I would, on occasion, see women and men rush from the camp to surround and confront a worker coming down the drive or a path from Upfumi. They were confronting them because the worker owed money to one of their group for goods he or she had bought from them. After the Upfumi workers were paid in August 1999, Chenjerai and Gutu, another male worker in the camp, snuck into the compound and confronted people who owed money to those in the dispute, including Precious who had a very profitable buying and selling practice (as discussed in chapter 2). Another of their members in the struggle, Enoch, was a carpenter, and he was grabbed by farm guards when he went looking for money owed to him. The guards wanted to fine him for entering, but Enoch managed to extract himself without paying, although his story circulated among those at the musososo about the risks of entering Upfumi.

Familial relationships were also severed by the lock-out. One man talked about the pressure he received from management when he was working at Upfumi during the war to divorce his partner, who was part of the strike. "Chapunga [the human resources manager of Zimfarm East] changed me from a good job in the workshop to the fields as I refused to put pressure on my wife to accept his offer to take some money and return to work. While in the fields, the supervisors blamed me for every mistake made by others, all because I refused to divorce my wife." A woman who was hired as a replacement worker at Upfumi after the labor dispute observed that many "'staying together marriages' [*kuchaya mapoto*][3] were broken because some men who had 'wives' at the musososo started to remarry women in the compound because they could not sleep with their wives who were at the camp." In turn, she continued, this rule meant that working women were caught between management laws and patriarchal family laws. "For instance, a man who was staying at the musososo would ask his wife to come and see him during working hours and when she failed to turn up the husband would accuse the wife of not listening and respecting his wishes."

Those engaged in the labor struggle also were treated as abnormal by other workers who could not understand why they did not accept the money initially offered by the farm. As Netsai remarked, "Workers on neighbouring farms call us *vapenzi* [crazy people] since we are fighting against the whites who have all the money and power. At times they taunt us when they walk by the musososo." Grace observed that "Other farm workers said us DRC[4] people were mad in the head as we had nowhere to go, but staying there. They said 'why waste your time staying in the wild instead of going to help your parents with work at the musha?'" Another worker said he felt ashamed for not working and needing to rely on his wife who worked at a neighboring commercial farm. He sheepishly said that people laughed at him, saying that he was the one who should be working. "I am so ashamed that I am going to ensure that we get at least Z$10,000 from Zimfarm." As Tapedza put it on August 1, 2000, a few months after the end of the legal struggle, "These other farm workers now say we were strong since we won, but at the time they did not help us. They only taunted us. Only our relatives really helped us. . . . And they were obliged to help."

The workers in the struggle drew actively on webs of obligation within family and kin; in so doing, their actions increased the strains and cracks within those relationships. Some workers in the struggle went back to their parents' musha. Others stayed with relatives. Most relied on borrowing from their relatives, promising, like Chenjerai to Mr. Mupungu, to pay back their debts after the end of the labor dispute, when, hopefully, they would be paid a significant lump sum. As Grace said, "When we were fired in October we still had money left over from our pay check but then it became smaller and smaller, yet we continued as we thought the war was going to end soon. We would then talk to our relatives who supported us by bringing us food or a bit of money for us to buy vegetables from others who have gardens. We would then resell those vegetables for more money, to make our money go further."

At the same time, many of these fired workers experienced much tension with relatives who counseled their kin in the dispute that they were foolish to join in such a long labor struggle against not only a white farmer but against a large company like Zimfarm.

Albert, who stayed at the musososo, said his brother who was the pack-shed manager at Upfumi almost cut ties with him after he had been evicted from the farm compound. Before that event, his brother had given him money so that his wife and child could go to their parents' musha in Buhera. Yet after Upfumi evicted the workers in the dispute from the compound, Albert said, "He took me as stupid, as someone who doesn't think. He said I should have taken the first offer of Z$200. But," Albert continued, "if I took that I would only have a three-month contract which would be a problem. After the three months, they would stop me from working for a few days and then have me start another one, like they are doing with their workers now, for they want to avoid treating them as permanent workers." His brother shunned him for a long time until "the day we went to court on October 27 and when he heard about the money they are talking about, that is when he said 'Your story seems to be going somewhere' and he is now giving me food and clothes."

Moreover, the tensions many single women had already experienced with their families were exacerbated by the new demands that they made because they no longer received regular income, even if it was low wages from farm work. Albert observed that the single women with children were especially facing pressure. Many of them were receiving letters from parents or siblings looking after their children saying that they needed to come home. "Seeing the hardships we are facing," Albert opined, "it is better for them to be here [at the musososo] so that if we win our case then they can carry something with them when they return to the musha. Some of their parents think they are engaged in prostitution, but it is not true." These relationships of affect and belonging on the farms were thus evaluated and transacted through moral criteria.

Overhearing Albert's account, Pedzi then took up the story. She explained why she decided to stay at the musososo and not return to her parents' musha at Nyamapanda, near the northeastern border with Mozambique: "If I go home and find there are financial problems, what will I do? I know I will be alone as my family does not agree with what I do. It is better for me to strive here by doing maricho and wait to get money at the end of our case. At home, I have two children who go to school. If I go home empty-handed, it will cause problems with my parents. So I can send a bit when I do maricho, though right now those jobs have disappeared as digging, planting, and weeding tasks are finished."

Now, she continued, she receives a lot of letters from her parents and her siblings, demanding that she return. "Their last letter said, 'We are going to sell your goats and send your kids to you because it seems you are enjoying yourself there. Why don't you come home?'" She said matter-of-factly that if that happens, she will accept her kids, observing that others had their children staying in the musososo. She also noted that she has a three-year-old son with another man who still works at Upfumi. But since she was evicted, this man now stays with another woman in the farm compound and their son stays with his father's relatives in Beitbridge near the South African border in the southern part of Zimbabwe.

These workers sometimes drew on these everyday hardships and concerns to understand some of their struggles and the wider political debates going on. The dramatic politics that were heating up on the national stage in 1999 were very much items of conversation and reflection for those staying at the musososo as they examined the topics through aspects of their own lives.

Rights, Land, and Citizenship: Views from the Musososo

Many of the women workers drew on marital metaphors in describing their conflict and in explaining their understanding of rights and justice. In early December 1999, I talked with a number of the women at the musososo about their next steps and whether they would stay at the camp or not. Pedzi said that in terms of rights, it was like being a wife chased away from home for being in love with another man: "She would know that she is wrong and would return to her family. However, if a wife is chased away because her husband wants another woman, she instead goes to her *tete* [her father's sister] to ask her to talk to her husband. They will then negotiate. And thus we are waiting for the court to come and tell us to pack our things and go home or to go back to Upfumi." In other words, she had a valid claim of belonging with her husband, and she could seek intervention by relatives to reinforce that claim. Agatha agreed and said, "If you know you are wrong, you leave. If you have been wronged, you stay, even if it kills you." To assert rights in marriage can be painful, they implied, but one had to do so to bolster one's claims in the relationship.

From this perspective, they saw management as negligent in its unequal relationship with workers. Rather than leave the relationship, they drew in the relevant interveners, the Labor Tribunal taking on the role of tete (father's sister) here, to try to repair the damaged relationship. The aim was not to sever the relationship but to persuade the dominant party to recognize the wrongs it committed against the weaker party.

Upon listening to this conversation, Nyasha reiterated a more liberal juridical view, asserting, "I know my rights. I acquired them through independence and learned about them through communicating with others and the teachings we got from GAPWUZ. Through all this I have learned my rights." Here, the workers qua "workers" have rights, and they need to assert them if they are being infringed upon. In other words, the subject (workers) has rights as a self-possessed entity. She then extended this metaphor of rights to make a more nationalist claim: "As a farm worker, I now know my rights. This land belongs to us and so we should stay here. It is our land." Nyasha was echoing statements made within ongoing wider public debates and actions concerning land redistribution and the rights of black Zimbabweans to land taken from them by white colonizers. Yet the subject position of "black Zimbabweans" has not necessarily included farm workers.

By the late 1990s, the demand that farm workers also were eligible for any land the government took from white farmers was part of wider policy and media discussions. Yet it rubbed against the dominant way in which farm workers were understood as a represented community: as foreigners with no rights to Zimbabwe other than being cheap labor. But, by the late 1990s, this viewpoint was being contested in various ways, as people involved in the Upfumi struggle knew.

The implications of the citizenship dilemmas facing many farm workers was an issue discussed more publicly in 1999. For instance, Chenjerai said that he had raised the issue of citizenship at a Constitutional Commission hearing. He told me that when he attended a hearing held nearby, he raised the problem of farm workers born in Zimbabwe getting proof of their citizenship. In response, he said one Commissioner observed that "Dual citizenship is more of a problem and that farm workers are mainly aliens who came here to work and should not be given land or benefit from the land resettlement scheme." Mr. Nzou of the Mashonaland East unit for the national Department of Labor also raised the issue of citizenship, farm workers, and land redistribution. He informed me in 1999 that he was on the provincial land acquisition committee, identifying possible farms for designation for resettlement. He said he had suggested include labor relations on the criteria used to evaluate if a farm should be so designated,[5] with those farmers with poor labor relations possibly being targeted for compulsory acquisition. In November 1999, he said his colleagues on the committee had not immediately accepted his suggestion, but he ruminated that this was a burning question of what to do with the farm employees on designated farms: "Should they be repatriated to their countries of origin, as many are aliens?" He also did not necessarily think that these alien farm workers were entitled to land.

This view was shared by the Goromonzi district administrator when I spoke with her in October 1999. She patronizingly declared that most farm workers could not grasp the key issues during the Constitutional Commission hearings she attended in the commercial farming areas in the district: "For example, there is the question on executive president versus a prime minister. To them, there is no difference and it took time to explain this to them." The main issue for farm workers, she observed, was resettlement. "Some of them do not have other homes. After they become too old, they will be kicked out of the farms. Most of the squatters are Mozambicans, Malawians, Zambians, though there are also some Zimbabweans." It was clear, however, that she did not necessarily see such "foreigners" as prime candidates for land resettlement. But not everyone agreed with her.

In November 1999, Councillor Banda said that similar debates were occurring within ZANU (PF) structures. He told me that for a long time farm workers were not being given land within the resettlement program (see Moyo, Rutherford, Amanor-Wilks 2000; Waeterloos and Rutherford 2004), but that he and MPs (members of parliament) representing commercial farming areas were making representations to senior ministers and ZANU (PF) leaders to try to rectify this inequality. He continued, "Those resisting us are saying farm workers are from faraway countries, are aliens. We reply that they are now full residents of Zimbabwe. Their children are citizens and if they are not resettled they will become squatters." As a son of a Malawian farm worker, he had a personal stake in this issue. This debate only increased after violent land occupations and the so-called fast-track land redistribution began the following year, as discussed in the next chapter.

The farm workers themselves also saw their claims to the farm as different from belonging to a musha. Working on the farm was "only a job, not a musha" was the common sentiment expressed when I asked these fired workers—as well as those still working on farms—about their ties of belonging to a farm. Those involved in the labor dispute with Upfumi said it was easier to motivate them to make the toilets and the rubbish pit at the musososo than, say, on a farm compound. They reasoned that at the camp their efforts were for their own struggle, whereas at the farm "our sweat is for the *murungu*." Attachment to land through one's own work for oneself (or one's family or, in this case, for others in a struggle) was stronger than working on land owned by another. The musha in a communal land was the contrast most frequently used by farm workers to differentiate their life on a farm; a concept, as Donald Moore (2005, 104) puts it, "gathers together the affect and materiality of home, hearth and huts."

However, while a few in the Upfumi struggle like Nyasha would speculate about getting a stand on Upfumi if it was ever designated for land redistribution, during late 1999 and early 2000, the main focus was finishing the labor struggle, which was not going nearly as quickly as they had presumed it would. Rita, who lived at Mupungu, talked of how those staying at the musososo suffered and that people felt sorry for them. "The Apostolic Church used to come and say we want to help you on your story, let us pray together. And we would do prayers all night or a *pungwe*. The church people saw the way people were living at the musososo and it pained and touched them. They had no water, people lived like animals, with no tent and nowhere to get food." Rita further reflected, "There were times when people would cry, especially the women. It was painful, for people were used to getting money at the end of the month, but that was now finished." One older woman said, "I did not want the money offered by Upfumi management at first as it is very little. The first offer was Z$200 and then raised to Z$2500. We do not know the truth now when we will get the money and how much." Mercy added, "I was taught by GAPWUZ my rights as a worker. GAPWUZ taught our leaders and our leaders taught us." One young woman agreed, saying, "I am staying here because of the rights we were told by our leaders. They read to us books from the labor office and so we want to follow those laws until we get our money. Had we not read those laws I would have gone home. I am anxious to receive my money so I can go back to my parents' musha in Zvimba because so many of my relatives have passed away without me able to go to their funerals."

The suffering in late 1999 for these farm workers was not mainly about land, unlike the "suffering for territory" by those living in Kaerezi poignantly discussed by Moore (2005, 2), in which he shows "the diverse ways land comes to be inhabited, labored on, idiomatically expressed, and suffered for in specific moments and milieus." For the farm workers in the labor war at Upfumi, it was a suffering of impoverishment, vulnerability, of not having a firm sense and sensibility of belonging to a territorialized sociopolitical form through which one could make various claims, even if it was as a farm worker. By this time, it was also a suffering exacerbated by growing splits among themselves; splits that were amplified by their increasing entanglement in electoral politics and a growing concern for how long they could continue their struggle. The bone marrow of the case started to shatter.

Whose Victory? Politics and Leadership

On November 4, 1999, I attended a small meeting in the Zimbabwe Labour Centre (ZLC) office within the International Socialist Organization (ISO) office. There were two representatives from GAPWUZ, Chenjerai, Precious, and two others from Upfumi, as well as Bhukurin and Gwisai from the ZLC. The latter gave a somewhat optimistic appraisal of the negotiations he had with the Zimfarm lawyer, Chagonda, saying that they had agreed that those working for more than eight months are permanent workers, despite Chapunga's contrary opinion, and that they will get paid for twelve months. Yet, Gwisai continued, those who were working elsewhere would have any money earned deducted from their pay-out. He said if Chapunga had evidence that these people worked elsewhere, then Zimfarm is within their rights to do so. He added that Chagonda informed him that they had evidence that around thirty of those people claiming to be part of the case actually were on leave when everyone was fired and thus left on their own accord. As a consequence, they would receive nothing from the company.

Precious responded that Chagonda was lying because when she and others returned from leave, the supervisors told them that they were all fired. Gwisai said that if the lawyer had evidence, he would have to agree with him "because I will not compromise the agreement for these thirty people." He also raised the issue of some type of levy on the award to help finance the ZLC (Gwisai later informed me that they were unable to represent workers involved in other labor disputes because they had no other funds). In short, it was clear that the framework of an agreement was there, yet it soon became hostage to the maneuverings of the main protagonists as each sought to increase pressure on the other; poritikisi was one such tactic.

Over the next month, a series of tactical moves were made by Zimfarm and the workers' committee representing the fired workers. Chapunga went to neighboring farms to ask the farmers and farm clerks to show him their books to see if any of the workers involved in the dispute had worked there. Chenjerai often went to the farms afterward to also talk to the clerks about this request and to try to convince them not to hand over any information to Chapunga.

The workers' committee also organized workers involved in their case to enter into Upfumi to hold a demonstration to demand a final settlement of their case to increase pressure on the company. They ensured that people who were part of their case but living in the townships or elsewhere entered, whereas those who had been evicted stayed outside the gate. Still, Chapunga got the police to charge those living in the camp for trespassing, and a court date in the Goromonzi magistrate's court was set to hear the evidence.

People in the camp, however, believed that these pressure tactics worked; on November 13, 1999, the people at the musososo finally received a copy of the Zimfarm offer. It was written by Chagonda, addressed to Gwisai, and brought to them by GAPWUZ. The company offer said that it does not need to reemploy any worker; that about forty workers, including the key people on the workers' committee, voluntarily joined the fired workers and were not part of the case; and that it would pay a one-year salary, about Z$14,000, to permanent workers involved in the case. The workers debated this offer, with those fatigued by the long struggle willing to take the money while others wanted reinstatement and additional money to cover the damages they had suffered. As Tapedza sputtered the day after they received the offer, "We were driven out like animals [in July 1999]—those [replacement workers] working at Upfumi were dismissed early from work at the packshed to see our things being moved onto the lorry to dump at the DA's office. I don't know where to start. It is like a person who was told his father is dead, mother is dead, wife and kids dead. . . . Where to start?"

By the end of the month, over the objections of those who wanted the package as well as the advice of GAPWUZ and Gwisai, the workers' committee instructed their lawyer to turn down the offer and go back to the Labor Tribunal. They asked if those in the case who wanted out—about a third of them—could take the Z$14,000, but Chagonda refused. Shortly afterward, they learned that Zimfarm changed lawyers, with Chagonda passing the case on to Brian Kagoro, another labor lawyer from the same firm, and someone who was very active in the National Constitutional Assembly (NCA) and the wider democracy movement. Chenjerai, Tapedza, and others convinced most of the others involved in the case that they could get a better package, but there was strong dissent, particularly from some of the women.

There was growing division between Chenjerai and some of the women at the musososo who were unhappy that he was advocating for them to stay in the labor dispute. They were concerned that he was monopolizing contacts with outsiders such as Gwisai, GAPWUZ, and myself, and, when they objected, Chenjerai threatened violence against them. Chenjerai's sense of leadership did not invite criticism, particularly from women.

As noted in the previous chapter, many Zimbabweans associate masculine leadership with the ability to command respect through one's ability to wield words and possibly intimidation. Although Chenjerai had the ability to command respect and support through his speaking skills, he was not adverse to intimidation, particularly against women involved in the labor struggle, as the following example nicely illustrates.

In October 1999, a bag of *matemba* (small dried fish) that I had bought for the people of the camp and a lunchbox in which it was kept went missing. Accounts differed regarding Chenjerai's next move. But, in all accounts, Chenjerai stressed his masculine prerogative as leader. Chenjerai threatened to burn the camp down, saying in the words Tapedza told to me in 2002, "Women are rude and don't listen to men" and that, if they did not listen to him, "I am going to burn down the camp." Grace's recollection was that Chenjerai was accusing women of stealing the matemba and that he would burn the camp down if no one revealed the thief. Chenjerai then set fire to the camp. Because he had forewarned them, the residents were able to get their belongings out. Tapedza continued his account, saying that Chenjerai said people could report him to the police, but no one did for they feared if they did so "they may fail in getting their money for which they have been fighting." Grace said Chenjerai threatened to beat up women and that "if anyone asks who burned the camp, say the enemy did so!" The women, she added, "did so as we were afraid of being beaten." As the acknowledged leader of the labor war, Chenjerai was asserting his masculine authority over the musososo, the site most closely associated with the workers' struggle, drawing on threats of violence to underscore his position. He was trying to assert sovereign power over those living there.

I did not learn of this incident until after their legal case was over. During one of my visits in October 1999, the men were putting thatch on the roof of one of the women's sleeping shelters, but they told me they were just preparing for the rainy season. Chenjerai was sitting next to me as we watched the thatch being put on, saying that he had no skills in thatching. Although I noted at the time that the musososo residents were somber that day and that there was tension in the air, I was ignorant of the growing dissension among those waging the struggle.

There was another fire just after Christmas 1999, this time caused accidentally, which destroyed the entire musososo, burning all the belongings of the women and men staying there. It also destroyed the beginnings of the book that Tawonga had started to write (although he told me in June 2000 that he had recommenced his writing project). The loss of their limited belongings and money was keenly felt by many involved in the Upfumi struggle. As Goodson said, he was at Mupungu "when I saw the smoke one evening. I and others ran there to help. We could not do anything and the camp burnt to ashes. We cried with the people of the musososo. It pained me because many were left with only the clothes they were wearing" and especially since "the musososo was the base of our struggle."

Exacerbating these divisions was a bitter contest between Chapunga and the workers' committee. After the fire burned down their camp, the residents and others rebuilt structures—one for men and one for women— although this time they were even more hastily constructed. Those involved in their case staying at Mupungu and surrounding farms also gave some clothes, blankets, money, and food to those who lost their belongings. Tawonga noted that a few workers at Upfumi secretly gave some clothes to those in the camp but that they "cautioned us do not publicly talk about it as 'We are afraid of Chapunga who was hunting for anyone at Upfumi helping those in the musososo.'" Archie observed that Chapunga assigned a guard to monitor anyone bringing clothes from the compound, "And if anyone is seen bringing anything to us they are fired."

Chapunga had long been approaching workers involved in the case, offering them money of varying amounts to return to work. Tapedza talked about how Chapunga would say to him, "You, Tapedza, are better educated than Chenjerai, and I will give you a management job, if you accept Z$2000 for coming back." Then Chenjerai said Chapunga would come to him and say "We never fired you—you are a good worker, smart man, come back for a better job." Chenjerai and Tapedza would tell each other about these attempts by Chapunga and once, in early 1999, they decided to trick Chapunga by staging a major dispute between themselves, knowing that the word would reach Chapunga. Shortly after Chenjerai stormed away from Tapedza after their putative argument, Chapunga arrived at Chenjerai's home at Mupungu, asking Chenjerai and his supporters to campaign for the fired workers to take a small package. Tapedza told me with a smirk, "Chapunga said that, 'We are now divorced and as a loving husband I will give you a small departure gift'": Z$1500 for those on three-month contracts, Z$2500 for those working for eight months or more, and Z$400 for those who had signed a disclaimer form. A few days later, Chenjerai told Chapunga and the farm's human relations officer, Mr. Madoro, that he convinced most of them, including Tapedza, and that "we want to be paid." Tapedza came up to them and said "Yes, we are tired. Life is difficult. We want to be paid today."

So, as Tapedza and Chenjerai recounted to me while chuckling, Chapunga went into the office to bring a table and a time-book out to the msasa tree outside the gate and asked a colleague to gather money for the pay-out. Tapedza told him that, "No, you cannot pay us here. You employed us in your office so let us go there so you can formally compensate us." So Chapunga went into the gates, and "all of us workers who were gathered there marched behind him singing how tired they were with his harassment and will not accept his bribes but want to be treated with dignity." Tapedza added, between laughs, that there were some European visitors in Schultz's office at the time, and, after hearing the noise, they asked why the workers were singing and dancing. Schultz reportedly told them that "They are being paid today and so they are happy." They said that Chapunga was scared to leave Upfumi that day in case "we attacked him for his attempt at forcing us to accept the company offer."

The story exemplifies the type of deception deployed by both sides, the maneuvers that management used to ensure it achieved its goal, and how management players could also be fearful of the workers. Chenjerai's leadership skills, discussed the previous chapter, were now not specifically geared toward the pedagogical project of educating farm workers about their rights. Rather, they were directed to the goal of winning their case. It was a war, and it played out throughout the Berkshire/Oxfordshire area. But the tricks that Chenjerai and Tapedza thought they were playing on Chapunga also were interpreted differently by some workers involved in the case. As the case dragged on, whenever workers saw Chapunga talk to Chenjerai or others, some thought they were possibly working on a deal together, with one of their leaders selling them all out for personal gain. This was especially apparent after the tribunal hearing on October 27, as the supporters split over whether to accept the negotiated deal or not.

As discussed in chapter 2, poritikisi as a cultural practice often included paranoia and deception and the possibility of violence. Starting in November 1999, a growing number in the struggle started to associate those traits with Chenjerai. The women critics of Chenjerai complained of being kept in the dark and of his unchallenged assertion of authority over them. Agatha drew on familial anecdotes to explain her perception of the imbalance in May 2000: "We are being treated like infants here. . . . People here are afraid of our leaders and we are just waiting to hear what they say. Whenever we say anything against our leaders we are labeled 'bad children.'" She talked about how only Chenjerai went to the offices in Harare and that, after November 1999, when he returned he did not tell them anything about what he had learned. That month, she gathered her belongings from the musososo and began to rent a room at the RDC houses for Z$100 per month, saying she was scared of Chenjerai, given some threats he had made toward her when he was drunk. In March 2000, she said she still contributed to the travel funds for Chenjerai to go to and fro between Berkshire and Harare, but she was eager for the case to end, noting that after the fire very few people were remaining in the musososo.

By then, those few remaining in the camp assumed that Chenjerai was favoring those in the case who stayed at Mupungu, where he still resided. They observed that most meetings he had were held there and that sometimes those at the musososo were not informed of these meetings. Echoing Agatha, Tapedza said in March 2000 that Chenjerai collected money to travel to Harare, "But when he returns he never told us what he learned, only telling those at Mupungu who then would tell us. And during the meetings, he would scold you." Precious came to visit from Harare where she was staying and listened to their complaints about Chenjerai. After her departure, Chenjerai visited the camp while drunk, berated them and claimed that, in Grace's words, "You people of the musososo, you now belong to Precious and I no longer represent you. He could even threaten some people, saying, 'I can beat you.'" As the labor struggle continued and tensions built up, Chenjerai's leadership increasingly drew on the threat of violence.

Chenjerai's women supporters explained Chenjerai's secrecy as due to strategic reasons, given the ongoing war. Patience said that there was a spy for Chapunga among them, for Chapunga would know of their next moves and tactics and he would boast to them that he knew everything going on. According to this paranoid logic, Chenjerai no longer could tell them what he was learning during his trips to Harare because Chapunga would then learn about it. She acknowledged, however, that this made "everyone mad at him, saying he has abandoned us and that they no longer trusted him."

In May 2000, only sixteen people remained in the camp, eleven women and five men. There was a sense of fatigue and pain. Hope said, "Most women are now tired and want their money and [to] leave. We are now entering winter and where do we get blankets? The ones we had were burnt." Ruth confirmed the sense of desperation, saying that their relatives were tired of supporting them. "We have no blankets and if we go home to our musha to collect some, our parents and relatives would say 'why do you not just stay at home?'" She also painted a picture of fear, noting that the snakes were very large and now, with so few men staying at the musososo, there were few protectors: "We can be raped or murdered here because we no longer have protection." Another woman echoed this, saying in a soft voice that "We no longer have the support from the big men of the workers committee. We are now scared of being raped since we don't have the support from Chenjerai, Tapedza, etc. We are now dying of hunger here. We cannot get food from anywhere now as we cannot work on other farms because it may lessen the money we get from Zimfarm. Our life here depends on the mercy of God." This loss of leadership led to a range of concerns and a palpable sense of uncertainty and vulnerability. An ethic of solidarity cultivated by previous practices of leadership had bled into a register of fear, suspicion, and resignation due to new divisions inculcated by some of the leaders and by the drawn out negotiations for a settlement—a register that many had associated with electoral politics before their struggle.

The Tribunal heard their case on March 24, 2000. After the hearing, Gwisai had a meeting with the workers to inform them that the judge once again counseled a negotiated settlement and that Zimfarm was willing to offer fourteen months' salary to those deemed to be permanent workers. Reinstatement was not an option. All but a few of those assembled agreed to accept the package. I was later told by a number of them that the majority talked about those among them who had passed away or were in need of money to cover health expenses and school fees and to pay back loans and the need to finish with the case. Chenjerai was one of the few who wanted to reject it; he was in favor of sending the case to the Supreme Court, despite the advice of Gwisai, who said they would possibly then receive even less money. Chenjerai's current leadership depended on the labor dispute to continue, even though the ties of attachment with many others who had been following him were straining. However, the majority opinion won out this time.

Divisive Victory

On April 11, the lawyers Gwisai and Kagoro agreed to a negotiated package that divided the 419 workers who were represented into seven categories:

1. Twenty-eight appellants who were deemed to be permanent but had already accepted packages from Zimfarm and thus had waived their rights.
2. One hundred sixty-two appellants who were deemed permanent, but who Zimfarm alleged had been employed elsewhere since being fired and thus should have any wages earned deducted from their packages. Of the 162, Gwisai admitted that 24 had been so employed. However, for the remaining 138 there had to be joint verification of time sheets and testimony from the clerks and managers of the alleged farm employers by representatives of Zimfarm and the appellants within three weeks.
3. The seventeen permanent workers whom management agreed were not employed elsewhere.
4. There were eighty-eight appellants who were deemed to be seasonal employees who had already accepted packages from Zimfarm and thus were not part of this case.
5. The fifty-eight seasonals who had not resigned and were not employed elsewhere were to be paid up to the expiration of their contracts. There was debate over the status of four of them, with the appellants arguing that they were in actuality permanent workers. Thus, a verification process of their status would occur, and they would then be paid accordingly as a seasonal or a permanent worker.
6. There were forty-seven appellants whom Zimfarm claimed were not on their payroll, and these would have their status reviewed to see if they were in the employ of Zimfarm on October 28, 1998.
7. Of the nineteen appellants whom Zimfarm claimed voluntarily resigned to join those dismissed rather than being dismissed themselves, seventeen were to have a hearing with a company human resource manager from a different Zimfarm division within a month, while it was agreed the two others were not to be part of the appeal.

The latter category referred to those who were off duty, on night duty, or on leave on October 28, 1998; it included Chenjerai, Tapedza, and Precious. Thirteen of the seventeen attended hearings at the ZimfarmEast boardroom on April 26–28, 2000; the hearing determined that all of the workers' committee members had left work voluntarily.

In agreeing to this settlement, Zimfarm showed that it had improperly fired the workers, particularly because nearly half of them were deemed permanent workers. Nonetheless, these legal distinctions exacerbated the conflicts among the workers. Chenjerai claimed that these "groups created by Chapunga are making people stick to these individual groups rather than acting as one workers' group which shares the same problems." He framed it in terms of the "war," placing responsibility on Chapunga and not on the legal distinctions to which even Gwisai agreed. As was occurring in Zimbabwe itself by this time, the register of poritikisi was taking on a larger role in shaping the conflict.

As the workers waited for the verification process and the determination of who would get what money, the division between Chenjerai and many of the women increased at this time, and the relationships among the three leaders also became more frayed. Those at the camp had many accounts of Chenjerai berating them, calling them "sellouts," and becoming angry with them if they ever talked to anyone when he was not around.

Neither Chenjerai nor the people in the musososo trusted each other any longer, accusing each of betraying the other. Mr. Gutu said Chenjerai hardly visited the camp between April and June 2000. Unlike many of the women staying in the musososo, Gutu still saw Chenjerai as their natural leader and said, "We are like blind people here as a group. We do not know where to go so we ask Chenjerai 'since you know where you are going can you please lead us.'" Expanding on this, he said, "We are blind as we do not know the laws and do not even know where the offices in Harare he visits are located," although he did acknowledge that Chenjerai had monopolized these contacts. Besides, he added, "We are afraid to get into the offices because we do not know who to talk to first and what to say. Also, Chenjerai told the people in the offices 'do not listen to any person who says he or she is coming from Upfumi farm except Tapedza, myself and Precious.'" Even those "among us who mistrust him do not tell him that," he admitted, "because we might lose all our money [coming to us from the case]."

By June 2000, Precious was living permanently in Harare and was not talking to Chenjerai. Tapedza was following Chenjerai, but no longer trusted him, while feeling somewhat betrayed by the fact that he was said to be not part of the case. In May 2000, Tapedza said with some anger that "People have the right to say what they think about us as their leaders, and in Zimbabwe, there is freedom of speech. If people can denounce Mugabe, the president, without fear, why can't they do it against me?" But divisions between Chenjerai and Tapedza grew stronger, leading the latter to resign from the committee and be replaced by Enoch, who had been involved with Chenjerai in ZANU (PF) and MDC activities. The tensions among those in the struggle were exacerbated by a delay in the Zimfarm payout.

After the March 2000 tribunal hearing, two GAPWUZ members, Gwisai and Chapunga, visited different farms to look at the time books. The majority of the cases were said not to be employed, but the ZLC and Zimfarm continued to debate about who was permanent and who was not. There also was a dispute about whether they should be paid the wage rate they had been receiving when fired or whether it should include annual increments given to farm workers since then and cash in lieu of leave days owed. All of this delayed the payout to the improperly fired workers. Thrown into the rumor mill was the sudden downsizing of Upfumi farm, with hundreds of seasonal employees let go as the pack-house was scheduled to be shut down. Any permanent workers remaining at Upfumi were asked to work in the fields, transfer to another Zimfarm enterprise in Harare or another Mashonaland province, or accept a termination package. The uncertainty, frustration, and disputes came to a head on May 29, when many of those involved in the case occupied the farm.

Patience said that, by May, there were so many rumors that Zimfarm was closing down Upfumi in the hopes to evade paying the workers that the women and men at the musososo had a meeting and decided to put pressure on the company to pay them. Moreover, Arianna added, the people living in Harare townships and other places far from Upfumi said they were tired of paying money for bus fare to come to meetings at Berkshire. Netsai said they then sent word to colleagues staying in nearby farms and in Harare townships about their plans, saying "Come with your blankets and pots." On Monday, May 29, a large group of the fired workers entered Upfumi farm. Some went to the pack-houses and, in Patience's words, "pretended to work with the other workers, mixing up the baby corn with rubbish and leaves, which forced Chapunga to come from Harare to meet with us." Netsai said the current workers were fine with the occupiers, informing her and others that "we have our own dispute with Chapunga. But they did not join us as they were told when their termination cheques were going to be ready."

Chapunga traveled from Harare and tried to ensure that the delivery truck left. The workers in the struggle closed the gate, preventing it and Chapunga himself from leaving. Mercy said that "We were now telling Chapunga that we want him to sleep with us here so he can feel how painful it is to sleep in the cold!" Chapunga phoned the police and, as Jane admitted, "Everyone was scared when the police arrived." The police told the workers to let the order go and open the gate. Rita said, "All of us went and sat on the ground in front of the gate. The truck with the order started to move, thinking we would move away, but we didn't. The truck came very near to us and all the women began to cry. We were crying because we were now thinking, 'Why does he want to kill us as we only need our money.'" But the truck stopped, and, as Rita continued, "The police gave up and left. They felt mercy for us." As Arianna put it, "The police told Chapunga, 'These people are right; give them their money.' The police told us, 'We are not going to chase you away—so stay until you are given your money.'" The workers then stacked firewood in front of the gate. When the police gave up, Chapunga phoned the riot police, claiming that workers were destroying the farm. But when these police arrived and found that not to be the case, they told Chapunga to stop complaining to them. As Rita recalled, "Riot police came at midnight and asked us what is taking place. We told them our story and they went inside to talk to Chapunga who told them that he was going to give us our money on Saturday. The police told us to let him go as he had promised to give us our money." They finally let the trucks leave the farm after, in Diana's words, "we heard that the plane that was supposed to take the vegetables to Europe had already left."

Eventually, Chapunga returned, but the workers refused to talk to him, as the built-up anger over their long war bubbled to the forefront. Rita explained it this way: "Many women wanted to beat him. I was among those who wanted to do so. We were so angry. Police, who Chapunga brought with him, told us not to do so, but we were pushing him a bit." She added, "We were singing 'Chapunga, you are a witch' while playing drums, taunting him." Chapunga then talked to the leaders, even giving some firewood to the occupiers. He even offered to pay the workers right there and then, "But we refused," said Rebecca. "We told the police that we want to get the money from our lawyer. Chapunga is a very cunning man and he could rob us." They remained, occupying the farm for more than a week until Zimfarm signed a check over for all their money to the ZLC and several had seen the check. As Diana put it, "Chapunga came to us and said 'I now surrender. I have tried all the tricks but you have won.'" He then gave some money to Chenjerai and Enoch on the Sunday, June 4, to travel to Harare.

Nevertheless, many of the women did not trust Chenjerai, particularly after he and Enoch did not immediately go to Harare without explaining the delay. Rita said, "Many women were complaining and asking, 'For how long are we going to be here?' What was now happening was so painful and some women said to Chenjerai 'If we were men, we would beat you!'" When Chenjerai and Enoch refused to bring a woman with them when they left on Wednesday, June 7, some of the women met and raised money for Netsai and two other women to also travel to Harare the same day to find out what was happening. These women were wondering why Chapunga was giving money to Chenjerai and Enoch. Jane said, "We were no longer trusting Chenjerai as we were saying why is it that he is now a friend to Chapunga, our enemy? Why is he talking to him when Gwisai and GAPWUZ are not here?"

This small group of women went to the GAPWUZ office in Harare and learned that the check had been issued. When Chenjerai entered the room and saw them there, the women later told me that he was very angry with the lack of trust they had shown in him. He then took them to Gwisai's office. There the women learned that the ZLC was proposing that some of them put a portion of their money into a trust fund—an idea that Gwisai was planning to bring to the musososo on June 11 to discuss. The women returned with Chenjerai and Enoch to Upfumi and informed the occupiers what had transpired. The next day they ceased their occupation.

On Saturday, June 11, Gwisai came to the musososo to explain "the project," saying that it was not compulsory, but that if the fired workers receiving compensation from the case put most of their money in the bank, it would earn interest. They then elected trustees, none of whom belonged to their previous workers' committee. As Gwisai put it to me in July 2000, "I was surprised that they didn't elect Chenjerai or any of their other leaders." Instead, they selected Agatha, Enoch, and four others to be in charge of the fund, along with the ZLC.

This project and the payout were quickly entangled in the divisions and despair overtaking those involved in this war. While the labor struggle was coming to an end with Zimfarm, they had been increasingly caught up in the electoral war on the national scale, which affected the dynamics during the end of their struggle and what transpired afterward.

The Fraught Potentialities of Poritikisi

In 2002, Brian Kagoro told me that when his firm asked him in late 1999 if he could take the Zimfarm case, he said, "I said, 'Oh, no. Not this one.'" He was aware of it through the media, and he wanted to make sure there was no potential conflict of interest given the role ISO was playing in it and how his own prominent involvement in the democracy movement via the NCA and other activities were entangled in some of the same forums as that of his former law professor, Munyaradzi Gwisai. And, he repeated, the Upfumi case was saturated in national politics.

If the workers were involved in a war with management, they were also entangled in the emerging *poritikis ihondo* (electoral politics is war) emerging on the national stage as some ZANU (PF) officials increasingly tried to become involved in their struggle while Chenjerai also actively sought greater involvement of the MDC. At times, the two sources of political power overlapped, complicating and amplifying the suspicions and fears commonly associated with electoral politics.

In the remainder of this chapter, I sketch out some of the maneuverings of different players in relation to the national political contest as it unfolded against the backdrop of the Upfumi labor struggle. I examine how the conduct of poritikisi from November 1999 to June 2000, including the start of land occupations, intersected with farm worker lives in this area and the specific events of the Upfumi struggle. The racialized territory of commercial farms became very politicized after February 2000, but the grounding of politics also depended on specific configurations of power and social projects, particularly in terms of the mobilization of supporters and resources.

When Chagonda and Gwisai were initially trying to negotiate an agreement in November 1999, the workers debated on whether to enter Upfumi to put pressure on the company. They alerted others involved in the case on surrounding farms and in the townships to come to the musososo on Friday, November 11. Many came, although some believed they were to hear the results of negotiations that day. They had received mixed messages from GAPWUZ and ISO about whether they should enter Upfumi or not, so they decided to march to the main gate, singing songs and threatening to enter the next day if the negotiations did not finish. While at the gate, Councillor Banda appeared to address them, talking about how they had won and that ZANU (PF) would assist them in ensuring they got their jobs back. Banda then suggested he accompany them to GAPWUZ to pick up the settlement and the court order from the tribunal, which stated that they had won. The workers discussed this proposal but thought it unwise because, in Tapedza's words, "There has always been a bitter relationship between Banda and GAPWUZ and now with the MDC formation, the relationship between ZANU (PF) and GAPWUZ is very difficult."

By November 1999, Banda and Mr. Mhanya were frequent visitors to the musososo. These men saw the workers as a mobilized, politicized group who could help reinvigorate ZANU (PF) structures in the area that they admitted had gone dormant. They also saw the fired workers as a base of support for Mr. Mhanya's ambitions to run in the ZANU (PF) primaries for the 2000 parliamentary elections. As promised when they had set up the ZANU (PF) structures in late October (as discussed at the start of this chapter), they brought soccer balls and got a team of musososo men to play in a ZANU (PF)-organized soccer tournament. Yet they were uncertain of their political loyalties—as ZANU (PF) people asked Tawonga when they brought him to do some errands for Mr. Mhanya in Harare: "We can't distinguish the Upfumi people—are you MDC or ZANU (PF)?" Tawonga smiled as he recollected this encounter to me, saying it was strategic to be a bit ambiguous, although he professed "We are ZANU" to his interlocutors in Harare.

Political party loyalties were very uncertain during this time as the MDC began building support throughout Zimbabwe. There were many media analyses, rumors, and speculations on the orientations of different factions in ZANU (PF) and whether some would move over to the MDC. As a main MDC organizer in Mashonaland East, Mr. Tashanda, who was then provincial chair, told me a lot of ZANU (PF) people were coming to join MDC, with "some saying 'we are king-makers, we are politically mature, we know secrets of government and will assist you to push them aside.'" He said one had to be careful as one did not know their real intentions—whether they would act to destabilize the MDC or were actually committed to the new party. So, one just had to "make an analysis and decide wisely." The themes of electoral politics—deception, dissimulation, treachery—were very clear.

The people in the musososo entertained thoughts about whether Banda would split with the ruling party, given his antagonistic relationship with the Oxfordshire structures and his support of their war, even with ISO and GAPWUZ involved. They also heard that others within ZANU (PF) structures suspected the same and that Banda was often questioned about his loyalties. This question about allegiances to political parties was woven deeply into the Oxfordshire ZANU (PF) structures themselves. As Carl noted to me, many of the leaders within Oxfordshire ZANU (PF) had once been strong supporters of Bishop Muzorewa's party in the late 1970s until

ZANU (PF) dominated the 1980 elections and then "they quickly jumped into the ruling party."

There always was uncertainty over people's general political orientation, especially given the intertwining of politics with violence and intimidation. Tapedza put it this way after Mr. Mhanya had established ZANU (PF) committees among the fired workers: "Yes we joined, but we are not sincere. The question is why did they come today and not yesterday? We are not the only people in the ward. Why not conduct lessons in the Upfumi compound? ZANU (PF) should combine us with those inside." Yet there were also assumptions that one actually supports a political party, no matter what one says. As Mr. Tashanda put it, the word "apolitical is not in the dictionary. You belong somewhere."

Although Chenjerai was eager for the MDC to come to the musososo and the surrounding area to encourage the fired workers and other farm workers in the area to belong to the opposition party, at least quietly, he was not getting much support from the MDC itself.

Since its launch in September 1999, Chenjerai had been actively asking MDC officials to establish structures in the area, but with no success. Many of those at the musososo were interested in the MDC, noting that not only had the ruling party failed to live up to its promises of providing "milk and honey," such as new schools and health clinics, while decent jobs were few and far between, but also because they were snubbed by their ZANU (PF) MP. Moreover, people were no longer afraid of talking politics. As Albert said in December 1999, "In the past, poritikisi was a scary word for most people and they did not talk about it." Reflecting on the term poritikisi ihondo (electoral politics is war), he said, "The people who have the power in ZANU (PF), running the country, had been free to do and say what they wanted. The rest of us just listened to those in power." But now, he declared, with nods from those sitting around the camp listening, "We are not afraid." Since ZANU (PF) failed to help them, "we are looking at other possibilities." Archie then noted, "Those in the top rank have seen our problems, seen our shabby shelters, and it is now raining and we have nothing to eat and are still camping outside." Yet they were not completely dismissive of the ruling party, given the support Banda initially gave them.

During this time, Chenjerai was still optimistic that the MDC could potentially offer assistance to farm workers and workers more generally, despite the lack of visible MDC structures being established in the surrounding commercial farming areas. He explained this lack of presence by drawing parallels to the relative weakness of the MDC on the farms to that of GAPWUZ, given that initially the MDC drew a lot of its personnel and structures from within the ZCTU. Because GAPWUZ had limited robust structures on the farms, Chenjerai speculated that the MDC shared that same weakness.

My interview with Mr. Tashanda, a key MDC organizer in Mashonaland East, bolstered Chenjerai's observation. When I talked with him in Marondera on November 30, 1999, he admitted that they had not done much work on commercial farms and had yet to set up structures in the Goromonzi area. He told me that he was using his other positions in the provincial ZCTU, NCA, and other NGO and member organizations (informal traders, residents' association, etc.)—and even for a while, his position as a soccer referee—to help establish structures, but these had so far been mainly in the communal lands and townships of Marondera. He said the main problem was getting permission from farmers to hold rallies on commercial farms. Some were not supportive: "One cannot just come in, but [one] needs to approach the farmer, who may say yes or no. It is his property. Thus the process is being delayed. Even the Farm Community Trust [a national NGO] is having a problem educating people in terms of health because farmers want their employees to work throughout the whole day. We do not have a mechanism to organize people." He respected the territorialized mode of belonging that sought to prevent outsiders from engaging with farm workers. By this stage, few white commercial farmers, at least those I knew, saw the MDC as a viable political party. Moreover, they were concerned about its apparent sympathy for workers, in contrast to the growth in their support of the new party in early 2000 (see also Pilossof 2012, 204–206).

Mr. Tashanda then reflected on the problems of what I call "domestic government," noting that some farmers "also think we are educating people to know their rights which will cause problems to the farm owners. Yes," he reflects, "some are abusing farm workers, with [hiring] kid workers. They want cheap labor, profits. Full stop." When I asked him about using GAPWUZ, he said that the union was helping a bit, but, as he had experienced trying to work with them in assisting farm workers who had approached him in the past, "GAPWUZ in general is a problem. The whole union. A lot of people are suffering [on farms] and GAPWUZ is not assisting their membership. Not sure what is their problem. Maybe because they are dealing with farmers who are property holders. . . . There is also a tendency for them [GAPWUZ] to be bought off." He then gave an example of a labor conflict in which he alleged that both the GAPWUZ officer and the labor relations officer were bribed by the employer so they would not assist the farm workers. Tashanda then echoed the dominant narrative of farm workers as a represented community in Zimbabwe, that their horizon of interests do not go beyond the boundaries of the farm itself: "They [farm workers] also lack understanding of what it is all about. What is politics? They are only interested in working on farms, staying there, being tied there." When I asked about any MDC policies directed toward farm workers, such as making it easier for them to receive identity documents, he said the only ideas he had heard being discussed within the MDC was to make sure farm workers got access to resettlement land if their places of employment were expropriated for land redistribution—a policy that many donors had been pushing and one that ZANU (PF) itself was also discussing.

Given the relative newness of the MDC and the demands placed upon it, farm workers were not at the forefront of its concerns. Like Tashanda, some within the ZCTU also told me that GAPWUZ was too organizationally weak to help the MDC and that farm workers were more pawns of the commercial farmers than necessarily players on the national stage. For those at the musososo, despite Chenjerai's efforts to set up MDC branches, nothing happened by the end of 1999. ISO had promised to come several times with membership cards, but representatives never showed up during this period.

In contrast, ZANU (PF) during this time increasingly saw farm workers as a politically significant group, though largely in terms of being a threat to the ruling party. And they had organizational traditions to draw upon in their particular form of farm worker (de)mobilization. This became painfully clear after the results of the national referendum on the draft constitution of February 12–13, 2000, were announced that showed the government had lost the vote.

The NCA's mobilization against the draft constitution drew in many farm workers. Although most of the "no" votes came from the urban areas, in Mashonaland East the voters in Seke district were in one of three out of twelve constituencies that voted against the government constitution in the referendum (Centre for Democracy and Development 2000).

A few days after the referendum, on February 19, 2000, Chenjerai said he had been somewhat active campaigning among farm workers to vote against the constitution, aligning himself with the MDC, NCA, and many others associated with the democracy movement. He observed that many white farmers were also advocating to their workforce to vote "no." But he did not see this as the main motivation for their vote: "Farm workers want a change and this is what the 'no' vote means."

Chenjerai then noted that ZANU (PF) was also busy trying to mobilize farm workers. He gave the example of Banda and Mr. Mhanya going around the farms near Rusununguko School "spreading false rumors." Chenjerai said they were promising farm workers who did not have their national identification cards that they would get a *chitupa* if they filled in a PDF—a personal data form. Chenjerai admitted that these ZANU (PF) officials recognized the real desire of many farm workers of foreign descent to get access to such official identification cards. Yet, when the mobile Registrar General office came around later to assist people in registering to vote and to take applications for official documents, they refused to accept the PDFs—"for these are forms used by ZANU (PF) to recruit people!" he exclaimed. So, people were angry at being lied to again by ZANU (PF), and they voted for a change. As Chenjerai continued his reflections, "The ruling party does not know there are now young, educated people working on the farms; it's different from what they assume. Politicians want us to vote for them but they do nothing to support us."

Immediately upon hearing the responses in the government media examining the causes of the government's referendum defeat, Chenjerai said he suspected that ZANU (PF) would not simply try to provide more support to the population and promise a better life. Instead, on February 28, 2000, he gave the prognosis that there was "now another war. ZANU people are wondering what caused the people to vote 'No.' So, they will be moving around in the farms, coming here to try and find out why we farm workers voted against them. . . . They are now saying 'we want to deal with farm workers.'" While observing that nothing had happened yet in their area compared to other farming districts, where occupations led by war veterans had started in the past ten days, he also went on to say that "As I was the district youth chairman [for ZANU (PF)] I know how we used to operate in the past. There will be some harassment done to farm workers by the politicians."

I am sure that Chenjerai, like most others, was unprepared for the type and extent of harassment unleashed by the ruling party and its allies on commercial farm workers and others whom they deemed to be pro-MDC and supporters of the "white settlers" and their "imperialist allies," to use some of the rhetoric publicly deployed by ZANU (PF) politicians, officials, and supporters. The unleashed terror that had begun to catch the attention of many international fora, leaders, and the media, however, differed in terms of its targets, perpetrators, and its timing from one locality to another. It was shaped by the particular territorialized modes of belonging it encountered and the social projects of its perpetrators and, at times, those who were its targets and others in the vicinity.

The occupations of commercial farms began on February 17, 2000, in Masvingo, two days after President Mugabe publicly accepted the referendum defeat of the government's proposed Constitution. The leader of the twenty ex-combatants who led the initial occupation lashed out against those in town who voted "no" in the referendum as well as those advisors who misinformed President Mugabe about the need for land for war veterans (The Herald 2000). By March 2000, the Zimbabwe National Liberation War Veterans Association (ZNLWVA) took over the organization, and the occupations had spread onto farms in much of the countryside, particularly in the Mashonaland provinces and on farms close to major cities like Harare. Between then and the announcement of the results of the June 2000 elections was a time of great uncertainty in the farm occupations; the objectives of the land occupiers were unclear, as were the types of support or challenges the occupiers would face (Scoones et al. 2010, 23–25).

Scholars disagree over whether the wave of land occupations was preplanned by different leaders within ZANU (PF) or allied organizations or whether they were more spontaneous, driven by both demand for land and promises of resources to unemployed youth and others in an attempt to get them to join the movement. What is clear is that state authorities not only allowed the occupations but often abetted them. Members of the security forces (army, police, CIO), in particular, assisted in the occupations of farms and then in making them prohibited areas for MDC representatives. At the same time, these land occupations were uneven, not occurring throughout the country or with the same consequences, but simultaneously instilling both possibilities and fears for differently situated Zimbabweans.

The district branch of the ZNLWVA that covered Berkshire was based at Rusununguko (ChiShona for freedom) School, where a number of the teachers and maintenance staff were war veterans. It was established after 1980, initially as a ZIMFEP school for ex-combatants.[6] It had since been part of the public school system, but its history made it the largest concentration of war veterans in the district. The war veteran leader for their district, Mrs. Chidzidzo, a sciences teacher, told me in July 2000 that after the demonstrations on farms began in February in Masvingo they met as a district war veterans' organization "and decided that we will be part of it and decided which farms to target first. We went to the farmers and they resisted and we said, 'This is a national issue, no matter what you think.'"

What she called "land demonstrations" were clearly part of a scale-making project entangled with national-scale actions and organizations. The support the ZANU (PF) government generally gave to the invaders emboldened them to carry out what she called "demonstrations" on commercial farms, with the aim being to demonstrate that *povo*, the masses, wanted land and that the government needed to speed up land resettlement (see figure 3.3). As she put it, "Any farm was occupied. The idea was to put pressure on so that people will be resettled fast, not necessarily on that farm. When farmers were educated about our intentions they said 'Fine, occupy that piece of the farm for demonstration.'" Initially, they only had the resources to occupy three farms in the district, putting up a few temporary shacks on each while dividing a section or the entire farm into stands for themselves, some of the farm workers, and others; she admitted that the "stand allocation was more of a demonstration as the idea is to have those given 'stands' moved from there to elsewhere [for resettlement], as they really need land. But if they are not given stands elsewhere, they may want to stay on these farms permanently." Ideally, Mrs. Chidzidzo continued, each of the farms would have several occupiers staying there, but as they increased the number of farms symbolically occupied, more farms lacked occupiers since "some of them are far from the school" where most of the members of the war veterans group resided.

Although she said that, "We told farmers they should assume all farms are occupied on paper," war veterans and others from "elsewhere" had also occupied farms in "our district." For example, she told me that two farms east of Ruwa and west of Berkshire, Chibhoyi and Lansing farms, were occupied by Ruwa-led groups. She said her group challenged these outside

Fig. 3.3. Sign Placed by War Veteran Occupiers of a Farm in Mashonaland East, June 2000

occupiers, but, in the end, her group of war veterans relented to allow them to stay because they did not have enough people to demonstrate on every farm. The question of who had the authority to allow occupiers to stay on the farm became a key debate issue in both the occupations and later when dividing up the actual farms, as discussed in chapter 4 (see also Fontein 2006; Matondi 2012).

Mrs. Chidzidzo emphasized that the government would follow its criteria established in the 1990s in terms of selecting farms for occupations—commercial farmers who owned more than one farm, had a farm next to the communal lands, or had an underutilized farm. Echoing what Mr. Nzou from the provincial Department of Labor had told me, she added that farmers who mistreated their farm workers should also have their farms taken. At Lansing farm, for example, "We went to the [tobacco] grading shed and they had no protective clothes or masks and there were mothers with babies on their backs [working there], so we asked, 'What about building a crèche?' The farmer replied he would do something about it. . . . If farm workers are subjected to such conditions so why not repossess it? We want farmers to treat them like humans." But she insisted that on the farms they symbolically

FARM LABOR STRUGGLES IN ZIMBABWE

occupied, she and the other war veterans did not want to disrupt farming operations: "Here in this area we don't want farm workers to lose work so we don't interfere in production; we don't want them to lose their jobs and end up occupying bush." In practice, this claim did not always hold up, particularly as the land demonstrations became land redistribution, as discussed in the chapter 4.

On March 19, 2000, Banda and Mr. Mhanya had a ZANU (PF) meeting at Karigamombe school, and Banda led some of the party supporters to symbolically occupy Upfumi farm. His supporters, as well as some current farm workers, were allocated portions of the farm, but, similar to what Mrs. Chidzidzo had declared, they did not disrupt farm production. None of the people involved in the labor dispute involved themselves in this land demonstration because they said they did not want to jeopardize the possibility of getting their payments. This did not mean that they would avoid entering Upfumi to pressure Zimfarm to finish the case with them, as noted earlier.

Part of the motivation for Banda's and Mr. Mhanya's continued involvement was to try to drum up support for Mr. Mhanya's campaign to represent ZANU (PF) within the constituency in the upcoming June 2000 parliamentary elections. In March 2000, Mr. Mhanya came to the musososo looking for Chenjerai. Once he found him at his home in Mupungu, he arranged for Chenjerai to come to Harare and see the minister of labor, Florence Chitauro, who was debriefed on the Labor Tribunal settlement.

Mr. Mhanya tried to demonstrate his ability to use his connections to assist the fired Upfumi workers in exchange for their support of his candidacy. However, his plans for becoming the ruling party candidate were dashed by what he and Banda claimed were irregularities in the ZANU (PF) primaries in Seke constituency. The voting initially never occurred in the Berkshire/Oxfordshire area, which was widely viewed as Mr. Mhanya's main base, in contrast to the other candidates. He and Banda managed to have the polling done in their area at a later date. According to them, it ended up taking place a week earlier than they had been told and so they said not many of Mr. Mhanya's supporters actually voted. A woman living at the council houses noted how a Banda supporter working for the council, Shuvai, forced everyone living there to vote in the primaries for Mr. Mhanya, even though most people there did not support ZANU (PF). A council truck came to these houses and drove everyone to Kunwa Doro to vote.

Yet all this organizing ultimately did not help Mr. Mhanya; Phineas Chiota from Seke Communal Land, a friend of the previous MP, won the candidacy. He was also supported by Nhongo of the Oxfordshire party structures. As Banda put it to me in July 2000, "We were very disappointed, but as loyal members of the party we will support the selected candidate who will stand for the party." The councillor's support was offered in the way the party usually conducted politics, by both making promises to help and uttering threats to the povo.

In terms of trying to help, in February and March, ZANU (PF) assigned a few people in Goromonzi to help farm workers get birth certificates. In addition to the PDF scheme that Chenjerai mentioned, Mr. Mhanya proposed a special system for farm workers, devised just for the elections. The main problem in getting birth certificates for those who were born outside of hospitals was to find witnesses to attest to the Registrar General's office that the person seeking a birth certificate was actually born in the district. However, as Mr. Mhanya observed, a farm worker may have been born in distant Mvurwi, Headlands, or Banket, and many of those who witnessed his or her birth may have moved away in the past twenty years. So, as he said, "Why not say the child was born here and not in Mvurwi?" For Z$200, ZANU (PF) would then manufacture witnesses to attest that the person needing the birth certificate was born in that locality. It saved the person the expense and trouble of traveling and allowed him or her to get a birth certificate and thus continue with school, get a chitupa, be able to vote, and more. "So when the Home Affairs officials call for a witness, one can easily find lots of witnesses in Goromonzi," he told me with a smile. He and others told me that quite a number of people were able to get their birth certificates through this scheme, which also helped to funnel money to ZANU (PF) supporters.

Although farm violence was not rampant in the Upfumi area leading up to the elections in June 2000, intimidation did occur. People at the council houses were told not to wear their MDC shirts, yet most of those staying and working there were sympathetic to the MDC. One of the council house guards was one of the few strong ZANU (PF) supporters staying there at that time. He said he felt isolated, given the political loyalties of his work-mates, yet "I have the courage to support ZANU (PF) because the majority of my seniors at Ruwa [the location of the main RDC offices] are ZANU (PF) supporters."

The leaders in the Oxfordshire ZANU (PF) structures viewed Mupungu farm as a stronghold of the MDC. ZANU (PF) held a number of rallies there and got Antonio, the manager, to go door to door to force everyone to attend. As Gutu dryly noted, "It was a must that everyone attend the ZANU (PF) meetings. It was impossible to refuse because [if you do] they will beat you." As Archie told me in June 2000, "If you don't go to a meeting, you may get hit by Antonio. So if you were washing, you finished quickly when you heard the knock from Antonio. If you were eating, you would have to leave the food and attend the meeting." Others said that Banda threatened Antonio to do so or, if not, Gutu said, "Banda declared 'We will say you and your people are MDC supporters and we will come and burn your compound.'"

Carl did the same on his farm and chased a few people away because of their politics. One was Patience, who was renting a house from him. Carl yelled at her, she recalled, saying "You and your MDC boyfriends from Ruwa have left their MDC papers all around here. Pack your belongings and go as I don't want to see you on my farm again!" She then managed to rent a house from Antonio. The cultural logics of electoral politics were on full display—since Mupungu was considered a stronghold of the MDC, ZANU (PF) ensured that its manager, Antonio, forced everyone to attend its rallies, where representatives would threaten people to vote for the ruling party.

The general consensus among the workers and some farmers in the area was that violence was not as bad in their locality compared to other locations in Zimbabwe in the run-up to the June election. This was surprising, given that most people involved in the case and on many of the farms were very sympathetic toward the MDC. Moreover, some of the neighboring white farmers were known to be strong supporters of the new party and were encouraging farm workers to attend MDC rallies. The actual dynamics of this period were often opaque to those living there, as well as to outside observers.

From June to August 2000, farm workers and former farm workers gave me various reasons why they supported, if not actually voted for, MDC. Some talked about the need for change. As Archie put it, "ZANU (PF) had been in power for so long, without improving our lives." Others talked about the lack of support they got during their struggle against Upfumi. For instance, Mercy said, "Instead of helping us, ZANU (PF) were being given bribes by our bosses. They never did anything for us." Or, as Rita put it,

"ZANU is saying they are leaders of this country yet out here there were people living like animals. People suffered when they were at the musososo."

There were no MDC rallies in the area, particularly after April 2000, when politicized violence became more intertwined with the land occupations taking place in other parts of Zimbabwe, including the killing of some white farmers and a number of black Zimbabwean MDC organizers and supporters (e.g., Hughes 2010, 107–108; Pilossof 2012, 205). Land occupiers increasingly prevented MDC paraphernalia from being carried by anyone, forced farm workers (and at times farmers) to "enthusiastically" attend ZANU (PF) rallies, and threatened and committed violence against MDC organizers and farm workers and farmers who were assumed to be MDC supporters. To compensate for the lack of rallies, the MDC would occasionally and discretely leave materials in the vicinity, doing, in Rita's words, "their campaign secretly, giving us papers to read." Or, supporters would go to the MDC rallies elsewhere.

As the June 2000 election loomed closer, the violence occurring elsewhere in Zimbabwe started to appear in the Upfumi area. At Upfumi farm, ZANU (PF) leaders like Banda selected workers to be part of youth groups, and they and the foremen would then "drive [read 'force'] everyone to rallies, no matter if they were during work hours or in the night," in the words Fadzai, a woman who had started working at Upfumi after the other farm workers were fired. Fadzai added that the workers "were given ZANU t-shirts, caps, and the like and if you were seen wearing any clothes of an opposition party, you would be beaten up until you could not walk." She claimed that "Workers usually followed [these orders] to try to avoid the invasion of their farm as we wanted to continue receiving wages and we were forced to vote for the party we did not want." She reflected in early 2001 that her only home as a single woman was Upfumi farm—she had no access to a musha or a place to stay in town—and "if war veterans invade the farms, what happens to us vagabonds who have no permanent residences?" Here, she was alluding to the growing concern of many farm workers, a concern amplified by growing numbers of media and academic reports on occupiers displacing tens of thousands of farm workers (Sachinkonye 2003; Hartnack 2005).

Some of the workers and people at the Council houses had their MDC T-shirts or caps taken from them by ZANU (PF) activists and burnt, and there were stories of a few young men from Ruwa who were beaten up while visiting wearing MDC-marled clothing. In early 2001, Prudence said she and her sister had left her parents' RDC house in June 2000 because they were perceived to be MDC and began working at a farm south of Harare; as discussed in the next chapter, like many others, she soon changed political affiliations. And then there occurred an incident as some people boarded a bus heading to a MDC rally in Ruwa on June 17.

On June 20, as I was waiting with the workers in the labor dispute for GAPWUZ to bring the money from Zimfarm to distribute at the musososo, I saw streams of workers leaving Upfumi and Mupungu—those not involved in the case—heading across the highway to the Council houses. They were walking to a ZANU (PF) rally being held there. Tapedza told me that most of the people staying at the council houses were MDC but there are a few who were strong ZANU (PF) supporters, including Mai Tendai who was a leader in ZANU (PF) Women's League and worked for the Council, who were seeking to "clean" the location of MDC supportors. He was now living there, renting a two-room brick house from a worker for Z$200 a month because he had wanted nicer accommodations for his wife and daughter, who was born at the musososo earlier that year. Another unspoken reason for the move was his alienation from the fired workers once he had learned he was no longer formally part of their claim, as noted earlier.

Members of GAPWUZ, Chenjerai, and some ISO members finally arrived from Harare at 5:30 p.m. as a dark, cool dusk was enveloping the area. Chenjerai told everyone gathered that, because they had not forewarned the bank, they could not withdraw the full amount of money to distribute. He suggested that those who were not part of the project (i.e., putting some of the money they were paid into a bank account to earn interest) be paid that day, and the others would be paid in two days' time. Ruva of ISO briefly repeated what Chenjerai stated. After shouting *"Chinja!"* ("Change!"), the MDC cry, she began the distribution of the money, using the light from the headlights of cars parked next to the remains of the musososo.

Two days later, I returned to the camp to witness the payout of the remainder of the money. Several told me what had happened at the ZANU (PF) rally at the council houses on June 20. Councillor Banda chaired the rally; and its main purpose was to act as a court for two council employees who were seen climbing on the bus for the MDC rally in Harare on June 17. On that date, someone had spray-painted "MDC" on the back of one of the council houses; by June 2000, this was typically the only public presence of the MDC in farming areas—brief signs and symbols left in public places such as buildings, roads, signposts—because they were effectively barred from being physically present by ZANU (PF) activists. The ruling party's activists and allies were exerting territorialized power over commercial farms, often setting up base camps on occupied farms, and presenting this embodied force of intimidation, if not violence, to prevent MDC from mobilizing farm workers and to threaten white farmers.

The Council employees denied making the MDC symbol. I suspect it was likely done by what the MDC support committee in Harare called "kamikaze drivers"—young men they sent at night to leave pamphlets and put party markings in the rural areas. Nonetheless, Banda threatened the two employees seen boarding the bus. In the words of Tapedza, who attended the last half of the rally, "They were given a warning for attending the MDC rally. Banda declared, 'ZANU (PF) built the council and it is a party institution, so going to the MDC is a sign of disloyalty. I won't beat you for ZANU does not beat people but makes them disappear. If you disappear, the police can't investigate because there is no corpse. We can easily make you disappear—beat you up, take you away, immerse you in acid and then you are gone.'"

Several others confirmed to me the tone of the threats made. Rudo admitted that she "was terrified and everyone kept quiet and listened to Banda boasting as though he was the only man in the crowd." A few threatened to "beat the sellouts," but Banda stopped them. According to other accounts I heard, Mrs. Tendai from the Women's League next led everyone in a revolutionary song, before Banda receited a Christian prayer and ended the meeting.

This is not the only example of Banda making threats. Rudo added that at an earlier meeting at Karigamombe Training Centre, Banda threatened "to burn Mupungu farm if ZANU (PF) loses the elections"; a threat others also told me they had also heard. Mercy, by then a worker at Black Forest farm, said she and other workers there were forced to go to another ZANU (PF) rally at the Council houses just before the elections. At this rally, she continued, Banda declared that he had given land to those in the struggle at Upfumi for their musososo, but "they have turned against him and are voting for the MDC and so they will pay for it at the end of the election." Patience talked about how a woman working for the council houses, Shuvai, was a vigilant ZANU (PF) activist who threatened others if they wore

MDC shirts and forced people to attend ruling party events. Even though her husband had MDC shirts that he had received from an Irontree farmer and was sympathetic to them, she attended and repeated after Banda *"Pamberi neZANU (PF) kufa ichitonga!"* ("Forward with ZANU [PF], which will rule until death!").

Tawonga also said that ZANU (PF) activists in the area had changed the popular development slogan, "Those who don't know should be taught" to "Those who don't know should be beaten at the back of the necks by knobkerries." He told me that ruling party activists said, "We have taught you long enough and if the povo still do not know [who to vote for], then we will beat them." Yet, Tapedza intervened, "If a father comes home drunk and beats his wife and kids, they don't respect him but fear him. People will go into the ballot box alone." Dissimulation was the performance stance closely associated with politics at that time. As Jane recalled in July 2000, "ZANU (PF) used to come and make us attend their meetings. But in our hearts we knew what we wanted. I voted for MDC." Agatha quietly told me that she would leave when she heard a ZANU (PF) meeting was to be held and come back when the meeting was finished.

On June 22, 2000, as we were waiting for the remaining money from their settlement to come from Harare—a smaller crowd since many had received money two nights previously—one of the older men said he had heard that ZANU (PF) would follow voters into the polling booths, so they would know "who we are voting for." Many of the young men and a few of the older men sitting next to him quickly disabused him of that notion. Others said ZANU activists were telling them that they had a computer to detect who one voted for, a claim that others were less vigorous in denouncing as a lie. The growing reach of ZANU (PF) since February 2000 onto the commercial farms, when combined with the widely known adage that electoral politics is dangerous—that, in the words of Archie, "One should not reveal what party you support, keep it in your heart, for if you tell them you could be killed"—created uncertainty about how to respond to such claims.

Darkness fell, and there was still no sign of the GAPWUZ and ISO vehicle bringing the money. People came up to Tapedza to ask him for his advice, and he replied, "Do not ask me. . . . If I tell you to go home and then they come from Harare, everyone will get mad with me. Remember I am no longer your leader." Women and men were gathering grass and small branches to start fires to try to stave off the cool air. Finally, after 6:00 p.m., a truck full of people drove past the camp and toward the gates of the farm. A few minutes later, Chenjerai and a Harare-based GAPWUZ official walked back to the camp and said that they would distribute the money by the Upfumi gates where there was light thanks to the entrance spotlights. After the assembled group moved there, the money was hastily distributed, with everyone anxious of possible thieves being out at night. Ruva and another ISO person distributed the money, while another who introduced himself to me as the guard stood by with his hand in his pocket—where he told me he had a gun in case trouble occurred. After 9:00 p.m., much of the money was distributed, although some still were not fully paid and others were complaining of not being on the list. A GAPWUZ official told them to talk to Chenjerai and Enoch, the latter now replacing Tapedza on the fired workers' committee, and have them organize a final disbursement of the Zimfarm funds. To those who were still owed a portion of their money, he handed some small change for bus fare to travel into Harare the next day to collect it.

The Color of Politics

Two days later, on June 24, 2000, I went to Mupungu farm for the first day of voting for the parliamentary election. Rinse and I arrived at Mupungu before 10:00 a.m. and found Chenjerai at a small bar on the east side of the compound. It consisted of a tiny, ramshackle wooden building with a narrow slot for a window and benches around a clearing in front of it. Antonio owned the bar but hired a woman to run it. Outside the wooden building, Chenjerai was sitting with some men and drinking scuds, containers of Chibuku beer. Chenjerai introduced us to the "big men" of ZANU (PF) in the area: Mr. Shoko, an older school teacher from Karigamombe. Also present were the security guard from the council houses, another man who rented a house at Carl's compound, and, sitting a bit away from the drinking men, Mai Tendai, who was the ZANU (PF) Women's League official at the council houses. Chenjerai stressed to them that I was not a Zimbabwean or a journalist and that "You should know him simply as Blair, not Mr. Blair or Baas Blair; just Blair." He was signaling my nominal connection to the then British prime minister, Tony Blair, who was in a long-standing rhetorical dispute with President Mugabe and ZANU (PF) over their rule and the disputed obligations of the British government to assist Zimbabwean land resettlement, given its colonial legacy. He also was noting my racialized identity.

As usual, I was the only racialized "white" on Mupungu farm. But, the day of the national election, I was more conspicuous given how ZANU (PF) campaigned on the theme that Zimbabwe "will never be a colony again," associating the MDC with white farmers and the UK government. Racial identification was always interlaced in party politics and quotidian life in Zimbabwe, particularly on commercial farms. Domestic government was predicated on racialized distinctions, and the land question was dominated by a sense of redress of racialized colonialism. It also was interlaced in the struggle at Upfumi, in that they were challenging whites who had money and connections, which led many other farm workers in the area to express that they were crazy for doing so.

The imbrication of whites with power was widely acknowledged and experienced in certain locations in Zimbabwe, particularly commercial farms (Rutherford 2001a; Hughes 2010; Kalaora 2011). Even after twenty years of ZANU (PF) rule and its African nationalist platforms and rhetoric, the widely felt sense was that, after the early 1980s, when party politics generally receded from farms, white farmers and domestic government had been reentrenched into the political economy and fabric of everyday life in these territories. This sense became more obvious under the Economic Structural Adjustment Programme (ESAP) of the 1990s, as commercial farming became the main beneficiaries of its policies while the majority of Zimbabweans saw their livelihoods worsen (Rutherford 2008). The very visible movement of some white commercial farmers into a supporting role in the MDC, starting in late 1999 but especially after the February 2000 referendum, not only led some to question whether this new party was really going to be a workers' party but also enabled ZANU (PF) leaders to characterize their new electoral challengers as those who supported "Rhodesians" and their "imperialist" and "white commonwealth" allies (Willems 2004).

This electoral campaign elevated the always present issue of race during my research. Tapedza, Chenjerai, Netsai, and others always told me that my mere presence and interest in their case helped to give them courage and strength. Partly, it was because they were keen on anyone being sympathetic to them; but partly it also was because I was viewed as a murungu, a white person. As they would say, "we are always surprised and curious" about my presence, sitting with them in the (relatively) dirty camp, taking time to hear their accounts and perspectives. Tapedza said that Brown, the white farm manager, only once shook his hand during their time working together, reluctantly and "as if he was in pain," he added with disdain in his voice. Chuckling, Tapedza said he would joke to women at the RDC camp that, after I returned to Canada, I would leave him my car since "we are so close," leaving the women shaking their heads in disbelief.

By June 2000, however, my racialized identification was also becoming a potential liability, if not a threat, to my interlocutors. Tapedza told me of an incident occurring a week before the elections. I had been sitting outside the musososo while he had been sitting in a truck parked alongside the highway, waiting for the driver to take him and another passenger to Marondera. The man sitting next to Tapedza saw me sitting and talking to people of the musososo, and, in a tone of disgust, Tapedza said the man declared, "Look at the murungu sitting among the poor black people there. He must be the one writing all those lies to the BBC!" Reverting to a conversational tone, but with some trepidation in his voice, Tapedza continued, "I just remained quiet as I didn't know who this man was and I was scared that he might beat me up if I said I knew you." As he said later, "*Poritikisi ihondo*. Best not to talk about it, especially if you don't know the person you're talking to."

Whereas race became a very politicized topic during the election campaigning, during election day in the Upfumi area my racialized presence was not the focus of tension. Rather, it was directed to the very real electoral challenge that MDC was mounting, leaving great uncertainty over who was going to actually win the vote.

At Mupungu farm's bar, the ZANU (PF) people were very tense, eyeing everyone who was wandering around the compound or going up the road to the Karigamombe Training Centre where the polling station was located. Chenjerai, however, was quite relaxed as we sauntered up to the polling station.

When we arrived, we saw a large queue going into the polling station. I recognized a number of the people in the line, a few even discretely holding up their palms to me in greeting—the open palm being one of the symbols of the MDC. I simply nodded in return, wary of being supportive of any political party. On the outskirts were eight ZANU (PF) youth who were glaring at everyone. The clerk from Berkshire farm later said they were telling everyone to "vote for ZANU (PF) and no one prevented them from threatening people." Banda was wandering around, dressed in a suit, and seen talking to a white farmer from the area who was a recognized MDC supporter in the area. A war veteran leader from Lansing farm was also there, as was Mr. Nhongo from the Oxfordshire ZANU (PF) structures. Sitting next to the party youth was a young man who Chenjerai identified as the election monitor from the Zimbabwe Council of Churches.

We later returned to the bar and chatted with the ZANU (PF) people. Chenjerai and Rinse were given ZANU (PF) hats to put on, which they did so with a smile. During tense times, it was clear that even Chenjerai was not overt about his political sympathies. I then talked a bit to the *vadhara*, the old men, who were part of the Upfumi struggle. One of them, Sakala, was quite drunk and went on for some time about their suffering under black rule and how their farm wages were able to buy more items during the colonial period. He said in a slurred voice, "The Europeans were just hitting us which caused us problems. Then the blacks were hitting back during the [liberation] war." He remarked that both the whites and the blacks "were taking us farm workers as fucking *mombe* [cattle] to do their fighting in the 1970s and since 1980. . . . Now they are saying we [farm workers] don't fucking think, but we think!" The other old men shushed him and tried to send him away, although agreeing that the situation for them was hard. Another old man asked if I could help him collect money he thought the NSSA (National Social Security Authority) owed him. I suggested that GAPWUZ or Chenjerai might help him, but Sakala said, "GAPWUZ never helps"; they had told his friend that "we are not NSSA" and that he should go to that office instead. "As for Chenjerai, he doesn't help either, especially since my old friend did not participate in the war against Zimfarm." Sakala then mumbled, "Chenjerai doesn't help us" before another of the old men, Tapera, warned him about saying bad things about their leaders. Sakala said, "Fine, as today Chenjerai seems to like us."

As I walked back to the bar, I was called to by Carl, who greeted me warmly. He pointed to a broken down brick house on his farm. He said that the man who had owned it had operated a small tuck-shop (a small store) on his farm. A month earlier this man had received a stand on one of the farms the war veterans were occupying and dividing up near Marondera. So, "he dismantled his house and hired a truck to transport all the bricks to his stand. But then," Carl added in a somewhat disappointed voice, "the war vets left that occupied farm and the storekeeper lost his stand and his bricks as he could not afford to hire another truck to bring them back." Now, he added, this former tenant was living with a friend on a farm that had been resettled in the 1980s. The uncertainty about the land occupations—the possibilities of getting land and the risks of having one's claim to it suddenly revoked—only became more profound over the following years, as discussed in the next chapter.

I sat back on the benches, as more men gathered. Chenjerai was still wearing a ZANU (PF) hat as he swigged from the scud when Tapedza walked by on the road coming from the training center. I asked him if he had voted, and he replied he had not because his name was not on the register. A few minutes later, Antonio, who was sitting next to me, leaned over and whispered into my ear with a broad smile that he himself was "MDC." My actions of support toward the Upfumi workers in combination with my racialized identity led many to assume that I was "MDC" as well.

Eventually, as Chenjerai escorted us to the car as we were preparing to leave, still with the hat emblazoned with the ZANU (PF) rooster (their party symbol) sitting snugly on his forehead, he opened up his well-worn jacket to show a red plastic card in his inside pocket. This was another symbol of the MDC, whose supporters often gave the ZANU (PF) government a red card during rallies and other public events, thus signifying that the government needs to be ejected, just as when a referee shows such a card to eject a player who commits an egregious foul during a soccer match. As I walked to the car, Tapedza pulled me aside and whispered to me that he had actually voted but that Banda had seen him outside the polling booth and quizzed him to see if he had voted. "I lied to him, responding that I couldn't vote for my name was not on the voters' list. I didn't want Banda to ask me who I voted for. Banda then told me, 'Come back tomorrow as the entire register will be here.'" When it comes to party politics, the wise thing to do, to recall Archie's words, was to "keep it in your heart" in terms of talking about your true affiliation or sympathies to a political party.

Conclusion

The uncertainty, tension, dissimilation, and excitement increased over the next few days after the closing of the polls on June 25, 2000, as Zimbabweans waited for the results to be announced. While waiting for the release of the election results, rumors flew through various channels about who won what seat, what type of corruption was occurring, and so forth. On June 27, the Registrar General declared that ZANU (PF) had won sixty-one seats to MDC's fifty-eight seats, with the remaining seat in the 120 constituencies going to the ZANU-Ndonga party in Chipinge. When coupled with the constitutionally provided thirty MPs appointed by the president, ZANU (PF) had a clear majority.

Many of the non-African electoral monitors and national and international organizations alleged electoral rigging and pointed to the violence and terror largely unleashed by ZANU (PF) against MDC that had occurred during the lead-up to the vote (Saunders 2000). Accordingly, the MDC legally challenged the victories of thirty-nine seats in the courts, a process that dragged on for years, in part due to increasing intimidation of judges by ZANU (PF) activists that led a number to retire (e.g., International Bar Association 2001). Yet most observers agreed that, by and large, MDC won the votes in the cities and in Matabeleland, and ZANU (PF) won most of the rural ridings elsewhere, especially in the Mashonaland provinces. One seat that the MDC did win in what was largely seen as ZANU (PF) territory was Seke constituency, the only seat for them in Mashonaland East province in 2000. Part of this constituency lies in what could be called the peri-urban area to the south and east of Harare, but it also covers a large number of commercial farms, including Upfumi. This, however, was also the only seat that ZANU (PF) challenged in the courts, alleging MDC violence and violation of electoral procedures; the court agreed to overturn this election result in January 2002.[7]

As poritikisi ihondo interacted with land demands as ZANU (PF) sought to assert what it took to be its sovereign authority over the state and national territory in the face of an emboldened and strengthened opposition party and strong condemnations coming from the Global North and various international bodies (although notably, criticisms of the 2000 elections were few and far between from other parts of Africa), many of those who had been involved in the war on Upfumi continued with their struggles for livelihood and were still involved with each other through their participation in the project established under the auspices of the ZLC. Issues of belonging and access to land-based resources took on greater importance as electoral politics became even more intense after the June elections. The suffering endured by those at the musososo became a touchstone in the debates over the project, my research, and access to the land and crops at Upfumi. All of this took place as the ground of politics became literal, as the ZANU (PF) government formally began to redistribute most of the white-owned commercial farms, and violence associated with this process and against MDC and its perceived supporters increased in the farming areas and elsewhere.

CHAPTER 4

POLITICS AND PRECARIOUS LIVELIHOODS DURING THE TIME OF JAMBANJA

Berkshire
July 28, 2000

"IN OUR WARD, there is no violence. Our war vets and the [white] farmers, we work together and when we get these strangers invading our area, I am able to control them, unlike south of us by Seke [communal land] where [war veteran] Mugwagwa is a bit violent. [Councillor] Chishiri and [ZANU (PF) leader] Mherera knew the war vets were coming down to Sky Farm today but they didn't go there because they were afraid of Mugwagwa. They have no control." So spoke Councillor Banda as I was driving him around on Friday morning July 28, 2000, as he performed his duties as chairman of the Oxfordshire East Peace Taskforce. The taskforce was put together before the June 2000 parliamentary elections and was composed of war veterans from Rusunguko School, white farmers, white farm managers, a black farm manager, members of a security company, and police from the Goromonzi station; although, George, one of the white farmers on the committee, informed me that the latter do not regularly show up, saying: "The member-in-charge is a war veteran himself and is good friends with some of the war vets in South Oxfordshire which causes problems. But also their hands are tied as orders come from the top; that's the problem, the orders come straight from Mugabe himself."

I will briefly sketch out how *poritkisi* was becoming a greater force and presence on commercial farms in the Berkshire area through two ethnographic vignettes concerning Councillor Banda; one from 2000 and the other from 2002. They nicely illustrate the erosion of domestic government and the rising influence of political leaders in the lives of people living and working in commercial farming areas. In the first example, Councillor Banda was willing to work with some white farmers to try to assert some control and leadership as land occupations were expanding in Berkshire. Two years later, he was now seeking to assert his authority over the lives of people on the farms.

On this July 2000 day, the Oxfordshire East Peace Taskforce was called to Portage farm to ensure that there was a peaceful "land demonstration," as Banda and Mrs. Chidzidzo, a leader of the war veterans in Berkshire, were still calling them. Yet there were competing land claimants on this farm, and it was unclear which authority should try to mediate between them. As noted in the previous chapter, Mrs. Chidzero sought to claim authority as the senior war veteran in the area, but she also sought to draw on the authority of Councillor Banda and the commercial farmers who were part of the taskforce.

Earlier in the week, on Monday, a group of war veterans from Marondera, led by a Mr. Shumba, arrived on the farm and claimed the farm for themselves. A few days later a group of war veterans from Harare, led by Mugwagwa, claimed some of the farm, including parts that had been claimed by Shumba's group. There was tension between the two groups and the farm management was at a loss about how to negotiate with both of them and how to reorganize their own use of (parts of) the farm. The aim of the taskforce was to ensure that peace was maintained and that everyone could "live together." One of the Portage farm's white managers was actually on the taskforce.

Yet, there were complicating factors to this conflict. The Marondera war vets claimed the company that owned Portage also owned three other farms. Mrs. Chidzidzo told me earlier that she was happy to go with war vets also from Rusununguko School to talk to war vets invading the farms from outside the district "to ensure production continues." But, she continued, if the "farmer doesn't reveal how many farms he owns and it turns out that the farmer is a multiple farm owner," then, according to official policy, the farmer should be giving up some of their farms. As Chidzidzo observed to the manager of the farm, "we have been put in an awkward position. We want to know if you have more than one farm. . . . The farmers need to be very honest or it can lead to violence." In the words of one of the women war veterans who went with Mrs. Chidzidzo to Portage farm on that day, "If the farmers resist, then watch out. There will be 'cross-fire.'"

When we arrived at the farm director's office, the director came out a bit warily when he saw Banda and me step out of the car. Once he was introduced to Banda, he smiled warmly and welcomed the councillor, clearly indicating that he saw him at least as nonthreatening. The director then told us that the meeting was being held at the Surrey Butchery on the main highway. When we arrived there a few minutes later, we saw members of the taskforce—Mrs. Chidzidzo and five of her war veteran colleagues from Rusunguko School; George, a white farmer; the Portage manager; and Trevor, a black manager on Dzemombe Farm near Rusununguko School—as well as a group of black men and women of various ages who had come from Marondera. Mugwagwa was to also attend this meeting but neither he nor members of his group showed up; likely busy, as both Banda and George speculated, intimidating white farmers, including making a death threat, in South Oxfordshire with his colleagues from Harare, according to some reports (see CFU 2000).

As a consequence, members of the taskforce spoke with Shumba and the ten others who had come from Marondera with him in a truck driven by a black commercial farmer who farms near the provincial capital. The farm director showed them part of the farm that he said they could peg out for members, a paddock with a water point. While the director was pointing this land out to the group, his white farm manager was quietly complaining that this disrupts Portage farm's production activities as they would have to move cattle and stop preparing the fields for next year's crops given this uncertainty. His opinion, however, carried no weight.

Seemingly satisfied with the allocation, the Marondera group pegged out small fields for each other, with one of the members who was quite drunk grumbling that "we want the entire farm." About an hour later, they boarded the truck and drove off, with the farm director looking around and asking with a hesitant chuckle, "Can I stop being nervous?" He then pondered out loud the uncertainty over whether the Marondera group will be coming back to start cultivating "or whether this was merely a pegging exercise" and how would the "Mugwagwa group respond to all this?" No one ventured an answer.

During the several hours we were at Portage farm, we waited around for the different people to talk to each other or to show up. The script of farm occupations and negotiations over them at this time was not clear-cut, with a lot of improvization and periods of uncertain waiting (Scoones et al. 2010). "No matter, people drink during these invasions because they are bored as it takes so long!" exclaimed Mrs. Chidzidzo, looking at her teacher and war veteran colleague pouring himself another whiskey and coke while we were at the farm. Banda and George talked about the uncertain events then taking place, with the farmer remarking to Banda that he heard other ZANU (PF) people were calling the councillor a "sellout" for working on the taskforce. In response, Councillor Banda smiled and said "I don't mind, as I am ensuring peace in my ward." He then pointedly asked George whether the commercial farmers in the area were going to abide by the call of the Commercial Farmers' Union (CFU) to halt farming on Monday, July 31 to protest the increased intimidation and violence on farms, despite, Banda stressed, "the end of [parliamentary] elections." Banda exclaimed that there was no need for commercial farmers to continue being "political" with their call for a national stay-away that took place a few days before another national stay-away called by the ZCTU to end violence against the MDC and to stop the continued occupations of white farms (Reuters 2000). George replied that their local farmers' association decided not to join in: "We are farming on Monday." This response seemed to please Banda, although he still looked skeptical.

In turn, George asked Banda if he knew anything about the Zimbabwean National Army soldiers who were going from farm to farm in the province, asking the farmer about the size of the farm, the number of workers, and "other details like that." Banda replied that he had heard about it but knew nothing about this "documentation exercise." George also asked Banda about when the council was going to fix the farm roads and Banda retorted "When the white farmers begin paying their council taxes," given that most had not paid that year. After a few minutes of back and forth about this, George informed Banda that "The council is sitting on my application to build an abattoir and I am wondering if you could help me?" Such banter and queries seemed both like an ordinary interaction between a politician and a constituent businessman and yet so extraordinary given the growing uncertainty, tension, and violence surrounding white-owned commercial farming at that time.

The disjuncture with the growing violence and intimidation occurring in rural Zimbabwe elsewhere, including on a number of the farms that I had done research, was made even starker when I was driving Banda and some of the teachers back to Rusununguko School. As we were driving, we spotted some land occupiers building a temporary structure to mark the "symbolic occupation." The war veterans in the car said I should stop and take a picture to document both the orderly process and to show that it was a peaceful exercise. I did, just as a tourist would snap a shot of an elephant they happened upon (which, indeed, I have done). Such events and similar encounters suggested to me that there was a possibility for negotiated accommodation concerning land redistribution, if only the divisive rhetoric being increasingly employed by both the western media and the Zimbabwean government stopped and all parties looked for possible solutions rather than fanning conflict, as I then argued in an op-ed article in a Canadian newspaper (Rutherford 2002). What I downplayed then was how the politics that Councillor Banda was deploying to "control rogue war veterans" as he was doing that day in July 2000 could also get actively involved in territorialized modes of belonging, drawing on the theme of poritikisi ihondo. The differentiated spatial experience of the land occupations and violence did not mean the same dynamics occurred in the same locales over time, as was very apparent during my next trip to the area with Councillor Banda two years later.

I did not return to Zimbabwe until the Zimbabwean winter of 2002, although I was receiving reports from my research assistants of the growing violence in the area around Upfumi farm, with Councillor Banda often at the center of it. I tried several times to meet with the councillor when I arrived in June, but only managed to catch him at his new home at the council houses on August 1, 2002.[1] As I walked toward his house, I was greeted by a tall man coming out of a pickup truck. Although I did not recognize him at first, it turned out to be Trevor, the manager of Dzemombe farm and a member of the Oxfordshire East Peace Taskforce in 2000 (an organization that had since been disbanded). I was then greeted by a surprised Prudence, who had been living between the *musososo* and the council houses (as her father worked for the council and had a room there) in 1999 and 2000. Although she told me of being a big MDC supporter in 2000, by the time I returned in 2002, others had already told me that she was now Banda's "girlfriend." She took my bag and walked me to the front of the house where Banda was seated facing a half circle of ten young men, while his wife was to the side cooking on an outdoor fire and his three-year-old son was playing with a ball.

Banda warmly greeted me, introducing me to the young men seated as "a good friend of mine, of Zimbabwe, and of ZANU (PF)"; he did so less because of any political loyalties or support I gave, but more because he wanted to try to disarm suspicion among the others of why a white Canadian man was visiting him. Once again, he stressed that I was "Blair Rutherford from Canada" and not "Tony Blair," the then British prime minister who ZANU (PF) leaders and media frequently portrayed as an "enemy" to Zimbabwe. Seven of the young men were wearing green shirts, with a small Zimbabwean flag patch over their heart. Five of them had green caps pulled down over their ears and two had red berets. Banda said these were Border Gezi youth graduates staying at the training center in Kunwa Doro that had opened in March; "These are not the fighting types and do not cause problems. It is just the western media that misreports what is going on in Zimbabwe," Banda informed me.

The National Youth Service training camps were established in late 2001 to help inculcate "patriotic training" in secondary school graduates. They were named after Border Gezi, who had been minister of Youth Development, Gender and Employment Creation and national political commissar for ZANU (PF) when he died in a car accident in 2001. Popularly known as "green bombers" for their green uniforms, private media and human rights groups had documented the terror tactics and violence, including rape, both used in the training centers, and, in particular, their activities harassing MDC members and others deemed to be "enemies of the state" (e.g., Reeler 2003; Ranger 2004; Grobler 2007). One of the green-uniformed young men eyed me suspiciously and asked if I wrote for newspapers and Banda said, "No, he is a professor," and I confirmed the answer. Banda's wife pulled out a chair for me and put it next to Banda's as he continued with his meeting.

After noting a complaint from one of the other young men that he was not being paid by one of the new black farmers and listening to a request for help in getting fertilizer from the Grain Marketing Board from a smallholder farmer in the area who was seated next to him, Banda then turned to the green-shirted youth to talk about "current problems in the area." This included a former Upfumi worker who beat his girlfriend, who was also a worker there, and a teacher at Karigamombe Primary School who was said to be a "MDC supporter." The discussion went on for a few minutes, before stopping when his wife offered everyone sliced bread and margarine and tea. After everyone ate the snack, the councillor directed four youth to drive with me while he, a leader of the ward's Women League, and the remaining youth climbed into Trevor's pickup truck.

As we drove the few kilometers to Upfumi farm, past the site where the musososo had been located two years previously, now seemingly just a field of grass and young trees, the four youth told me that they had just graduated from training in Mt. Darwin in Mashonaland Central province, although they themselves came from homes in Manicaland or Midland provinces. They entered the program after completing their O Levels as they had heard it was a guaranteed path to get a job afterward. Like Banda, they also stressed that they were not violent, only "causing problems when people give us trouble."

At Upfumi, Banda and the youth entered into the manager's office; management had arranged with Banda to detain their former worker when he had arrived earlier in the day to pick up his last paycheck. A few minutes later, Banda's youth roughly escorted a young man out of the office, put him in handcuffs, manhandled him into the back of the pickup, and then surrounded him while he was standing in there. A young woman in a work uniform followed behind and nervously talked to Banda for a few minutes. I then talked with the white manager who followed. When I asked the type of relationship he had with Banda, he replied that Upfumi, like all farms that are still operating, is "120 percent ZANU" and "completely abides by their rules to continue farming." It was clear that party politics shaped more actions on operating commercial farms than they had previously.

Banda explained that he kept "an eye" on what was happening on the farms in the area, as any other territory in his riding. This was exemplified by our next stop at the nearby primary school where he had to threaten a teacher said to be disrespecting him and, by extension, ZANU (PF). A few hours later we arrived at the Rural District Council (RDC) office in Ruwa.

When we arrived at Ruwa, Banda told the two remaining youth to take the prisoner grabbed at Upfumi farm to the police station. He then began dealing with a variety of issues inside and outside the RDC office. This included receiving a delegation from a communal land in his ward, who showed him letters they had received from him and others from the council's land committee saying they were given "stands" on a recently resettled commercial farm. Yet when they went to the resettlement farm they were then told by the DA's office that they did not have the right to settle there. They were asking Banda to talk to the DA's office to make sure they could stay on "their land." The confusion and uncertainty surrounding the land resettlement exercise was evident in the delegation and in their demeanor, which alternated between pleading and defiance; an uncertainty that plagued the process for the next ten plus years given how political decisions tended to trump bureaucratic ones (see, e.g., Moore 2005; Alexander 2006; Matondi 2012).

In the meantime, Trevor had told me that he and the white farmer for whom he worked were still farming a portion of Dzemombe farm, with settlers farming on the remainder of the farm. These settlers "weren't causing any problems," he added, but he said the farmer recently learned that the farm had not actually been given a Section 8 (compulsory acquisition order),[2] although some of the settlers had shown them a document purporting to be one. Trevor thus was seeking to determine whether or not their farm had been legally allotted for redistribution. He had previously visited the provincial administrator's office in Marondera who then had asked him for a letter of support from the councillor, which was the reason he had been with Banda all day. In Ruwa, Banda left the delegates from the communal land and handed a hand-written letter to a staff member of the RDC to type it up and told Trevor to return tomorrow to pick up his letter of support. Banda then started to enter into other private discussions with various ZANU (PF) officials, war veteran leaders, and council staff members, and I departed.

These two ethnographically depicted encounters of mine with Councillor Banda over a span of two years provide some insight into how the postelection *jambanja* violence and uncertainty affected the Upfumi area, indicating how it played out differently in particular locales and at specific periods in time. Jambanja is a word that quickly became part of Zimbabweans' vocabulary in the 2000s; as a phrase initially used in a popular song, it became known as a reference to the violence, uncertainty, and chaos, particularly associated with the conflict over land (Pilossof 2012, 44). The first example of the Oxfordshire East Peace Taskforce suggests that one of the reasons why, before the end of June 2000, most farm workers and farmers around Berkshire were talking about how they were largely spared from the violence was the role played in part by some of the ZANU (PF) leadership in the area. Although Councillor Banda had been implicated in threatening violence and intimidation during the 2000 electoral period, he also was credited by some white farmers and farm workers for seeking to minimize some of the violence on the farms, particularly if carried out by "outsiders," those who did not reside in the area. The farmer's authority on the farm, the domestic government, required support from a ZANU (PF) leader against alternative sources of power, also from within ZANU (PF).

Two years later his actions were very different, as he had taken land himself and was more directly involved in some of the violence on the farms in the area. Now Councillor Banda readily used intimidation to help define his leadership in the area. He also asserted his authority within the remaining commercial farms. The intended result of such violent actions was to ensure that the people in the area remained "loyal" to ZANU (PF) as well as other authority figures within the ruling party who may want to have influence in the area. Threatening physical attacks was more explicitly part of the repertoire of political authority figures by this time.

The councillor drew on his authority within electoral politics, a discursive practice that became more deeply entangled in the lives of farm workers in Berkshire as elsewhere in Zimbabwe. This entanglement increasingly made many of them "former farm workers" with even more precarious livelihoods, as the mode of belonging of domestic government was directly attacked and undermined. Farm workers and former farm workers had to attach themselves to territorialized forms of power that were even more conditional as they operated through the extremely precarious landscapes of jambanja. Electoral politics began to reshape the grounds of everyday life throughout Zimbabwe, but nowhere as dramatically and effectively as the lands and social landscapes of commercial farms.

This chapter explores some of these dynamics for the former Upfumi workers as well as other farm workers and farmers in Mashonland East from 2000–2002, highlighting how the power relations between farmers, farm workers, ZANU (PF) activists, and government officials shaped much of the actions and narrowed the scope of action. Such politicized dependencies deeply shaped livelihoods and forms of authority for farm workers and farmers, as well as ethnographic practices of anthropologists, as I continued to carry research on those who had been involved in the war (labor dispute) at Upfumi and other Zimbabweans who were living through the precariousness of being a farm worker during the time of jambanja.

"A Small Victory": Realigning Ties of Dependency

Immediately after the simultaneous end of the labor conflict and the June 2000 parliamentary elections, the "war against Upfumi" shaped and marked many of the workers involved in it, particularly those who had spent time at the musososo. Being from the "DRC" was something that distinguished them from others living in Berkshire, which some sought to downplay and others emphasized, as they differentially assessed the monetary and symbolic capital they (the Upfumi workers) earned through their struggle, and as they inserted themselves into the fast-changing landscape of rural Zimbabwe as jambanja, the chaotic land occupation, and land resettlement processes continued.

Many of the workers who had been living in the musososo continued to live in the vicinity, renting places to stay at Mupungu, Carl, the council houses or in the nearby small-scale farms, or finding jobs and staying at some of the nearby commercial farms. After their lengthy struggle, these workers had earned a reputation of being tough, of choosing to fight Upfumi and "living in the bush (musango)" rather than giving up and leaving the struggle. For a few, it earned them an admirable reputation, of the ability to hold the murungu to account. Prudence even mentioned in July 2000 that a foreman from a farm south of Harare whom she knew had wished many of the former Upfumi workers would come to his farm to "stir things up" as the farmer there was oppressive. Yet, the majority of the workers from the war who I knew, they were more apprehensive and uncertain after their lengthy struggle.

In August 2000, Tapedza noted that the majority of the people staying at the council houses avoided him and others involved in the struggle. "If a woman talks to my wife, the other women chastise her for talking to 'one of them.' Men see Tawonga carrying a newspaper but they are nervous about asking him to borrow it. We are outsiders here, we people of the musososo." The negative evaluation was partially informed by the wariness of talking to those who were viewed as "MDC" during this period of uncertainty, when the people of the victorious ZANU (PF) party were continuing to attack perceived supporters of the MDC, including in the cities where soldiers were beating people in the bars and other township sites where the MDC had won most of their seats (e.g., Daily News 2000). Occupations and violence on commercial farms continued even more so as the ZANU (PF) government began to legislate a massive land redistribution exercise, now calling it the Fast-Track Land Reform program. Belonging to Zimbabwe, as I will discuss in more detail later, increasingly meant belonging to ZANU (PF) which strongly influenced livelihood options available to many in the country, including (former) farm workers. More pressing for the fired Upfumi workers was the question of whether they actually were given sufficient compensation for their struggle; a discussion that the participants in particular continued in earnest during the winter of 2000.

On July 1, 2000, Arianna looked around Mupungu farm, taking in the largely dilapidated mud and pole huts and said "We won. . . . But it was a small victory." Elaborating, she said, "We are glad because the company admitted that it was wrong and managed to give us our money, although it was little." As Archie then put it, "During our case people saw us as crazy people fighting for nothing. Even our relatives did not want to visit us because they did not understand why we were causing ourselves to suffer. But now because we have got our money, we have now regained our friends and relatives as they now know we were fighting a right cause." The money the workers received from Zimfarm went largely to pay off debts of various sorts, the purchase of consumer goods, and for investment into economic activities.

Many of the women to whom I talked brought much of their money to relatives, particularly those who were looking after the children. They brought money in part, as Jane put it, to prove to their relatives that their struggle was just and worth it, and also to pay back money to those who had been financially looking after their kids during the lengthy struggle. They also bought clothes for their children as well as food items, seeds, and fertilizers that they brought to parents and other relatives at the *musha*. Some of the men bought calves with the money. Both women and men also used money for their own personal consumption—one purchased a bed, another bought a wardrobe, for example—and often to buy items for trading or petty commodity businesses. A number of the former workers bought clothes, clocks, shoes, or food items such as vegetables, meat, cow fat, and the like for resale in the farming areas.

The amount of money received and its allocation were constantly under scrutiny and critical reflection during this period, with much debate and suspicion over the public decisions made over the allocation and investment of the payment. There was widespread disgruntlement over the actual amount of money received for different categories of workers—permanent workers received around Z$9000[3] and seasonal workers around Z$3000. Seasonal workers would have received only Z$1500 according to the court-sanctioned settlement, but through the persuasive suggestion of Gwisai and the leadership of the strike a decision was made to deduct money off the payment given to the permanent workers to increase the payment given to seasonals to around Z$3000. Given that minimum wages in the farms in 2000 was now Z$710 (about US$12) per month, there was a sense that their year-and-a-half struggle was not fully or justly compensated.

For example, many of the seasonal workers felt aggrieved, particularly those who had been staying at the musososo. Mercy bemoaned this "discrimination," observing that

> This really pains me because we seasonal workers are the ones who really fought this war. Most permanent workers never stayed at the musososo. We suffered alone.
>
> I lost my things such as clothes and pots when the houses were burnt. I was there then, but it was difficult to remove things. Most of the permanent workers lived in Harare and Marondera. They were even working where they were getting money at the end of the month. Each time Chenjerai went to Harare, us people at the camp paid Z$5 [to cover his transport costs] and yet when he would have meetings people from the towns and elsewhere came to hear his account, but they never paid the money to send him. If I think about this, it really pains me.

The financial project arranged by the ZLC was a lightning rod for these anxieties. There were strong inducements for the workers involved to participate in the project, with seasonal workers getting more money if they joined the project. Others joined the project because they did not want to spend all the money they had received in a lump sum and they did not have a bank account as they did not have a national identity card to open one up or found it too difficult to deal with banks. In total, 155 of those who received funds invested money into the project. But the expectations varied, and its mode of governance was obscure.

People entered into the project thinking they would receive about Z$600–Z$800 after a month based on what the ZLC officials had told them. Yet when they received their first payment August 5, 2000, of Z$430 for permanent workers who did not work during the struggle, Z$300 for permanent workers who had been identified as working during the struggle (and had received less money from Zimfarm), and Z$150 for seasonal workers, there was widespread disenchantment. As Tapera spat out, "a bucket of maize costs Z$120, rent costs Z$200, not to mention other expenses. We do not understand why we only got Z$430 when our money has been there for nearly two months. We expected Z$1000, not this!" he fumed. "We thought that by putting our money into the bank it would help us! But this is not the type of help we expected. We now have to start running around looking for jobs because we cannot survive from this Z$430."

The differing expectations over the amount of the money they would receive had amplified greater concerns over its management and who was actually involved in it. There were two main concerns. Although a committee was selected to manage it and was tasked with monthly visits to Harare to collect interest, there was tension between its members and Chenjerai, who was not a member of the managing committee. The second concern was that there was general uncertainty over the role of ISO, GAPWUZ, and the former workers' committee in this fund. The two concerns were interlinked. Through advice given from ZLC and GAPWUZ officials, the workers decided to give some of the funds they received from Zimfarm to Chenjerai, Tapedza and Precious to recognize their leadership role and since they were found not to be legally part of the case. However, how much was actually given to them was unclear to many of the workers in the case. Tapedza said later in 2000 that he was told to come secretly to the ISO office to collect his money so no one saw him receive the funds. He did not tell me how much money he ended up receiving, "for the sake of my privacy," as he put it.

Although none of the three leaders had any money involved in the project, Chenjerai appointed himself as the keeper of the register of names and saw himself as one of the leaders of the fund, even though he was not on its elected managing committee. At a meeting concerning the project held on July 30, 2000, at Mupungu, Chenjerai berated the ignorance of everyone, noting that they still had to figure out payment to Gwisai, as GAPWUZ did not pay him much and, he added, GAPWUZ was also demanding a high fee for the support they gave them. He thus was declaring that his role in the project was vital as he had this knowledge of various debts made through this struggle. As a consequence, he declared "I think I am entitled to go to Harare [with the leaders of this committee] even though I am not a member of this project." He demanded to receive money to travel to Harare along with two members of the managing committee, Agatha and Gutu. He also lashed out at those who were "spreading rumors" about him, sarcastically observing that "people are saying I am eating their money, drinking their money and doing everything using their money. If I am able to, why shouldn't I? Look, I am drinking this scud," pointing to the container of Chibuku in his hand, "with your money!" He said that those spreading rumors should leave the project, threatening that "if you do not submit your name [to withdraw from the project] while you are well-known for spreading rumors, the next step will be that I will just take all your money and chase you away from this project!"

Such threatening behaviour was in keeping with what many of the former workers had been telling me about Chenjerai's characteristics as a "politician"; his inexhaustible will to rule, even if he did not have any mandate. He was also trying to squash the rumors about his actions. The rumors about Chenjerai centered on the actual amount of money he had received from the Zimfarm payment and the practice of him collecting money for the six people in their group who had passed away during the course of the labor dispute and for a few who had not yet arrived to collect their money, mainly because they were residing in a musha far from Harare. People told me about several instances of relatives of the deceased trying to claim the money from the ZLC who were having difficulty doing so. Whereas Chenjerai claimed his authority to look after the money of those who had yet to collect it because he was their "leader," others were increasingly unsatisfied with those claims, both among the women who had sent a delegation to follow him to Harare in June, and others. And as their labor struggle was now over, many felt no need to be beholden to him.

By August 2000, among those who had lived in the musososo, there was a widespread distrust of their leaders as well as ISO and GAPWUZ, in part because of the conflicting messages concerning the project and in part because of the tensions and divisions that had emerged in the last few months of the struggle. This was not only directed toward Chenjerai but also against Precious. The fired workers said they both received preferential treatment from the various Harare-based organizations. Tapedza, the original nominal leader, but long marginalized, noted the unequal reception of their group by those who are supposed to be aiding them, "You know there are people who are heard when they go to the Labor Centre, while there are others who are not heard and so this money is at the mercy of the small group of people who are listened to at the expense of those who may really need the money. Maybe we are not able to convince the people there but the moment you mention the Labor Centre around here people would begin not to trust you because of this experience."

Their claims indicate how the relations of dependency entered into by these farm workers were susceptible to severe power imbalances and great uncertainty, even among those that are seeking to assist them. There was an opacity in their transactions to the majority involved in the struggle, who were supposed to be satisfied with what their leaders and members of these organizations told them. When followers were told many different, often contradictory, accounts or when leaders threatened them when they asked questions, resentment and suspicion were common responses.

I too was pulled into these rumors. Chenjerai and others had falsely claimed that I was investing money in the fund to help the people of the struggle, particularly those of the musososo. I learned about this in late July 2000, with some of the workers declaring that many became involved in the project on the assumption that I not only made a significant financial contribution to it but that I, through Rinse, my main research assistant, would manage it for them. Tapera spelled out the logic: "We have been told that you are the ones who have helped us continue our fight while we were still at the musososo; you helped us with food and so you organized our money so that we can put [it] into a bank project. Everyone here praises you." The rumors about my involvement mutated, with one account suggesting that the money that I (allegedly) intended for the Upfumi workers ended up with the MDC and another story claiming that GAPWUZ and I received a farm south of Harare through the fast-track land resettlement scheme to which all the former Upfumi workers would be relocated. The ties of solidarity that I assumed I was presenting and contributing toward were clearly viewed through the lens of racialized hierarchy and ties of dependencies.

The rumors and claims were both purposefully told and speculated on, as I was placed into the role of possible benefactor, to which many would willingly enter into relations of dependencies under me. My research was implicated in these dependencies, as these former Upfumi workers were often keen to talk with me or my research assistants, since they no longer had to abide by Chenjerai's constraints on what they could say and to whom, as their struggle was finished. Although claims of my largesse proved to be chimerical and of which I denied, these former Upfumi workers were not simply hoping for their investment to cover their economic needs and aspirations. Most were busy involving themselves in other activities to seek income or other forms of remuneration. These also required continuing or forging new forms of dependencies as well as a whole new set of vulnerabilities and fears.

Livelihoods in Times of Uncertainty

As it was before 2000, the people who had been engaged in the Upfumi struggle and others living around Upfumi farm combined a variety of livelihood strategies—from farm work to trading, petty commodity production to sex work. The difference was the growing scarcity of jobs and increasing prices as the effects of the politicized land occupations and resettlement programs undermined much of the previously normalized, although often precarious, economic activities and, concomitantly, the greater presence and interventions of politics in people's lives.

Many of those former Upfumi workers still living in the Berkshire area after the struggle continued to find work on commercial farms, although the jobs fluctuated with the tempo of land invasions and the type of arrangements negotiated between the occupiers and the farmers. A number of the workers went to Black Forest, a large flower farm south of the highway from Upfumi that was still in operation. To get a job there, one needed connections, or working through what workers called a "color bar" or "racial discrimination"; terms that did not refer to hiring decisions rooted in racialized identities as was institutionalized in the colonial history of Zimbabwe and elsewhere but rather selection based on who knew the foremen and other senior workers who made the hiring recommendations. "Color" here referred to the power to decide, not assumed phenotypical or genotypical traits.

A few of the former Upfumi workers had worked at Black Forest during the labor conflict. After the payout was made many more got hired there through their links to senior workers, so that there was a division between what they called "Upfumi" workers and the rest. Many also worked on other farms in the area. Farmers in the area saw the people living in the Mupungu/Carl area as a reliable short-term workforce, as they had been when they were residing at the musososo, and would send tractors or other vehicles to this area in the early morning to pick up workers during harvesting time. This was also the case for some farms outside the Oxfordshire-Berkshire area.

In September 2000, a former Upfumi supervisor who had since become an assistant manager at a farm in the Rusape area, about 150 kilometers away, came down and posted a notice at the rest camp off the highway near Mupungu advertising jobs for women pickers and graders of peas, saying a lorry would come to pick them up on Sunday, September 10. Tens of women from the Mupungu area, including some who had been involved in the struggle, boarded the lorry and went to the new farm. But many came back a few months later, complaining about abusive treatment by the murungu and the foremen. The returning workers said management were using "the usual tricks," as Nyasha termed it—trying to lower wages by using a *mugwazo* (task work) system in which people often would be paid for only a half-day's work, no overtime was paid, no workers' committee was in operation, and the workers were compelled to buy most of their goods from the farm store owned by the farmer, despite the inflated prices. "The murungu offered credit to the workers to buy from the store but when he assessed that not many were buying from the store on credit, he would delay paying wages to make sure people would be forced to buy things from the store on credit," Nyasha explained.

In January 2001, one former worker, Thomas, characterized the effects of this practice by saying one was always hungry given the late payment. He continued talking about this farm where he had been working the year before, noting that "The boss would say go and borrow [on credit] from the shop because everything was there. . . . The boss really hated anyone who wouldn't borrow from the shop. I found it very difficult to work for groceries all the time and decided to quit. These things should not be happening in our country." Such attempts by farmers to reacquire the wages by giving credit at farm stores had been a common practice on Zimbabwean commercial farms (Rutherford 2001a; see also Bolt 2012, 2013, 2015).

What was new in the early 2000s landscape was that farm workers could easily get implicated in the land occupations. Some farmers used their authority to direct workers to defend the farm, as what had happened on the Rusape farm. Thomas alleged that the boss ordered everyone working for him, including women, to attack occupying ex-combatants who had planted maize on part of the farm—threatening to fire whoever did not go with them. Nevertheless, he observed, in December 2000 the farm was closed down "because it was in debt to the Zimbabwe Fertilizer Company." He continued by noting that the boss had left in the middle of the night, abandoning the workers, making "the workers upset and desperate as most did not have money for bus fare."

This was a common pattern for many of these former farm workers; they would labor for a short period on farms, then leave for various reasons; either the working conditions were poor, there was no work, the farm closed down due to debts, or, more commonly as the months continued, due to acquisition for compulsory resettlement. A common strategy was to combine farm work with other economic activities, like *maricho* (piecework) for black Zimbabweans who needed short-term agricultural workers or brickmakers, including new settlers as the "land demonstrations" turned into the Fast Track Land Reform program. As before 2000, many also engaged in petty trading. Buying and selling meat, cow fat, clothes, vegetables, and so forth, or making and selling beer were common pursuits, typically earning a bit of profit for the trader.

In February 2001, a woman explained how she used some of her Z$2800 (US$28) per month salary at Black Forest farm to help subsidize her husband's buying and selling business. Her husband had bought a bicycle with the money he had received from the Zimfarm payout and used that to buy cow fat from Surrey butchery about 15 kilometers away and vegetables from a smallholder farm. He then sold them on farm compounds on credit, returning on payday to collect debts. Enoch's activities are another example. Enoch would run his carpentry business only around payday so he could demand the money up front. Otherwise, he would buy and sell vegetables, thatching grass, and the like. Others, for instance, sold cooked mice at the beer hall.

Living on the farms meant that one was close to a market for small-scale purchases of goods and services (see also Bolt 2012, 2015). But as a renter or occupier one had to be wary of the rules of the farmer. For example, by early 2001, Antonio forced anyone working on a farm but living with a friend or relative at Mupungu farm to rent their own individual huts. This was a way for Antonio to increase the rent coming into Mupungu. At other times, Antonio would prevent people from brewing and selling one-day beer as it competed with the bar that he controlled. He also forbade lodgers from raising chickens as he himself was breeding them to sell. The unwritten rules of renting on the farm narrowed the scope of actions, and attachments of belonging, for the renters.

A similar conditional belonging affected those living on smallholder farms as they were commonly expected to do certain work as a form of labor tenancy (similar to what Antonio demanded of some of those involved in the Upfumi struggle in 1999, as discussed in chapter 3). In December 2002, Agnes was paying rent to a plot-holder near Kunwa Doro who began demanding that she and her husband work for him for free or for very little payment. When they did maricho labor for the plot-holder by weeding his two-hectare maize field, he only paid them a quarter of what they charged. And when her husband told the plot-holder that he was too ill to fix a fence, he replied, in Agnes's words, "There is no need for you to stay at the plot so I can give the house to another person who is well and who could do some work around here." So they left their lodgings and her husband was given accommodation on another plot in exchange for being a "garden boy" with a small salary. In the meantime, Agnes was doing maricho labor, such as weeding and tending a plot, in which a black farmer grew maize and flowers, in exchange for cash. She was trying to save some money to renew her business of buying and reselling cow fat. By June 2003, she was working as a "house girl" at the plot where they were living as a condition of residing there. Her husband, who was the gardener, had been told by the plot-holder that he had to find someone to look after the kids and to do the housecleaning or he would be let go and evicted from their house. The plot-owner was a black businessman who lived in a posh northern Harare suburb.

Agnes's husband was much older than she was. She had lived with men before but the relationships inevitably ended, in part because she did not get pregnant and the male partner deemed her to be barren. The man with whom she was currently living and whom she called her "husband" was at least twenty-five years her senior and had adult children from a previous marriage. He was born in Malawi and did not have a musha. Although she would occasionally visit her parents' musha in Masvingo, she had no claim to land there. By 2003, to continue living in the area thus meant they had to rent land and then negotiate the likelihood of plot-holders making additional demands on them over and above the monetary relationship. Plot-holders, like others, began to take advantage of the massive reduction in wage-earning jobs in the area as more and more commercial farms were shuttered. Even those who had been living on farms for decades, like Tapera, who had been growing a hectare of crops by the railway line for the last ten years while renting a hut from Mupungu, started thinking about looking for a more secure place to live.

More and more farm workers I knew were becoming anxious about finding a place to stay as some sort of security, particularly if they were in their thirties or older. As a foreman on a neighbouring plot explained,

> I do not feel a sense of belonging on this farm. I do not feel as if I am at home. I feel being at work. You know, being here there are rules which govern you— for example, the murungu [meaning, here the black plot owner] does not want people to keep chickens, to do small businesses like ordering matemba [dried tiny fish] and other things. The murungu says "I have a shop here, so everything you want you can get it from here—so shop here." So people get everything on credit from the farm store to such an extent that they do not get any pay at the end of the month and need to get credit for more food for the following month. So I would prefer to have my own stand close to a town where I have the freedom to do my own things.

Nonetheless, getting such land, a stand or a musha, could be difficult. Some approached the new land-giving authorities—war veterans, politicians, and other government or ZANU (PF) leaders—to try to get a stand on the occupied commercial farms, but many faced discrimination because, as farm workers, they were viewed as "foreigners" and unworthy of getting land in the massive resettlement exercise—while others were uneasy about investing in such land (Waeterloos and Rutherford 2004).

Although land is not alienable in the communal lands, there has been a growing practice of selling access to a musha—either from the person who had been living there or, more frequently, the "traditional" land authorities there, particularly the *sabhuku* (kraal/village heads) (e.g., Chimhowu and Woodhouse 2010; Rutherford 2001a, 201ff.). Although some of the (former) farm workers I knew were able to get land in a communal land without paying and to which they had no previous claims (for example, one worker shared the same totem as the chief, which led the latter to give him a musha), it was often difficult to find a large enough musha with sufficient land to grow crops. More commonly they only found a piece of land on which to build a home and have a garden. If they wanted to farm, they would have to look for other land to borrow or lease. Like the Mozambican refugees in Vhimba in the 1990s discussed by Hughes (2005), many of these farm workers were subject to the discriminatory politics of land-giving authorities as they operated through the unequal ties of dependency to acquire a claim to belong to these other land categories.

The example of a couple who were farm workers at Berkshire farm is instructive. Although she was born in Hwedza in Mashonaland East province, her husband came from Malawi and as a married woman she had difficulties finding a musha for them in Hwedza. She explained in October 2000 that as they were getting older, they had been looking for a musha for some time, but found it difficult to find land in a communal land that they could afford. Finally they found one in Chinyika communal land in Goromonzi and with help from some of their adult children were able to pay for it. The woman commented, "It only cost Z$2000. But the land, I want to tell you, it is too small to cultivate it for a yield that can feed the family for a year. It is a musha, which we can only use for accommodating us in the meantime. Then we can find a bigger place as time goes on." To make ends meet, her husband was working as a "dairy boy" at Berkshire farm, even though he was not happy about the working conditions. In explaining why they did not acquire land through the ongoing fast-track land resettlement process, she noted "We bought the land from the sabhuku, not from the war vets. If you are given the land by the war vets you are not sure that you are not going to be sacked from the land. A lot of people have paid money to them and then they are sacked from the land." She drew on the same metaphor used for being fired from work—"sacked"—which also entails losing one's access to land on a commercial farm. The uncertainty of where the (former) farm workers can claim a toehold, a contingent belonging, continued to grow.

The majority used whatever access to land they had, as farm workers or as renters, to engage in multiple livelihood strategies, not only wage work. This was emerging as the new norm for those living on commercial farms and, increasingly former commercial farms, as farm workers, former farm workers, and others use these often contingent claims to land "as a base from which to attempt a number of other livelihood and social reproduction strategies" (Hartnack 2015, 127).

For some, their livelihood activities also risked legal sanction. For instance, some of the women involved in the Upfumi struggle would buy and sell marijuana, known as *mbanje*. In September 2002, police searched three homes of women at Mupungu, looking for mbanje. According to one of these women, the police were tipped off by another woman staying there as she was angry with them. The police did not find any mbanje, although she reflected afterward, "it was a close call." Mercy said she has just stopped selling *mzee*, another name for mbanje, as she was worried about going to jail. She said she and a few other women used to buy an envelope of mzee and sell it for a Z$200 profit, selling it to people from the Berkshire area or to others who came to drink beer. "Apart from selling mzee, we also sell small items such as maputi [popcorn], freezits [plastic sleeves of sugared, flavoured water], tomatoes and matches." Then, while laughing, she added, "In the process, we also do not forget to sell *beche* [the vagina]!"

The Farms as a "Hiding Place": Sex Work

Some women engaged in sex work as a livelihood strategy. As other paid jobs disappeared, a few of the former farm workers noted that more and more women in the Upfumi area were engaged in sex work, which was increasingly common elsewhere in Zimbabwe given the economic downturn (e.g., Saunynama 2015). These women reflected on the relative advantages of practicing sex work in the farming areas, compared to other spaces, while recognizing the very real risks involved in this livelihood strategy.

As others have noted, there can be a fuzzy boundary between boyfriend-girlfriend relations and sex work in the region (e.g., Campbell 2003; Hunter 2010). Although the former entails more permanence than the latter, it also can involve prestations, including money. A relationship that began as one involving a client and a sex worker can turn into a boyfriend-girlfriend one. For some of the women living at Mupungu, both could be a source of livelihoods as well as a source of particular risks. It was also a livelihood practice enabled by a mode of belonging through paying rent, which allowed them to live at a place without necessarily relying on family or kin dependencies.

In the evening, it was common to see expensive cars driving into the Mupungu compound as men came to visit their girlfriends. There were at least a dozen or so women in their twenties and thirties I knew who were quite open about being "prostitutes." They mainly sought clients who did not live in Mupungu, to minimize problems they may have with the men's wives or other girlfriends. Maria added that many men in the Mupungu area just want to "have free sex" so "we single women informally tell each other that a man should pay first before having sex. We also feel that we should just have boyfriends from outside the farm who do not stay on this farm to avoid problems here and by doing so we can be able to communicate freely with any women staying here." Rita chimed in that there is a danger that if their "boyfriends" from outside the farm come to the compound "looking for them and don't find us then they will be taken by another single woman. Single women here just want money; if you have money they just come to you." Patience also talked about occasional times when men from outside "conquer" the compound and do not pay for having sex with many women:

> Although we women talk among ourselves that "so and so has money and doesn't want to pay for sex and so don't have sex with him," some single women will ignore the message, thinking others are just jealous of her. But when women take another's boyfriend, we have a saying: *tsungu nanungu mubako rimwe abayiwa ngabude* [with a rabbit and a porcupine in the same cave, whoever gets pierced should get out]. This means that if your boyfriend has been taken by another woman, you should not feel the pain and continue with the relationship even though you know that your boyfriend sleeps in the next hut with my friend and if you feel bored you just get another boyfriend, just like that.

Rita later echoed this point, saying the single women don't fight among themselves because of "the system" they use of *"wainditorera saka ndichaku-torerarwo* [you have taken mine so I will take yours too]. This makes it fair game."

Patience identified three types of sex workers at Mupungu farm depending on where they search for their "catch": those who go to Ruwa and Harare; those who go to nearby areas; and those who remain at Mupungu. Those who traveled to Ruwa or Harare made the most money, but one could not always afford to travel there, she noted. She also recalled that before when they were working on the farms full-time they would be too tired to travel. Since they had been fired from Upfumi some of them have been doing it more regularly, with two women earning their full-time living from sex work. Yet, at the same time, there was fear that if they traveled to towns then they may be observed by relatives who live in the nearby areas, Ruwa or Harare.

Rita made this point explicitly, stating that Mupungu was a "good hiding place" from her relatives so she can continue this "silly business": "It is close to the main tar [road], a school [for our kids] and we have cheap accommodation." It was not a perfect place as the houses were not of good quality, the water quality was quite poor and Maria noted that some of her boyfriends were scornful of her living conditions when she brought them back to her somewhat dilapidated hut. Yet, as Rita pointed out, like any other men the "rich business people who come here to Mupungu are able to fit in very well in these small huts." Other than the living conditions, she continued, "Here we live a town life; we do not care what others say. We are all lodgers here and we rent like those in the towns do."

Rita had come to the farm because she was chased away from her deceased husband's musha as she did not want to be "inherited" (*kugara nhaka*) by one of his surviving brothers. Living a "town life" meant that one could be independent of the webs of power and financial dependencies of families or spouses. As another woman, Rudo, observed, if she can no longer stay on the farms because of the jambanja and evictions of farm workers by war veterans and new settlers, "I will find another job and will not go to my parents' musha. I do not want to go there as I am accustomed to getting money on a monthly basis and am old enough not to stay with my brothers at the musha. You know, as a woman, your brothers can restrict you. They may say "We do not want to see you with any man" and stuff like that. This is not good for an adult woman like me. I need the freedom to have my boyfriends."

Indeed, a few of the other women celebrated the "freedom" they had of not being married. Rita explained that "I fear a person who has paid *roora* [bridewealth] to my parents, but not a boyfriend. The latter has no right to tell me what people I can speak to. It is up to me. And as a boyfriend is not the last man in Zimbabwe, I can leave him as there are many guys out there who want to be loved. And if he leaves me, I don't mind either."[4]

The money received for sex work was usually not much. In 2000, the women I knew charged between Z$30 to Z$50 for a "short time" at the beer hall and Z$200 if they go home with a client. Moreover, Patience said that if "I see that his health is not good I charge an amount so high you know he can't pay. That is how I reject some men. It is my secret because if I tell him the truth then he would become violent." The women were very cognizant about the combined risks of sexually transmitted diseases, including HIV/AIDS, and male violence. For the former, the women said they insisted that their clients use condoms and most complied. Although, as Patience put it, "There are times when the men just remove the condoms without your knowledge and you find yourself with an STD or pregnant." She and others noted that many suffered from STDs in the area, including herself, but she added that she had suffered from them even when she was married "because my husband too much liked *kupinda-pinda* [screwing around]." Many would go to a n'anga (traditional healer) living in Carl's compound as well as to the clinic for treatment.

Some also become pregnant unexpectedly, leading some to have the child and others preferring an abortion. Rita's experiences are telling. She had been married to a man working for the Ministry of Health in Harare and they had three children. When he married another woman, she was not happy about this new polygynous relationship; so she left him and the children in Harare, arriving at Upfumi in 1995 where the mother of her "sister" (cousin) was working and helped her get a job. She said that she continued to visit her children and had a good relationship with her former husband, much to the chagrin of his new wife. She then had another child "with a man she did not love." She tried to abort, but it did not work, and, after giving birth, she sent the child to live with her mother at their musha in Mutoko. She frequently had to balance different relationships, noting that she would have different boyfriends who would pay her money. For example, she said one day one boyfriend gave her Z$800, out of which she bought clothes for her daughter, and the next day another boyfriend gave her more money, which she used to collect her kids in Harare to go visit the musha, where she hoped to buy a heifer for herself.[5]

Balancing these different relationships could pose difficulties, especially if the men involved encountered one another. Rita gave the example of one boyfriend who had moved to Bulawayo the previous month who then unexpectedly arrived in the compound in the middle of the night and found her with another man. So she talked to a neighbour, "who agreed to accommodate the visitor" and everything worked out. Neither man was really angry—"I was lucky that none of the guys wanted to beat me." She said as both of them had wives who had died, she did not want to marry either of them for fear she too would die. She rather preferred to stay in a boyfriend-girlfriend relationship.

Then in January 2002, she became very ill after using some self-practice method of having an abortion (see, e.g., Bhachi 2011). According to Jane, in so doing, Rita's womb shifted over and her stomach became so swollen she could not eat or move. Amai Mike and Ambuya Lydia heard her cries and washed her and moved the womb to its proper position, tying a belt around her waist, and contacting her former husband in Harare to come and stay with her for a week. Jane remarked somewhat sarcastically, "That was fun because some of Rita's boyfriends would come to visit with her and were chased away by her husband, or one of us would warn them to go away." Her husband then took her to her mother's musha in Mutoko and that was the last I heard of her.

Sexual relations were implicated in the risk for violence in the area (e.g., Armstrong 1998; Tom and Musingafi 2013), like in many other places of the world. It was not uncommon for huts to be destroyed or burned down, men attacking women, men attacking men, women attacking women, over alleged or identified improper sexual relations. Grace talked about her neighbour at Mupungu needing to flee in July 2001 after her boyfriend was caught by another boyfriend. Both were married men and the one who came to the hut at night stabbed the woman, yelling, Grace reported, "I am the one who keeps you [by providing you with money and gifts] and you sleep with other men!"

Sometimes these conflicts turned deadly. In February 2003, Antonio, the manager of Mupungu, died after being stabbed by another male farm worker in a drunken fight that started over a woman—one of Antonio's girlfriends. People were saddened but not too surprised, noting that his philandering had caused much conflict on the farm.

Others died from what others thought were HIV/AIDS, although the diagnosis was not always widely accepted or publicly discussed. Carl died in late 2000 after suffering what was called "pneumonia" for some time, although most suggested that he had succumbed to AIDS. As others have noted in studies elsewhere (Campbell 2003; Chazan 2015), HIV/AIDS was deeply stigmatized, with the assumption that if someone had HIV/AIDS then his or her close relatives could also be infected with it—either directly or because they too were morally weak and "irresponsible." Archie explained it this way:

> People hate the word "AIDS" because if you say, "my sister died of AIDS" and in that family there are other girls who are not yet married people will begin saying that these other young sisters are likely to be infected as well as they could be doing the same activities of prostitution which the older sister likely was doing. These young sisters will not be able to get married as people will think that [they] are likely to be contaminated with AIDS. So one avoids saying the word "AIDS" to protect the whole family from being looked down upon by others.

The link of moral licentiousness and infection was strong and women bore the brunt of it, hence the desire of many of the young women who engaged in sex work to "hide" out at Mupungu, away from the possible gaze of their relatives. People also said that Carl's brother refused to bury Carl at the farm, in case his "diseased body" infected the water supply.[6]

Moral condemnation and attempts at regulation were common after 2000 as before, but they were channelled through existing gendered power relations. The single women who engaged in sex work as part of their livelihood strategies sought to minimize violence toward themselves, including getting STDs or HIV/AIDS and nominally tried to look after each other, although not always successfully if customers or boyfriends thought otherwise. Like in many Zimbabwean households, domestic violence was common (e.g., Shamu, Abrahams, Temmerman and Zarowsky 2013; Chipunza 2013). As Patience explained her sore back in February 2002, "My boyfriend has a problem when he is drunk, and he had beaten me using a bottle in the attack." I also knew a number of married women who had confronted single women who were involved in relationships with their husbands, but then they themselves were beaten by their husbands or chased away or told to leave the household and go to his musha.

For example, Martha, who had been involved in the labor struggle, was married to a man who then left her to be with another woman, Batsirai, at another farm. As she was not working and no longer getting money from her husband, Martha travelled to that farm and confronted Batsirai, where a fight ensued. The husband was alerted of the fight and came to the compound where he began beating both of them. As Martha admitted, her husband was violent—"my husband can beat. When he wants to beat you he uses an electrical cord to whip you. He can beat you to such an extent that he can leave you half-dead." As a result, the husband returned to his home at Mujiba farm where Martha was living and brought Batsirai to live with them as a second wife. But the situation remained very tense. One day in early 2001, the husband discovered that Martha had stolen a pair of pants from Batsirai and put *muti* in it—medicine to try to make her husband divorce the second wife. He then beat her, and although she went to the police, he just had to pay a fine. Two days later he sent Martha to live at his musha in a nearby communal land.

Whereas women found men difficult to control if they were violent, other than possibly going to the police, both women and men found male leaders even more difficult to stop. Just as foremen and managers would at times sexually harass and abuse women, making demands for sex in exchange for jobs or perks at work, male leaders did the same. Chenjerai started to get a reputation for going after teenaged girls and having a number of girlfriends, as did Councillor Banda; although, the latter was taking himself to be a regulator of moral virtue, arresting men accused of involved in domestic violence, as the man at Upfumi in August 2002 recounted at the start of the chapter, and thrashing women accused of being "prostitutes." Those involved in political leadership also often assumed the role of morality police, while occasionally adopting a "sovereign exception" (Agamben 2005) to following the same rules and codes.

In October 2002, Mai Tendai, the ZANU (PF) Women's League official who lived at the council houses, pleaded with Chenjerai to try to reign in Banda. She said the week before, shortly after he was reelected as councillor in the 2002 RDC elections, he and his youth heavily assaulted four women at Upfumi farm. She explained that this violence was troublesome, unlike the more explicitly political violence carried out in the name of her party:

> I am not worried about people who were assaulted before and during the council elections, but I am worried about people assaulted after the elections; why assault them now? I watched him assault these women and I did not want to intervene but after I had seen how terrible it was, I had to intervene. I asked Comrade Banda why he was doing this and he replied "these women are accused of *chihure* [prostitution] and so I am disciplining them." This is bad. People who assault so violently in the manner he was doing are a disgrace to the party. Besides, who is disciplining Comrade Banda? He is the worst male prostitute in this area and he is not ashamed of himself!

By this time, Chenjerai was once-again quite close to Banda, and both were deploying and organizing violence against others as a way to assert their political authority—an authority based on being part of ZANU (PF) which Mai Tendai supported, although in this instance she was not keen on the violence entering into punishment of those accused of sexual immorality. Yet she was downplaying the broad form of moral authority that poritikisi can take. Similar to what the ex-combatants based at Karigamombe Training Centre in the early 1980s were doing in terms of regulating domestic disputes, intervening in labor conflicts, and vigilantly guarding against the rise of opposition political parties (see chapter 1), by 2002 Councillor Banda and his allies were carrying out similar activities as a way to assert their authority over their territory. They were doing so in a way that was much more ruthless than before and it now also included intervening in the occupation and distribution of commercial farms.

The mode of belonging to "the nation" was trumping other modes of belonging, but there were multiple people making such claims, seeking to engage in scale-making projects that bolstered their authority over others. This was occurring as much within ZANU (PF) as between it and those who belonged to the MDC or no political party. The result for many of the farm workers and former farm workers was greater insecurity as they were subjected, and subjected themselves, to these even more conditional modes of belonging.

Shaky Ground: Poritikisi and Labor Relations

The Upfumi war was sustained through its linkages to poritikisi. The fired farm workers' leaders drew on a range of extra-local organizations and individuals from across the political spectrum to assist their struggle. Although Chenjerai had taken on elements of a politician in terms of his strong words, intimidation, and occasional violence, he did so largely as a way to support the workers' struggle. This changed after February 2000 ushered in a very different political landscape in Zimbabwe. I will provide some examples from the Upfumi area to show how poritikisi became more pervasive in people's lives, leading to a variety of struggles as different leaders sought to assert their authority and power over people and resources, all largely done within ZANU (PF). Whereas the particular power/sovereignty dynamics and socio-economic relations in the locations formed the grounds that shaped how these practices of electoral politics played out, at the same time considerations of electoral politics were substantially reworking the social footings in many such places.

After the June 2000 parliamentary elections, politics became even more entangled in the lives of the people living on Upfumi farm and in the surrounding area as in Zimbabwe itself. The struggle against Upfumi and the victory of the MDC in its electoral district definitely marked the workers involved in the labor struggle, their leaders, and many of those living at Mupungu and Carl farms as "MDC." Yet, that allegiance soon shifted for most as ZANU (PF) continued its offensive against perceived and real MDC structures after the parliamentary elections. To explain this shift, one needs to understand the increasing repression of any scale-making projects outside ZANU (PF) networks that led people who had leadership claims, like Chenjerai, to reconsider the relations of dependencies through which they would attach themselves. Attachment to ZANU (PF) not only increased one's authority, but it also helped to ensure access to resources, including land, as state agencies overturned unequal racialized relationships institutionalized through the colonial and postcolonial history of land settlement. And leadership in these structures could allow one to distribute resources, including land.

Although the primary aim of electoral politics in the Berkshire area was to ensure people voted for ZANU (PF) in this period, one of the key means of practicing politics was through territorializing power as different leaders sought to assert control over demarcated areas and the people living in them. Whereas the thrust at the national scale may have been to assert the ability of sovereign power to define what politicized categories of people are viewed as part of the state or not by "determining who qualifies for inclusion to the legal protections of citizenship, and who is excluded or banned from the law's purview of application" (Worby 2003, 59), the violence unleashed in the name of the ZANU (PF) state actually generated more openings for competing territorializing projects. These projects often were in competition with each other as different individuals with varied claims to authority, although nominally within ZANU (PF), sought to demonstrate control over the same or overlapping territories. Commercial farms and farm workers became key targets of these ambitions, as the boundaries around these territorial spaces were breached.

As before 2000, working conditions continued to fail to meet the minimum regulations on many commercial farms and grievances were many. Conditions on black-owned farms were typically no better, if not worse, than found on white-owned farms. Mupungu was a case in point where Antonio typically paid wages after they were due, sometimes months afterward, and often less than what was owed. As Tapera's wife, who worked there for eighteen years, said in January 2001, "When you complain to Antonio, saying, 'What are we going eat?' he replies, 'Go and get maize on credit.' Even if I take the maize on credit, where will I get the money to go to the grinding mill? What will I use to buy cooking oil, soap, and other things? He says, 'Just wait.'" Nevertheless, in my research in the Berkshire area no one working on black-owned farms actively sought outside intervention to improve working conditions or to demand their rights. But that was not the case on white-owned farms, as after June 2000 there were more actively willing interveners. It is here that the reduced presence of organizations not actively linked to ZANU (PF) and the shift in Chenjerai's own affiliations become readily apparent.

By 2000, ZANU (PF) officials in Berkshire/Oxfordshire once again started to actively advertise that they and unions associated with it—not GAPWUZ—were the only ones farm workers should approach for labor disputes. This was part of a wider national-scale strategy of trying to counter the MDC and its support from the ZCTU (Raftopoulos 2003). The Zimbabwe Federation of Trade Unions (ZFTU), formed as a rival to ZCTU, and actively supported by the ZANU (PF) government, became the loose umbrella for small preexisting unions or individuals who would seek to intervene in agrarian labor relations. One example from 2001 is when one of the widely known, if not infamous, Harare-based leaders of the war veterans, Joseph Chinotimba, who also became a leader of ZFTU, led a number of demonstrations for higher wages on farms around Harare ("Rabble-Rousing Union," *The Farmer* 2001). In contrast, GAPWUZ officials were persona non grata on farms that were increasingly falling under ZANU (PF) control after early 2000. In the run-up to the 2000 parliamentary elections, GAPWUZ officials were threatened on a number of occasions and some were even detained by ZANU (PF) activists and land occupiers. GAPWUZ's main official in Marondera, Justice Watchi, was forced to flee to Harare because of his active support for the MDC.

After June 2000, Chenjerai still had the cachet of being a leader in the Berkshire area who assisted in farm worker struggles, but many were turning more to ZANU (PF) structures. On July 1, 2000, twelve farm workers were let go from Dryvalley farm in Oxfordshire without compensation. A delegation of them tracked down Chenjerai at Mupungu farm and asked him to intervene. As a worker later told me, "We know Chenjerai helps farm workers—he was involved in ZANU (PF) in the past and then with GAPWUZ. He knows the laws." Chenjerai went to the farm and after talking with the workers, the clerk, and the manager he said that six of them should be treated as permanent workers as they had worked more than eight months and thus their firing was illegal. He wrote a letter addressed to GAPWUZ and told the workers to bring it to their Marondera office. Instead, a few of the workers on the workers' committee went to see Mherera, the ZANU (PF) official based in Oxfordshire, with their complaint. Chenjerai later explained to me this decision by observing that this workers' committee had also been the farm's ZANU (PF) committee since 1998, for he had helped to establish it during the local government elections when Banda was first elected.

A few weeks later, I travelled to the farm with Chenjerai and we talked to some of the workers involved in the dispute and then to the farm clerk. The workers told me that when they went to Mherera, he told them "Do not go to GAPWUZ as we in ZANU will solve this issue." He then wrote a letter for the workers to give to the clerk demanding that he come to Oxfordshire to meet with the party committee the following weekend or "you will be sorted out by our people." At the meeting, the workers continued, there were ZANU (PF) officials like Mr. Chishiri (the councillor for the ward in which the farm was located), Mherera, almost ten war veterans and three members from the youth brigade. The clerk told us that the war vets were intimidating him, saying, "We know what happens on farms. You MaBharani [the clerk], you sit with the murungu. You tell him to fire these farm workers and then you will take their money at the end of the year. We know these farms."

When a war vet asked the clerk where the farm workers voted in the parliamentary elections and he replied at Karigamombe School, he said, "They snarled at me, saying, 'That box mostly was for MDC.' Ahhh, it was terrible." The clerk said if it was not for Councillor Chishiri, he would have been beaten up.

The clerk said he managed to convince them that the six who were seasonal workers would still be dismissed but they would be paid a week's salary and the rest would be rehired, as Chenjerai had suggested, since they were permanent. He said it was difficult convincing his boss, the murungu, to rehire the six as he had wanted only to pay them out as they were "bothering" him, but the clerk managed to show his boss the legal, if not political, need to do so. As the clerk reflected, "If this happened last year, people would have simply gone to GAPWUZ as before ZANU (PF) never came here. And if ZANU wrote a letter, I would have simply ignored it. But now because of the elections. [I cannot ignore ZANU]"

Quickly, more and more farm workers began to realize this newly reassertive, and threatening, power of ZANU (PF) officials and allies in the Berkshire area was becoming the only authority in the area. When I went to that farm in July 2000, Chenjerai also talked to a group of over twenty workers at the Dryvalley farm compound about this case and he asked for and listened to their problems and violations of working conditions, which included: they do not sign contracts; there is no disciplinary committee; many of them lacked zvitupa (plural of chitupa; national identity cards) because they are seen as foreigners; GAPWUZ would never come even before it was declared an enemy by ZANU (PF); "the government only sees us as sheep"; and so forth. After hearing these complaints for some time, Chenjerai reiterated many of the same themes that I had heard him talk about during the Upfumi struggle—that farm labor is not a ZANU (PF) or an MDC issue and that farm workers need to be proud of who they are and work together to put pressure on GAPWUZ, their MP, the government, and so forth. When Chenjerai suggested that the workers' committee should have a meeting with management to present their concerns and complaints, one of the men present responded that "the murungu will simply tell us to 'fuck off!'" Undaunted, Chenjerai urged them to elect a stronger workers' committee and recruit more workers for GAPWUZ—"the union is poor, it only has one truck for all of Zimbabwe. But if a million farm workers pay them dues, the union will be strong." To which, another man replied, "The union officials only live in towns and we cannot afford to travel there to see them." Although Chenjerai seemed to be sticking to his well-worn script from the Upfumi struggle, I sensed many of the workers, like the clerk, recognized the postelection situation was changing significantly. Even though the 2000 parliamentary elections were finished, ZANU (PF) was not going to remain stationary given how close they came to losing (if not, as critics averred, actually losing the election save for its rigging [see Carver 2000, 20–21]). Over the next ten months, Chenjerai too would be taking a very different approach to these issues.

Despite occasional letters sent and other entreaties from Chenjerai, no GAPWUZ official showed up on the farms. Leaders in the area who wanted to invoke ties to extra-local organizations had their choices narrowed considerably by 2001. In the months immediately after the election, people involved in the Upfumi war were viewed largely as MDC. As Banda was involving himself in the Oxfordshire East Peace Taskforce over the winter months of 2000, and violence was increasing in the cities and on some farms in other areas of Zimbabwe, there was a strong sense that it was impossible to openly identify themselves as MDC by donning their party's shirts or hats around the council houses or elsewhere. Chenjerai would occasionally visit Gwisai in Harare who by then was an MDC MP, but as the year progressed, he spent less and less time with him. The MDC MP for the riding of Seke East never appeared and no MDC structures were made or established in the area, largely due to the siege made by ZANU (PF) activists and structures against the new opposition party. Yet even by early 2001, many residents in the Berkshire area, including those in local leadership positions, saw Chenjerai and many of the farm workers involved in the struggle as MDC sympathisers. This was evident when the ZANU (PF) leaders at the council houses chased away Tapedza, his wife, and Tawonga from their homes there, in January 2001, because they were viewed as members of the opposition party. Another example was the cessation of casual work for former Upfumi workers living in Mupungu at nearby Nyamhanza farm because the war vets who camped there told the white farmer in February 2001 that these workers were "MDC" and should not be employed.

This political uncertainty began to limit Chenjerai's own actions during this period. He publicly entertained thoughts about running for councillor in the 2002 RDC elections for, he said, "farm workers know and respect me and they say I should run." There were more open disputes with him by those who had previously followed him. As Grace put it in October 2000, "Now that we got our money we are no longer afraid of him." These included occasional brief physical fights. Most people had more nuanced views of him, as they did of many of their leaders. As a former female Upfumi worker explained on Berkshire farm in March 2001, "Chenjerai is a strong and brave man. [Although] he has been cheating us on several occasions and we have been angry with him during these times, but in the end we won our case." Others assumed that he used strong *mishonga* (medicine) to avoid long stays in jail when he was arrested for various reasons and cited his apparent immunity from HIV/AIDS given his frequent sexual partners; a supposition bolstered by the fact that his mother was a *n'anga* (healer) in the area.

Nonetheless, for the most part during this period Chenjerai focused his leadership on issues that never left the scale of the farm, unconnected to any scale-making projects, other than his own. As he admitted in November 2000, a "group of farm workers came to me this morning and asked me what they can do because they had been given a mugwazo [task work] and when they failed to finish it they were not marked for their ticket [pay] that day. But I am scared of giving them any advice as I cannot do anything to help them." In other words, he had no viable access to extra-local interveners.

A few months into 2001, he was openly regretting his decision of leading the struggle, and declared several times that he "wished he had been bribed away from the struggle by Chapunga." By April 2001 Chenjerai lost his battle with Antonio over nonpayment of rent and left Mupungu. He moved to a place on a smallholder farm near the bar, Kunwa Doro.

In the meantime, ZANU (PF) interventions and those of the councillor, in particular, increased in the area. The Oxfordshire East Peace Taskforce slowly stopped operating and instead Banda became more involved in threatening to lead farm invasions and to inflict violence against those who either directly challenged his authority or were seen as outside of ZANU

(PF) control. A good example comes from his intervention at Black Forest farm in mid-January 2001.

New management arrived at Black Forest farm in late 2000 and began to disrupt some of the past practices, irritating a number of workers. Moreover, the new white woman manager told the daughter of Shuvai, a ZANU (PF) activist living at the council houses, that she could not wear her ZANU (PF) T-shirt to work as the farm "is not ZANU (PF) property."

The next day Banda and Shuvai arrived at the farm at lunch time and met with the main farm manager for awhile before addressing the workers. After leading with party slogans—"Pamberi neZANU (PF) kufa ichitonga [Forward with ZANU (PF) which rules until death], Pamberi naComrade Robert Mugabe, Pasi neMDC [Forward with Comrade Robert Mugabe, Down with the MDC]"—Banda quickly moved into the main purpose of his meeting: addressing farm worker grievances, in particular about the new murungu manager. According to one of the workers, Sipho, the new management, was "'hot,' not interested in listening to the workers." He and the other gathered workers listed a number of grievances concerning access to fire wood, leave days, rations, number of uniforms they receive from the farm, contract status, and her propensity to fire workers for what was perceived as the smallest mistake. Banda then declared that if anyone sells out those who had complained to him by telling the bosses, they would have to meet him face to face, and that he will take the problems to the bosses and if they do not change things "I will invade the farm."

A few hours after Banda's departure, the manager organized a meeting for the workers, demanding to know who called the councillor to the farm. As Nyasha put it, the "boss said why not use the workers' committee? 'Is it good to destroy the committee and use Banda as your representative at this farm?'" As a member of the workers' committee at Black Forest, Sipho explained afterward, management never had meetings with workers because "when we ask for the time to have a meeting, the murungu says the farm is busy and has no time to allow the workers to have a meeting." Yet, the farmer did initially address some of the concerns raised by the workers in their meeting with Banda, who did not return to the farm for some time afterward.

Sipho said those Black Forest workers who had been involved in the Upfumi war were the ones who had called Banda, since they knew him from their struggle and they had been telling the workers' committee that "we know the rules and laws regarding farm workers' rights better than you." She observed the growing number of these Upfumi workers at Black Forest: "The previous management of this farm never wanted to employ people who worked at Upfumi but this new management just recruited people on the basis of job ability and that is why we have people who had been camped at the roadside [in the musososo] working with us now." Although shortly after Banda's visit, some of the workers were saying things have not improved dramatically and Sipho observed that management still ignored many of her committee's suggestions, nonetheless many were happy that Banda had come and threatened the bosses. As she said, "We all here appreciate Cde. Banda's visit because this is what led the murungu to calm down and understand us better. If anything goes wrong with management again, we will call Cde. Banda but we will not let the murungu know that he has been invited by the workers' committee because the murungu might start hating us."

The double edge of party politics was now very visible during the time of jambanja: it is a source of power that can help in some struggles and, as a form of strength, *simba*, it can also be a source of fear and occasional terror. By the start of 2001, Councillor Banda, war veterans, and others within ZANU (PF) structures were targeting farm workers, both in terms of trying to help them and by threatening them. Those who had been talking about wearing their MDC t-shirts a few months earlier were no longer doing so. No visible sign of the MDC could be shown, including the open palm, which was an MDC sign. Increasingly, people would only raise their arm with their fingers clenched in a fist to greet each other. The danger of politics was on the ascendancy again. As a Black Forest farm worker explained in February 2001, "I am a ZANU (PF) supporter, attending the meetings at Goromonzi turnoff. I am also an MDC supporter because I don't know what will happen tomorrow. It is my secret though. Most people know me simply as a ZANU (PF) supporter. I am also the chairman of the ZANU (PF) youth on our farm." The necessary duplicity of public political affiliations was increasingly important for the sake of personal security.

The growing control of ZANU (PF) in the area was exhibited during the Independence Day celebrations on April 18, 2001, held at Karigamombe School. A teacher noted that usually it was the school that was in charge of organizing these events for the area. Instead, Councillor Banda organized the event. "In the past, the school was informed of its responsibilities in a letter from the district administrator for Goromonzi district and as a school we were supposed to make all the preparations in the form of school choir, traditional dances, and other forms of entertainment. . . . But this year, we have been left out of the loop, regardless of the fact that the celebration is being held at our school."

Neighboring farmers, as well as individuals living on the farms, were forced, as some put it, to donate food and money for the celebrations. One resident of Mupungu bitterly recounted that on the Sunday before the celebrations, "ZANU (PF) youths from the council houses came to Mupungu telling people to donate Z$50 for the celebrations. These youths were carrying sticks and whips, telling us that those who fail to attend today's celebrations will be beaten. Moreover, they said only those who had the money and contributed will be able to get food and beer today."

According to my research assistants who attended the April 18, 2001, event, the Independence Day celebrations in the Upfumi area clearly marked the nation as belonging only to ZANU (PF). Farm workers were located in a particular way to this politicized nation.

Pressured by ZANU (PF) officials to attend, many in the surrounding farms came for the celebration. After everyone was searched by party youth upon entering the school grounds, the event started. Banda ordered all the workers to join groups according to the farms they belonged to and served each group one plate of sadza and meat—not nearly enough for everyone to have a taste, leaving many disgruntled. Then a ZANU (PF) official from Goromonzi addressed the crowd. Recognizing that most attendees were living, if not working, on a commercial farm in the area, he not only shouted out the now standard ZANU (PF) line that "the war of liberation will be over when people are given land," but he also added that "the time has now come for people to be given land and not to be made to work on the farms by the whites." After urging everyone to vote for President Mugabe in the presidential elections scheduled for the following year, he observed that "all those who support MDC have lost direction. Supporting the MDC means that you want the whites to rule this country one more time!" Banda echoed these thoughts in addressing the large crowd, declaring that "the government was fighting another war with the whites and the MDC. It is a way of getting back land and giving it to its rightful people—the blacks, who also include farm workers."

In this speech, at least farm workers became part of the ZANU (PF) slogan "the land is the economy, the economy is the land." Although Banda was trying to include farm workers in the nationalist script, others were not so generous in their definition of whether or not they belonged to Zimbabwe.

For instance, the teacher quoted above also noted the difficult situation faced by the majority of the students at the school who lacked birth certificates. He said only about 200 of the 640 students in the primary school at the time had birth certificates and yet the Registrar General's office was indifferent to the teachers' attempts to assist the students in getting their documents. As a result, he said teachers tended to guess the date and day of birth for these students when they write their Grade 7 national exams and these dates become official dates of birth for them within the records of the Ministry of Education. Nonetheless, these students were unable to enter secondary school without birth certificates. And without birth certificates, they would be unable to get a national ID card, vote, and be officially recognized as citizens of Zimbabwe. He partially blamed the nomadic lifestyle of farm workers, which, for him, included "nomadic" marriages with the man having children with many women. He saw them as vulnerable to abuse by their murungu and having their scale of attachment being narrowly defined to that of a particular farm or a farming area rather than to the nation. As he observed, "This is how this Berkshire farm community is like because you can see that even those who were fired from Upfumi are still staying here long after they were given their terminal benefits."

However, after 2000 it was the ZANU (PF) government and its cadres, more than the varungu [plural of murungu; white farmers], who exploited the lack of documented citizenship for farm workers and their insecure belonging, both amplifying their vulnerabilities and channelling it for their own political objectives of forcing white farmers off the land and preventing farmers and farm workers alike from providing support to the MDC. By 2001, it was becoming clearer to many farm workers that the "land demonstrations" of the 2000 parliamentary elections were becoming the fast-track land distribution exercise, which meant the likelihood that they could lose their job and the access to wages and whatever land-based resources that their configuration of domestic government enabled. And it was uncertain if they would be able to get access to land in this resettlement program, given the discrimination against farm workers by many of those who were distributing land (Sachikonye 2003; Waeterloos and Rutherford 2004).

Most farm workers I knew were eager to get access to land. As Patience told me in July 2000, "I am for MDC but I would not refuse getting land for me and my children." Tapera, one of the *vadhara* who had worked at Upfumi, even asked me in August 2000 if I could assist in getting land for them: "Look, this [Mupungu farm] is not a secure place. Anytime the farm owner can come to us and say, "Guys, I want to lock my houses; please find somewhere else to go." This will really make us suffer more. Because you have helped us a lot, I think it would be better if you complete the help by finding a piece of land for us to stay and start farming. We would appreciate it if we could get some form of resettlement, where we feel we belong, as this is someone's land and we just rent here."

This was a request others had asked me directly or indirectly through Rinse, mistakenly assuming that I had some influence over the very uncertain process and resources to assist in securing their access to a plot or a stand. My minimal support to their struggle had placed me into a presumed web of dependency relations with some of the farm workers.

Even farm workers who had a musha elsewhere were keen on getting land through the fast-track redistribution exercise. A farm worker living at Mupungu farm had come from Bikita were he could get access to land via his family. But, he said "I cannot go there and stay on a piece of land as the soil is very poor and the land plot would be quite small." Moreover, he did not want to live near his relatives. As he identified himself as a "true citizen of Zimbabwe" (unlike, he implied, many of the other farm workers whose ancestors came from afar), he felt entitled to get land. Still, he reasoned, "it is not wise to claim land on the farm where you are working because the boss will be against you. To get land, go to other farms where you are not known." He was thus attending all the ZANU (PF) meetings that he could and registering with as many official land redistribution authorities to try to ensure that he would be able to get a stand on a farm.

Yet, it was rare for farm workers to get the land in the immediate environs of Upfumi at that time. In 2000, war veterans occupied a neighboring farm, Burton farm, and distributed land to war veterans. As recounted by Jane who was working there at the time, the war veterans said "They had come to take the farm because the land belonged to the people." But they did not give any land to the farm workers. She said that half of the farm workers were keen on trying to get land, while the other half were scared of losing their jobs. "Especially people from Malawi and Mozambique did not support the idea of the farm being taken because they said they would have nowhere to go if the farm was taken." The attachment of farm workers to the farm often was intimately tied to their perceived ability to be attached to Zimbabwe itself, at least those who were viewed, legally or not, as foreigners.

In the next two years, the only people in the Berkshire farming area that I knew who received land through the various routes sanctioned by what the government called the Fast- Track Land Reform exercise were mainly nonfarm workers: Mai Tendai of the ZANU (PF) Women's League; Councillor Banda; Tawanda, a former National Railways of Zimbabwe worker who rented a shack on a farm and was active in ZANU (PF); and a few other nonfarm workers. Archie got access to land via his wife's brother who was a war veteran in Macheke, but he was only loaned the land. In mid-2001 when Agritex officials came to peg out land at Lansing and Irontree farms, the farm workers from the farms were denied land. People talked about how farm workers remaining on these farms who did not get land, as well as those still working or staying on other farms, were stealing the irrigation pipes and cutting them up to sell as scrap metal in Harare. "Everyone is trying to survive," muttered Archie at Mupungu farm. The lack of planning was evident in similar accounts of chaos and uncertainty on other farms being distributed for land resettlement (see Matondi 2012, for a thorough account). In the meantime, farm workers continued to register for land through their councillor and with individual war veteran groups.

Farm workers were generally discriminated against in the land redistribution process, although they were not completely denied access as others have shown (Sachikonye 2004; Waeterloos and Rutherford 2004; Scoones et al 2010; Moyo 2011; Chambati 2011; Sadomba 2011; Matondi 2012, 28), and that I discuss further in my conclusion. Though some have pointed to these examples to suggest that farm workers were not consistently excluded from land redistribution, they were consistently subject to the growing weight of a mix of sovereignty, power, and violence associated with electoral politics. The ground of politics was now underfoot in more and more places most of the time.

In the Berkshire area, compounding the insecurity was the growing violence as war veterans and ZANU (PF) activists intervened more and more into the lives of those on the farms, both for acquiring land and to address labor issues, as they sought to assert their power to rule over them. This was also part and parcel of the growing campaigning for the 2002 presidential elections. Let me give one example.

In April 2001 there was more worker unrest at Black Forest. Management started to lay off workers, one at a time. They argued that European buyers were uncertain about the ability of Zimbabwean commercial farms to remain as consistent suppliers and thus they were no longer ordering many flowers. With the drop in sales, the farmers reduced production and retrenched farm workers. In March 2001, they began forcing some workers to take leave and when eight of them returned from leave they fired them, one of whom was a permanent worker who had been there for nine years. Other workers said the boss was not keen on giving the fired workers much money as leave pay, which incensed them, particularly the one who had worked on the farm for the long period. A woman worker said that one of the fired workers went to the GAPWUZ office in Marondera who confirmed that the amount management was offering was sufficient according to industry regulations, but they refused to come to the farm to address the workers about the law because war veterans had threatened GAPWUZ officials in the area. Instead, other fired workers went to the councillor and war veterans in the area.

According to a number of workers, Banda returned to the farm and talked to the manager, telling the workers afterward that the murungu refused to hire back the workers or increase the amount of money he was offering them. Shortly afterward, two war veterans and a number of youth came and ordered the guards away from the farm gate. As one guard later put it, the "war vets said if 'we see you at the gate we are going to beat you.' And the guard on duty was told to 'open the gate, surrender the keys to the murungu, and leave!' which he did." The war veterans then had a long meeting with the farmer who, clearly under duress, had agreed to increase the payout so that the permanent worker received six months' salary, the seasonal workers received four months' salary and the casual ones received two months' salary.

The chairman of the workers' committee said the war vets also met with the workers' committee, berating them for being "too weak" and "not doing your job." A few days later, Banda had a meeting with the workers and said that they had to listen to his orders now. As the chairman explained, "Banda said 'you are the ones who selected me to represent you so listen to what I am saying.'" Banda also ordered the vice chairman of the workers' committee to leave the farm for selling out the workers, with a guard suggesting that the councillor later beat him. Banda threatened, if not physically punished, the vice-chairman because he had accompanied the farmer to the police station after the councillor's first visit where he had submitted a complaint of harassment against Banda. The vice-chair acted as an interpreter for the murungu, and thus in the eyes of some of the workers and of the councillor he was a *mutengesi* (a sellout).

Banda was reliant on his ZANU (PF) position to stake a sovereign claim to intervene in the labor affairs of the farm. He also relied on the threat, if not the actual meting out, of violence associated with electoral politics to support his interventions.

Whereas actions by the government and ZANU (PF) cadres increased the livelihood insecurity of farm workers, underlying their conditional belonging to commercial farms and uncertain claims to resettlement land based on how they are represented as a community on the scale of the nation, the government also sought to channel some of this anxiety against their employers. The classed and raced attributes of domestic government were amplified through the passing of statutory instrument 6 (SI 6) early in 2002, entitled *Labor Relations (Terminal Benefits and Entitlements of Agricultural Employees Affected by Compulsory Acquisition) Regulations*. According to an official with GAPWUZ, SI 6 of 2002 was largely based on a document Munyaradzi Gwisai had written up for GAPWUZ, which they had submitted to the government in 1999, concerning the situation of farm workers during compulsory land acquisition—as a response to the designation of almost fifteen hundred commercial farms in September 1997.[7] Entitled *Farm Workers Rights on Compulsory Land Acquisition*, Gwisai provided a legal argument that "compulsory land acquisition does not relieve employers in the agricultural sector from their obligation to negotiate an appropriate retrenchment package with their employees," suggesting that the employers could even argue for the inclusion of such costs in the compensation they would receive from the government (Gwisai, 3). Although Gwisai did not specify in the document the precise mechanism to determine the amount farm workers on acquired farms would receive, he reasoned it should be "fair compensation" similar to that found in retrenchment regulations, with the qualification that "compulsory land acquisition is much stronger than in the typical retrenchment scenario because the farmer would after all have been paid 'fair compensation' for his/her property" (Gwisai, 8).

In SI 6, compensation was generously defined as "severance pay equivalent to the full wages of their employees for a period of three months prior to the date of termination of employment and also wages in lieu of notice under the contract of employment of the agricultural industry agreement" and "an amount equivalent to twice the employee's current monthly wage for each completed year of continuous service with the employer as well as Z$5000[8] in respect of the relocation of the employee." Moreover, farmers were asked "to pay the gratuity on termination of employment payable to the employee . . . and the cash equivalent of any vacation leave accumulated by the employee in the year in which the termination of employment occurs" (The Farmer 2002). In other words, for a farm worker it was a relatively substantial package, particularly those who had long-term service.

Although it was to be predicated on the farmers receiving their compensation for the confiscated land, very few farmers actually agreed to the typically low compensation offered by the government to some of them, while the majority had yet to receive an offer of compensation.[9] This legislation amplified the class and political divisions between workers and farmers. Given the growing evictions of white commercial farmers, farm workers increasingly wanted to ensure they received their "fair compensation." Made aware of the new legislation on the radio and from activists including ZANU (PF) cadres and war veterans and officials from GAPWUZ or the ZFTU and seeing farmers fleeing their farms, if not leaving Zimbabwe, many farm workers became more militant in their demands, even if there was no immediate sense that their farm was closing down. But their militancy often was supported by outside interveners, which by this time meant essentially those associated with ZANU (PF).

ZANU (PF): The Rule of One, the (Competing) Authority of Many

Such militancy was a factor in Chenjerai's reconversion to ZANU (PF) by the middle of 2001, as was the fact that this was more or less the only remaining avenue for political leadership in the area. By this time there was a complete cessation of scale-making projects associated with GAPWUZ, ISO, and MDC in the Berkshire area in terms of social projects concerning farm workers through which he had previously forged and bolstered his position of authority. There also were no further possibilities for him to mobilize people at Mupungu farm, given both the hostility toward him by some and the end of any direct link to their struggle against Upfumi. The continuance of any sort of leadership position thus required him to insert himself into the main source of scale-making projects remaining in the area: ZANU (PF). But this was far from a highly structured or univocal vehicle of leadership. Chenjerai reactivated his old relationship with Councillor Banda in order to play a contributing part in the refashioning of the farm landscape through ruling party activities and conflicts with a variety of actors and groups, including those within ZANU (PF) itself.

In early June 2001, Chenjerai talked approvingly about a meeting he attended in Oxfordshire earlier in the year in which "Hitler" Hunzvi, the then ZANU (PF) MP and leader of the Zimbabwe National Liberation War Veterans Association (ZNLWVA), told farm workers that they needed to participate actively in the land distribution exercise. Chenjerai now stated that this was a cause with which he could sympathize, particularly given the greater involvement of ZANU (PF) officials, councillors, and war veterans in farm labor issues: "I think farmers will only understand labor negotiations if there is an element of militancy involved in farm labor issues. This approach should continue to give the farmers an awareness of the existence and power of the farm workers." He paused before simply stating, "I like the approach of Comrade Banda. He approaches every grievance given to him by farm workers politically."

Poritikisi became the discursive field to enable one to challenge various aspects of the existing order on farms, if not seeking to completely overturn it. If electoral politics had played an important supplementary role in the labor struggle on Upfumi, enabling the fired farm workers to garner wider forms of support as they sought to achieve what they saw as their labor rights, it became the only potentially effective domain for labor relations on farms by 2001, even though it could easily be used for other social projects, including the removal of farm workers themselves as well as the white farmers.

Chenjerai now claimed that the support for the MDC in 2000 was a "protest vote" as at that time ZANU (PF) had been "hijacked away from being a revolutionary party"—aside, he added, from Mugabe and a few others who "seek to help poor people." He even criticized Banda for only helping farm workers working on white-owned farms, ignoring the lack of pay and abuses on black-owned farms. But he also said the MDC was diverted from being a workers' party as it had been at its birth. "It was hijacked by the rich class and the fact that the MDC is against the land issue, the resource of the poor, makes it no longer a party of the poor people. It is the rich who have land and they do not want to release it to the poor. I am not yet satisfied with the restructuring exercise going on within ZANU (PF), but I look at ZANU (PF) as being once again a revolutionary party after this exercise."

In June 2001, Chenjerai also noted that he had made a rapprochement with Banda by becoming his vice chairman of the ward committee of a community-based orphan care program run by Hear the Word, an international Pentecostal church. He added that there was some financing involved in ensuring orphans have their school fees paid and they are being fed. Shortly afterward, he became political commissar for the ZANU (PF) structure in the area.

Chenjerai also mentioned that Hunzvi had told farm workers that those born outside of the country or whose parents or grandparents were born outside of Zimbabwe had to go to the embassies of the countries where they were born to be able to get their Zimbabwean identity documents. Chenjerai did not dwell on the matter, other than saying the government was trying to clarify the situation of foreigners in the country.

Such a "clarification" took the form of virtually eliminating claims to citizenship for many current and former farm workers and others whose immediate ancestors held non-Zimbabwean citizenship. The July 2001 amendment to the Citizenship Act further refined the 1983 ban of dual citizenship in a way that required citizens who held foreign citizenship, or had an entitlement to it because either or both of their parents held foreign citizenship, to formally renounce the other citizenship in a process validated by the laws of that foreign-held citizenship or else to forfeit their Zimbabwean citizenship and to be removed from the voters' roll. This led to much confusion as many embassies in Zimbabwe, particularly those from Malawi, Zambia, and Mozambique where many farm workers had potential claims to citizenship, did not have any process to allow formal renunciation of citizenship. Moreover, many in the farms did not know the details of the amendment and did not try to renounce, unlike some located in cities—some of whom challenged the amendment in court. As a result, thousands were disenfranchised.[10]

To try to ensure success for the 2002 presidential election, the ZANU (PF) government was not only introducing legislation by undermining those who were viewed as MDC supporters, like white farmers and farm workers, it was also channeling various resources, including confiscated land marked for redistribution, through party structures to bolster patronage networks (Sachikonye 2011). The continuing disruptions, violence, and confiscation of commercial farms when combined with a poor rainy season, fast-declining economic growth, and rapidly rising inflation led to growing food shortages for many Zimbabweans. As a way to manage this growing crisis, the ZANU (PF) government began what Moyo and Yeros (2007) define as a "heterodox development plan" to centralize control over many economic activities. This included tighter controls over maize sales, reversing its previous policy during the neoliberal times by making the Grain Marketing Board (GMB) the monopoly buyer and seller of maize, and, by September 2004, employing police set up roadblocks to confiscate any maize being transported to the cities and not to the GMB depots (IRIN 2004). Whereas Moyo and Yeros largely applaud such efforts as positive indications of the "revolutionary situation," they also downplay how such centralization was also explicitly used for political gain and for personal rent-taking (Bond and Manyanya 2002).

By 2001, Banda received a wide range of resources going through local government and political channels and he became a gatekeeper of their redistribution. In addition to the AIDS Orphan Care program, Councillor Banda also received funding from the National AIDS Council to distribute resources to people with HIV/AIDS. A large number of people registered to receive this funding, which led to Banda threatening them to provide proof of their HIV+ status. He also was running food-for-work schemes. Moreover, he tried to muscle into food distribution carried out by NGOs for former farm workers on farms, according to both staff of some NGOs and former farm workers in the area. Although some alleged that the councillor was gaining some extra resources (rent) from these activities, Banda's main use of these resources was to control their distribution so they went to those who were deemed loyal to ZANU (PF).

By 2002, Councillor Banda was distributing GMB maize. To get the maize, people living in the ward had to register with the councillor. It was made very explicit that to receive the maize one had to attend ZANU (PF) meetings. By mid-2002, he had a system of maize distribution whereby the people queuing to buy the subsidized maize were vetted by the ZANU (PF) chairman and youth leaders of their farms to determine if they actually lived in the ward, which was a way to ostensibly ensure no one from outside the ward received the subsidized maize. More importantly, it helped to ensure that no non-ZANU (PF) member received it. If they were said not to be from the area or not attending local ZANU (PF) meetings, Banda would refuse to sell them maize.[11] Patience was prevented from buying the maize as she was still viewed as an MDC member, although she was now denying it. At such distribution exercises as elsewhere in Zimbabwe (see, e.g., HRW 2009), a number of people were verbally harassed and those found to be not giving "proper answers" to questions about ZANU (PF) were threatened with violence.

Violence was increasingly threatened as a means of transacting more and more social practices as party politics seeped into an increasing number of social domains and places. As a Upfumi youth leader said to one person waiting to receive food on October 12, 2002, "The time to persuade with words is over, now we do it through violence!" Even people in the party structures harassed police constables who were watching this food distribution exercise. In the October meeting, for example, the then youth chairman who worked at Upfumi farm, challenged the Zimbabwean Republic Police (ZRP) officials to release one of his friends, who they had handcuffed as a suspected pickpocket. He threatened to beat them up, with Chenjerai and other youth members backing him up. The police just stood there, seemingly unable to defend themselves from the verbal abuse and threats until they ultimately released the youth. Police, as the officers themselves often said, were subservient to politics (Sachikonye 2011).

By 2002, the violence that had been growing in the Berkshire area increased even more with the introduction of what soon became known as the "green bombers," the graduates of the Border Gezi youth training camps, and the passing of statutory instrument 6. As noted in the introduction to this chapter, by July, green bombers were working with political leaders like Councillor Banda. The Border Gezi training camps emerged in late 2001 and quickly became notorious as vehicles of political and sexual violence. The government claimed that Zimbabwean youth were lacking knowledge of "patriotism" and thus proclaimed that they had to be further trained at the Border Gezi training centers after finishing secondary school (Ranger 2002).

These youth became notorious in meting out violence against those they perceived as enemies of Zimbabwe, and, as documented by NGOs as well as a parliamentary committee dominated by ZANU (PF) MPs, the conditions of the camps where they were trained and lived were grim and there were many allegations of sexual abuse of women occurring there (e.g.,

SPT 2003; Manyukwe 2007). Nevertheless, the ZANU (PF) government had made it clear that such training was mandatory for youth to receive jobs in the public service, including the police, as well as in private companies owned by those allied with the ruling party.

In the Berkshire area, the green bombers began to make their presence felt, even before a training camp opened up at Kunwa Doro in March 2002. At the end of December 2001, Mercy talked about a group of Border Gezi youth stationed in Ruwa who travelled around the area, including Berkshire, in groups of four to six terrorizing everyone. As she described:

> At times these youths are in their green uniforms and at times they are in plain clothes. When you meet them, they ask you for your ZANU (PF) membership card. They want people to produce a party membership card from 1998 as well as one with a current membership for 2002. If you fail to produce the 1998 ZANU (PF) membership card, they will call you a traitor, a *mutengesi* (sellout), and then start beating you. They also ask you to do ZANU (PF) slogans and if you fail, you become their meat. We are being threatened with *kunyangarika* [disappearance], if you are found out to be a MDC member.

During the run-up to the 2002 presidential elections people in the Berkshire area became increasingly terrified. The green bombers and some of the ZANU (PF) youth were randomly stopping people, asking for ZANU (PF) cards, which virtually everyone by then had purchased, and also giving tests to assess their loyalty to the ruling party and willingness to vote for President Mugabe in the upcoming March elections. Patience explained some of the tests: "The youth used to ask what one plus one equals. If you say 'two' you will be beaten for you should say 'one,' for there is only one man who can be president in Zimbabwe." She then continued by noting, "Some of the youth may also give you a riddle, telling you 'say you have many cocks [roosters] at your home and one very big one. If visitors come to your place, which one would you kill [to feed them]?' You should say 'the small ones' because the big one resembles Mugabe." As noted above, the symbol of ZANU (PF) is the rooster.

In the middle of the night of March 4, 2002, two young women and a young man came to Mupungu, asking where Antonio's house was. They could not find it, so instead came to another house, doused its grass roof with gas, and lit it on fire. They did the same to a few other houses, while shouting *"Chinja maitiro! Pisa utize"* ("Change your ways! Burn [the house], run away"). The first slogan was an MDC one, but the women whose houses were burnt or living nearby did not think it was the MDC. As Patience said, "The MDC in the past simply left pamphlets and perhaps painted their slogans around the place." Although these women had been MDC activists for the 2000 election, they not only reported this to the police but also to the ZANU (PF) structures—to Tawanda, who was chairman of the ZANU (PF) branch in the area, and to the ZANU (PF) youths staying at the base camp at the nearby health clinic behind the Mashco store. In the words of one of the leaders of the youth, this event "led us to increase our patrols at night to ensure things like that did not happen again." ZANU (PF), more than the police, were the main security structures in the area. Whereas no one was ever caught for carrying out this act, the association of the burning of the huts with the MDC was interpreted by many of the people staying at Mupungu as more of a warning that they needed to vote for Mugabe at the upcoming election to overcome the perception that their farm was "MDC," or else violence would befall them. The dangers of poritikisi hit home for many of those living in the area.

The election that took place March 9–11, 2002, was peaceful in the Berkshire area like the rest of the country. Robert Mugabe defeated Morgan Tsvangirai with 56 percent of the votes to 42 percent. In Seke constituency this time, ZANU (PF) drew more votes than MDC, 14,667 to 12,551. Even though ZANU (PF) won in the riding, after the election, groups of youth came to Mupungu taking individuals back to their base camp to interview them. A number of people who answered incorrectly in the eyes of their interviewers were beaten up. Patience, who had been chased from Carl's compound in 2000 in part for being a "MDC" supporter, was taken to their base camp on March 13. She said, "I was asked to hand over my MDC cards, *zambia* [print cloth that can be used as a wrap, a skirt, baby-carrier, blanket, etc.], T-shirts, and binoculars that I was alleged to have had in my hut. I told them nervously that I had none of these items. After awhile, they did not beat me and let me go."

Politics, White Farmers, and Farm Workers

The results of the 2002 presidential election helped to weaken the MDC and the resolve of the remaining white farmers, leading to an acceleration in the dissolution of the bonds of domestic government in many farms. The MDC had been counting on winning the presidential elections and did not seem to have any backup plan to put in place in case they lost due, according to many observers, to intimidation and violence—if not actual rigging (Bond and Saunders 2005). White farmers I knew who had been active in the MDC were devastated by the results and were growing dissatisfied with what they saw as the lack of resolve of the opposition party to put pressure on the government. Moreover, many white farmers remaining on the farms began to lose their own sense of strength and solidarity; a sense of isolation that increased as administrative and confrontational take-overs increased after the presidential election, particularly after the return of the Zimbabwean army from the Democratic Republic of Congo whereby officers were promised farms as compensation for their efforts (Hartnack 2002).

Angus Selby, a member of a farming family in Mashonaland Central who wrote a very insightful Oxford PhD thesis on the dismantling of white commercial farming in Zimbabwe, provides figures that show that the number of white farmers remaining on their farms started to decline dramatically during 2002. Whereas the numbers of white farmers went from about 4300 to 3200 from January 2000 to January 2002, they went down to 2600 in July 2002 to about 1200 in January 2003. The numbers of white farmers in Mashonaland East province went from about 1000 in January 2000 to 800 in January 2002, to 600 in July 2002 to about 200 in January 2003 (2006, 320, derived from figure 6.3).

Selby analyses the changing political dynamics after 2000 which led many farmers to see the "hopelessness of the situation," particularly the lack of responsiveness of the police to their concerns, or worse, the active police involvement in the occupation of their farms, and the different messages they were getting from various government officials, ZANU (PF) politicians and activists, and those occupying their farms. Psychological trauma, threatened and actual violence, and uncertainty were also important factors adversely affecting many white farmers and their households (see also Buckles 2001; Hellum and Derman 2004; Holtzclaw 2004; Hughes 2010; Fisher 2010, Kalaora 2011; Pilossof 2012; Hartnack 2014). By 2000, many had established "reaction units" of farmers and farm workers to respond when neighboring farmers were besieged, to try to chase away and outnumber the invaders and to ensure there were witnesses to any events occurring. Selby (2006, 300) observed that after "the 2002 election when the process of evictions sped up and the army became more involved, such interventions were more risky, and the dwindling numbers of remaining farmers increasingly opted for lower profiles." Many farmers sought to negotiate agreements with different parties to continue farming, but often such concords would fall apart as another powerful actor refused to recognize it. As I briefly witnessed with Trevor (and noted at the beginning of this chapter), the farm manager from Dzemombe farm who was trying to get letters of support from Councillor Banda to allow the white-owned farm to continue operating, many white farmers and their managers were desperate to try a variety of tactics to continue farming some portion of their previous commercial farm.

What is of interest here is the ambivalent roles played by farm workers in the territorial rule of domestic government. If the land occupiers and many in ZANU (PF) saw farm workers as ultimately belonging to white farmers, many white farmers were unsure of the loyalty of their farm workers in this period of jambanja. The bonds of domestic government were tested and often broken, leading some to question the loyalty of farm workers,[12] demonstrating the shaky presumptions of sovereignty in the microcolonialism of commercial farms.

Selby also observed the gratuity packages (SI 6 of 2002) for farm workers played an important role in breaking potential or existing alliances between farmers and farm workers and in breaking farmers' morale. In July 2002, a white farming couple, Bill and Violet, who were very active in the MDC in the Berkshire/Oxfordshire area explained similar reactions. Unlike other high profile white farmers working with the MDC, their farm had not yet been taken, although they did not hide their support for the MDC.[13]

They were not sure why they had been spared up until that point, although they chalked it up to simply being "lucky." For instance, they told me they heard that people had stood up for them at ZANU (PF) meetings in the province during which they were being denounced. These black Zimbabweans had praised their school or their generosity or that of Bill's parents who had previously farmed there. Nor was either of them openly running for the MDC, unlike Iain Kay from nearby Hwedza who lost his farm and nearly lost his life in early 2000 for doing so.[14] Bill and Violet were ultimately evicted in 2003.

In 2001, Bill received a Section 8 and their 1400 hectare farm was divided into 51 pieces, ranging in size from 25 to 140 hectares. The farming couple retained one of the larger plots from the original farm. In June 2002, they told me that only fourteen of the new farmers came to look at their allotted pieces and six of them had started to do some farming or depasturing livestock, including Councillor Banda, who was grazing three cattle on part of the land and had a young man looking after them. Violet said that they had no conflicts with them, but that she and her husband were busy trying to figure out how to maintain a proportion of their farm. Bill said he had talks with Banda and senior ZANU (PF) leaders in the province who said if he legally subdivided his farm, the farm would not be taken. But he continued by saying that he then had contacted David Coltart, the then MDC MP and justice critic, who advised Bill that if he did so and handed over the title deeds, then there would be no chance to claim back his farm if and when an MDC government emerged. They also explored connections with people in the Department of Lands to get their farm delisted, but it went nowhere. They had a lawyer looking into legal challenges to the designation of the farm as well. Like many white farmers during this time, they tried every channel they could find, but none ultimately helped them.

As I talked with them, what Selby identified as the feeling of hopelessness was very apparent, as they were not as animated as they had been the previous years. They were expecting to be evicted from their farm, although hoping against hope that it would not happen. They had begun planning for it, diversifying their economic activities by opening up a shop in Harare, planting most of their crops on land leased from neighbors whose farms were not (yet) listed, including black farmers, and looking at moving into the city.

Both Bill and Violet mentioned how shocked they were that ZANU was able to drive a "wedge between us and the workers" through SI 6. Bill told me in a puzzled voice that it was a stunning surprise to him early in 2002 when 80 percent of the workers told him that they wanted compensation at a meeting they demanded to have with him. "At that time," Violet continued, "we thought it was over. For we had said we will win if we stay united but it looked like this was no longer the case. But at the next meeting a few days later, which we called, most of them elected to stay on the farm as seasonal workers. A few had threatened to 'phone Chinotimba' and Bill replied, 'go ahead, contact him.' Then," she added with a smile, "what did they do? They asked us if we could phone him up for them!"

The farm workers knew that the threat of bringing in war veteran leaders like Joseph Chinotimba to exert pressure could act as leverage for compensation but none of them had the means to actually contact him given that many farm workers at that time could not afford cellphones and the lack of cellphone coverage in many of the farming areas. Although amusing to the farmers, the request for the means of communication typified the extent of dependency relations that dominated the lives of farm workers, even on farms operated by self-identified liberal whites (see also Hartnack 2015).

During the meeting Violet had mentioned, which Bill had organized with his workers, he offered three choices to his permanent workers: leave the farm and receive three months' terminal benefits and Z$5,000 relocation money; receive three months' terminal benefits while changing their contractual status to seasonal worker; or remain as a permanent worker and get the day off. They told me that the majority (80 percent) chose the second option. He said other farmers were asking him how he had done this, as he had avoided the stipulated payment of two months of salary for every year worked in the SI 6 formula.

Bill and Violet contrasted themselves with their neighbor who, as I talked with them on July 26, 2002, was being besieged for the last two days by his farm workers demanding full compensation, to which the neighbor had just agreed to pay. Bill and Violet were not completely sympathetic, saying that their neighbor had never talked directly to his workforce and generally had "poor communication" with his farm workers. When the neighbors had decided to leave the farm because it was designated for redistribution and started moving equipment, Bill told me that these plans were never communicated to their workers, enabling rumors to start and passions to rise. All this, Bill added, was stirred up by the "ZFTU folks" who were coming to the farm, encouraging the workers to demand more while they themselves, the ZANU (PF)-aligned union officials, demanded a percentage of the payment in exchange for their leadership (see also JAG and GAPWUZ 2008, 15).

During our conversation at their farm, their barricaded neighbor actually rang them on the phone to ask if they could come over the next day to visit; after hanging up, Violet said quietly, "What a way to finish your fifty years on the farm."

Bill and Violet were self-identified liberal white farmers and had told me several times over the previous years that they had often felt like a minority among other commercial farmers. Their perspective assumed a natural link between those white farmers who actively sought to "develop" their workers and those farm workers who are keen to be improved, a form of governmentality that built on a style of edification found within routinized domestic government. They sought to improve the situation of farm workers through their actions and with support of NGOs and other relevant outside actors, seeking to enable farm workers to be part of the wider national public and, theoretically, not dependent on white farmers (Rutherford 2004, 132ff.). Such liberal sentiments and, often practices, were often deployed by farmers active within the MDC, often with a subsidiary aim to recruit farm workers to participate in MDC activities. Selby (2006, 298) also observed that, "Close relations between younger farmers and farm managers with black managers, assistants and foremen, had encouraged and promoted political alignments that carried through to the referendum debate." Often, farm workers who became active in the MDC did tell me they did so on their own accord, although others later complained to me of being forced to join the MDC due to the pressure from their employers; but it is unclear how these latter sentiments were influenced by the terror unleashed by ZANU (PF) activists against the MDC by then. Indeed, politics often depends on dissimulation and duplicity; as did operating through domestic government.

In an interview I then had with Melissa, Bill and Violet's domestic servant, she explained some of the dynamics that influenced the decision-making of the farm workers in terms of which "package" to accept. She said, "In the compound one had to be careful with whom one talked as rumors could spread and if you heard anyone speak for or against one of the parties it was best to stay quiet and not be spreading rumors." Before the presidential election, she continued, Banda and other ZANU (PF) leaders came to the farm and threatened that ZANU would go back to the bushes and start a war if Mugabe lost, thus literalizing the saying poritikisi ihondo (politics is war). She continued, saying ZANU (PF) also "duped people, saying they had computers that would identify how each person voted based on the numbers on the ballot. It was only when we had voted that we had realized that each ballot had the same number on it. These ZANU people stood outside the polling booth on the farm, intimidating people while they were voting. And a number did vote for ZANU this time."

Melissa said that the farm workers ended up demanding compensation because people were anxious about the farmers' plans to go on holidays in the winter months, thinking if the farm is closed down when they were away then the workers would receive nothing. She identified closely with her employers, at least to me. She fingered new hires as the agitators, observing that a small group of people hired in the last four or so years started pushing people in the compound to demand compensation. She added ruefully,

"Many complied because we were afraid that these people would go to nearby base camps and get war vets and ZANU cadres to come here and beat us up." When Bill, the farmer, then offered his options, she and other domestic servants initially were the only ones who had said they wanted to remain permanent, while the majority asked for compensation and became seasonal workers. When others began heckling them "that we were too close to the murungu and that is why we went into that group, so we too moved to the group to get compensation and become seasonal workers." When I asked why, she quietly replied, "We were afraid what may happen to us in the compound afterward."

Domestic servants, like foremen, were commonly viewed by workers and farmers alike as being closer to management than labor. After 2000, this often meant they were targeted for assaults by land occupiers, war veterans and ZANU (PF) cadres who were trying to intimidate the workforce not to vote for the MDC or to support their white employer. But like all farm workers, the belonging of domestic servants and foremen to the territory of commercial farms was also very conditional, which informed their actions during this time of poritikisi.

Conclusion

The world shifted quickly for many Zimbabweans in the first decade of the twenty-first century, particularly in the first few years as jambanja characterized life throughout the commercial farming areas as well as other parts of the country. Everyone was trying to find their bearings. Some farm workers partook in the violence. Others were its targets. Others fled. The majority tried to cope and figure out a strategy to move forward or, more typically, not "move backward" too much, by trying to find land through what was becoming the Fast-Track Land Reform program or through the "vernacular market" operating in the communal lands; looking for work, seeking to maintain former dependency relations with more powerful or more resourceful individuals, or striving to forge any type of relations to make claims to some sort of livelihood practice, tenuous as it may be.

This period also saw the crystallization of the two dominant narratives to explain the unfolding Zimbabwean events. For some, President Robert Mugabe's ZANU (PF) government was (finally) completing the anticolonial struggle, using its political control of the state to forcibly redistribute the land to the (black) Zimbabwean people, while countering any counter-revolutionary forces such as the MDC and its imperialist backers (e.g., Moyo 2001; Moyo and Yeros 2005). For others, the Mugabe regime was using state violence and ignoring its own laws to violate the human rights of the MDC and its supporters, hurriedly changing its own laws (and much of the senior members of the judiciary in the higher courts) to expropriate land from white farmers to give to ruling party allies and elites (e.g. Sithole 2001; Hellum and Derman 2004). Two contrasting views became dominant in the mass-mediated public space within Zimbabwe and about Zimbabwe in transnational spaces (e.g., Willems 2004, 2005; Ranger 2005): politics as liberatory or politics as oppressive of human rights.

Yet, as shown in this chapter, the politics on the ground were not necessarily so black and white. Councillor Banda shifted from being a key person on the Oxfordshire East Peace Taskforce in 2000, where he sought to at least mediate some of the ongoing land occupations and conflicts between farmers and different groups of occupiers, to imposing his authority over people living in the Upfumi area, including Upfumi farm itself, in 2002. Even starker was Chenjerai's shift. Despite his various efforts to mobilize in the name of workers' rights, seeking to demonstrate their independence from political projects, while drawing on networks of support through both political parties, he became more authoritarian when he returned to ZANU (PF).

Such a shift signals both the changing circumstances of the national scale and the dynamism of asserting political leadership. The state-supported massive land occupations and then land redistribution and the simultaneous attempt at crushing the MDC and its allies, real and imagined (including most trade unions, teachers, white farmers, farm workers, and many NGOs operating in the rural areas), meant that ZANU (PF) was the only nonreligious vehicle around in the early 2000s with leadership ambitions. Moreover, the end of the Upfumi struggle meant that Chenjerai had lost his specific channel for asserting his leadership ambitions and his pedagogical project of organizing farm workers as his flexing of masculinist authority, not to mention that by the end of the struggle he had alienated many of his erstwhile supporters. Meanwhile, the meaning and practices of being a "farm worker" in Zimbabwe were being substantially transformed.

The land occupations and subsequent land redistribution undermined the social hierarchies of dependency and power relations of the mode of belonging of domestic government. White farmers were increasingly displaced and former farm workers were trying to figure out strategies to seek out livelihoods. Many sought to ensure they received compensation from farm owners who were being forced to flee or likely would be soon forced to leave. Many others looked for jobs on commercial farms that were still operating or forged relations of dependency with others looking for labor through maricho arrangements or via some form of labor tenancy; still others turned to trade, sex work, or other typically precarious forms of livelihood.

The farm workers who had engaged in the long labor struggle in the name of upholding workers' rights at Upfumi saw the force that had sustained their struggle, the linkages to electoral politics made by Chenjerai, become a means to radically change the economic and power arrangements of the microcolonialism of commercial farms. However, this transformation of the power/sovereignty nexus of white-owned commercial farms has opened up more fundamental questions of belonging, livelihoods and dependency relations for current and former farm workers and farm dwellers in Zimbabwe.

CONCLUSION:
REPRESENTING LABOR STRUGGLES

WHAT ARE SOME of the implications of my analysis of this momentous farm worker struggle for understanding current and possibly future dynamics in Zimbabwe, for labor struggles elsewhere, and the politics of representation when conducting ethnographic research during unsettled times? Examining the key components of the ground of politics, my brief thoughts focus on the questions of sovereignty, livelihoods, and belonging. Let me begin with perhaps the most iconic figure of Zimbabwe: Robert Mugabe.

Poritikisi and the Weight of the Sovereign

When discussing Zimbabwean politics, Robert Mugabe quickly emerges as a key object of attention and subject of conversation. Regardless if one is speaking inside or outside Zimbabwe, talking with those who are knowledgeable or admittedly know very little about the country, "Mugabe" has become very much iconic of the state of politics in Zimbabwe, if not of the Zimbabwean state itself. Recall the anxious silence after Chenjerai declared "Pasi na Mugabe" ("Down with Mugabe") at the meeting after the October 1999 tribunal hearing, as such verbal attacks on the sovereign in Zimbabwe were and still are dangerous. Robert Mugabe has been the only government leader Zimbabwe has had thus far since it became a country in 1980, more than three decades since I write this, and has always strived to be visible in a variety of international fora (Chan 2003).

From longstanding rumours about his physical and mental health spread in hushed conversation, diplomatic cables, or media outlets to scholarly assessments of his influence over government vis-à-vis the "securacrats" (those leaders in the military and CIO who influence the deployment of the means of state coercion), different factions within ZANU (PF), and now his family, the two dominant narratives used to explain Zimbabwean politics, which I have called in shorthand fashion "politics as liberation" and "politics as oppression," also are expressed through an understanding of "Robert Mugabe."

For many, Mugabe is the articulate proponent of African "sovereignty," the one willing to use state power to "liberate" Zimbabweans from the economic remnants of colonial rule in defiance of Western opinion and actions. This has made him an important, if controversial, figure among other African leaders, many of whom have supported Mugabe, or felt they had to support him, against sanctions imposed by Western powers (see, e.g., Tendi 2011, 316–317; Raftopoulos 2013). He garners much praise from Africans at large as well, as demonstrated by the "big cheer" he received when he attended the memorial service for Nelson Mandela in Soweto in December 2013 (Business Day 2013). For many others, Mugabe represents the prototypical "African tyrant," who uses all available means to remain in power, including abusing the human rights of his own citizens, deploying coercive politics for the benefit of a few, while enabling resources, including farms taken for resettlement, to go toward his family and allies (e.g., Muronzi 2014).

Both narratives fixate on the sovereignty effect of power, the ability of certain positions to rule over subjects within a territory, deploying violence if need be in the name of preserving that authority. The difference lies in the evaluation, in how the portrayals assess the actions of President Mugabe (and the Zimbabwean government) through appraisals of their consequences for Zimbabweans. To draw on an insightful essay by Eric Worby, both narratives pivot around "the point at which 'biopolitics'—the calculation of the life-chances of theoretically discrete populations—becomes linked to the question of sovereignty, by determining who qualifies for inclusion in the legal protections of citizenship, and who is excluded or banned from the law's purview of application" (Worby 2003, 59).

As Worby shows, at the center of much of the debate over recent Zimbabwean politics is differing appraisals of who should be viewed as truly belonging to the nation, regardless of their actual citizenship status, and how they benefit or not from the actions undertaken by the sovereign authority. For the politics as liberation narrative, Mugabe's Fast-Track Land

Reform program rightly transferred land from white "settlers" to black Zimbabweans, ensuring the achievement of "economic sovereignty" for (black) Zimbabweans two decades since political sovereignty was won through the armed anticolonial struggle. In contrast, for the politics as oppression narrative, Mugabe perverted the laws of the land—if not the "laws of economics"—by disregarding the rights of white Zimbabweans, and those of farm workers whose livelihoods were derived from working for them, to distribute land to mainly benefit the ZANU (PF)-connected elite and to cause misery for the majority of Zimbabweans. A dichotomy emerges: either the sovereign as challenging the (imperialist) West and returning land to the "*vana vevhu*" (often translated in a gendered way as "sons of the soil," although literally meaning "children of the soil") or the sovereign as tyrant destroying the life-chances of his people for the benefit of holding onto power for the benefit of himself, his family, and the *chefs*, the elite connected to ZANU (PF).

White-owned commercial farms thus have become a fulcrum in this argument. Given the history of white farms as a microcolonialism, a similar link between biopolitics and sovereignty has often been made in the evaluations of their worth to the nation. The lives of farm workers have been used as a crucial measure in evaluations of this link. Varied Zimbabwean and international actors and commentators have provided evidence of how white farmers had treated farm workers in comparison to the situation of farm workers under the Fast Track Land Reform program. Moreover, the differing commentators have deployed the opinions and actions of farm workers toward white farmers since 2000 as evidence of whether white farmers have value or not for the nation and thus should, or should not, gain the benefits of full citizenship.

From this calculus, the authority of white farmers over farm workers and the uses to which white farmers have put it have become the measure of their value to Zimbabwe. For the politics as liberation narrative, white farmers had oppressed black people since the colonial era and did not want to share any economic power with them and therefore they have forfeited any rights to the postcolonial nation. For many who promote the politics as oppression narrative, white farmers provided jobs and "looked after" hundreds of thousands of workers and their dependents, thereby demonstrating their commitment to the wider society. In such equations the value of farm workers to the Zimbabwean nation has been defined largely through evaluations of their dependency on white farmers.

Although such evaluations and debates are all about politics, what they generally have not analysed is the practice of politics for different farm workers. Without such an analysis, farm workers become merely a cipher for some larger political position on Mugabe, democracy, sovereignty, workers, oppression, citizenship, and so forth. This is not inherently problematic, for political discourse, like all narratives, traffic in allegories and questions of representation. As Luise White expertly shows when analysing the varied and contradictory confessions to, and explanations for, the murder of Zimbabwean nationalist Herbert Chitepo in Lusaka, Zambia in 1975 during the liberation struggle, these narratives do not need to be adjudicated in terms of their veracity. Rather, they can be investigated in terms of how their framing speaks to the "contests over national narratives and histories" (White 2003, 9).

Both politics as liberation and politics as oppression narratives are able to mobilize divergent empirical examples to provide evidence for their arguments (e.g., farm workers protecting or attacking farmers during the *jambanja*) to construct or reinforce national and international narratives and histories. Yet, they do not provide any understanding of how *poritikisi* can both buttress and challenge relations of dependency, which I have sought to show through analyzing the practices of electoral politics in relations to the power relations involved in the livelihoods of farm workers.

The labor struggle at Upfumi clearly demonstrates the contradictory uses of politics. My analysis suggests how the organizations and networks that could be mobilized through poritikisi in the late 1990s enabled a group of farm workers to sustain their remarkable struggle against management. The leadership of the workers was able to draw on these networks and the *simba* (power) found in them to not only educate and mobilize many workers around the promise of labor rights but also to challenge their dismissal. Although the challenge was ultimately successful in the Labor Tribunal, the result was bittersweet for many of those involved. They were dismayed at the limited compensation they received and that the company was not required to hire them back. Moreover, they were disquieted about the threats, violence, and intolerance coming from their own leadership. Ties to electoral politics provided strength to these farm workers, but its attributes were not unproblematic.

It is important to examine the weight of sovereign power—be it President Mugabe in Zimbabwe or white farmers in their "microcolonialism"—

and how it intersects with biopolitics, disciplinary power, and oppression. The particular configuration and articulation of these forces in the late 1990s was very different from what they were like after 2000, as pursuits and uses of legal avenues were greatly limited because the ZANU (PF) government greatly politicized state institutions, including the court system. The legal route taken by the Upfumi workers in 1998 would have been a more difficult enterprise in the 2000s as the "rule of law" became seen by many activists and commentators as something that was actively undermined by ZANU (PF). Yet, at the same time, it is also crucial to understand how they all interact with the conduct of electoral politics itself in particular social spaces to better understand the differing and, at times, changing stakes for varied Zimbabweans. As I have shown, the legal route taken by the Upfumi workers in the late 1990s was very much enabled by their involvement in party politics. Moreover, gendered livelihood possibilities and practices are often integral to such changing stakes.

"Farm Workers": Changing Livelihoods and the Fraying of a Category

Anna Tsing (2003) has discussed how "peasants" and "workers" were key categories of thinking about politics in the twentieth century in the Global South, examining in particular how "peasants" became a key allegory in understanding rural social life in Southeast Asia, shaping administrative policies, academic programs, advocacy agendas, and schemes of different rural peoples. Social science scholarship foci such as "peasant studies" brought a specific analytical attention to rural populations, economies and struggles in what was known as the "Third World" in the 1960s to 1980s in particular and contributed to understanding these populations in certain ways. Yet, it also "universalized and naturalized core peasant dilemmas, making it difficult to see what else was happening in the Third World countryside besides the reproduction or dissolution of allegorical peasantness" and overlooking the "histories of how these particular populations had become central to national storytelling" (Tsing 2003, 153, 155).

In Zimbabwe, "farm worker" has become an important category to "national storytelling." Although farm workers increasingly became an object of policy attention and development interventions during the 1990s, the breadth and reach of this category grew dramatically after 2000. It emerged as such not only due to the violence of the land occupations but also due to the role farm workers played in the link between sovereignty and biopolitics in the debate over these events. Since 2000, many Zimbabwean and international groups and journalists have written reports, accounts, and studies that have focused solely, or in large part, on the situation of Zimbabwean farm workers, largely indicating how the land occupations and Fast Track Land Resettlement program have displaced and discriminated against many of them (e.g., FCTZ 2000; ZINISA 2001; Amani Trust 2002; Sachikonye 2003; ZCDT 2003; JAG and GAPWUZ 2008; GAPWUZ 2010). This generated a discursive field to which some of my writings and discussions have made modest contributions. In turn, the Zimbabwean government carried out a survey of farm workers to ascertain their preferences for land resettlement (MPSLSW 2001) and "farm workers" became a category of analysis in Parliamentary reports on land resettlement (e.g., Parliament of Zimbabwe 2003) and on a rare occasion, farms were designed specifically for them, although often they were given smaller plots than other settler farmers (e.g., Marongwe 2004; Matondi 2012, 221).

Even in publications that endorse the violent fast-track land distribution exercise, there is still typically a brief acknowledgement that farm workers generally did not benefit from it and their economic conditions have largely worsened. In *Zimbabwe Takes Back Its Land*, for example, the authors lay the blame for the worsening situation for "farm workers" on GAPWUZ supporting the MDC and being aligned "with international agencies who are seen as wanting to reverse land reform" (Hanlon, Manjengwa, and Smart 2013, 196). Despite squarely acknowledging and ultimately supporting the discriminatory political environment whereby (alleged and declared) support for opposition politics justifies exclusion, the authors boldly suggest "GAPWUZ, NGOs and donors" could try to organize the new farm workers and assist former farm workers by finding land for them and by better organizing some of their new-found livelihood practices such as gold panning (Hanlon, Manjengwa, and Smart 2013, 197), as if electoral politics no longer matters. Yet, this elision of the power relations of poritikisi is not unique. A number of studies that seek to provide empirical data concerning social dynamics in rural Zimbabwe downplay the importance of politics in shaping the agrarian landscape and the possibilities and contours of change (Rutherford 2012, 2013, 2014).

At the same time, actions in the name of politics on the national-scale ultimately have led to the transformation of property and labor relations on most commercial farms in Zimbabwe to such an extent that the meaning of "farm worker" in Zimbabwe is no longer as self-evident as before, at least for those who currently provide farm labor. The few empirical studies of rural labor practices in Zimbabwe that have been done in the last few years suggest significant changes in the organization of farm labor and the relations of production. Most farm work is done by casual workers, by contract work gangs, and by those working through kin relations of dependency. Although those favoring the Fast-Track Land Resettlement celebrate the greater number of farm labor jobs available due to the increased number of settler farms compared to the previous number of commercial farms, even these scholars acknowledge the working conditions are generally quite poor, remuneration is very low, and social services are almost nonexistent (e.g., Chambati 2011; Hanlon, Manjengwa and Smart 2013, 194–197; see Rutherford 2014). It seems that currently at least there are few farms with a sizeable farm worker population. There is almost negligible presence of any union or government monitoring of labor relations or working conditions. The *maricho* labor combined with the buying and selling of a variety of goods and services, often for limited remuneration, is more widespread for many living in rural Zimbabwe. As Scoones, et al. (2010, 145) note, much current farm "labour is casual, informal, seasonal, underpaid and often female. . . . This is not well-paid employment by any calculation, and the conditions are nearly universally poor, but the scale of employment opportunity has certainly increased dramatically" (see also Hartnack 2015).

The situation facing many of those laboring on farms is similar to the trend that those engaged in the struggle against Upfumi encountered as they waited for the Labor Tribunal ruling and after their labor dispute ended in June 2000. Although there were attempts by Chenjerai and GAPWUZ in the early 2000s to represent farm workers in the area, ZANU (PF) structures were playing greater roles on the remaining commercial farm operations. These also became the main vehicles of administration on the newly resettled farms. As Prosper Matondi (2012, 249) observes in the conclusion to his book on land reform in Zimbabwe, "decision-making rests with partisan committees bent on protecting and promoting political interests rather than ensuring that agriculture moves forward to feed the nation."

While the empirical focus on the agrarian changes since 2000 has generated rich insight into the changing relations of production and forms of remuneration, there is limited analysis of how these rural livelihoods intersect with politics and power. There may be some acknowledgement that decision-making has been politicized, but then such observations would be subsumed by a hope expressed about policy-makers (e.g., Scoones, et al. 2010, 252–253; see Rutherford 2012), technical experts (Matondi 2012), or even civil society organizations (Hanlon, Manjengwa, and Smart 2013) playing a bigger role in ensuring that greater development benefits emerge for some of the varied people involved in these new settlement farms. Yet, politics and power at different scales have been integral to the formation of the agrarian landscapes, both before and after 2000, and have directly shaped, typically by limiting, the presence and activities of such bodies of expertise in these agrarian spaces, as these authors and others have also shown. Nonetheless, such power and politics tend to be expunged from the analysis when proposing to "make things better."

Although most commentators and scholars of rural Zimbabwe since 2000 feel compelled to have at least a brief section on "farm workers," they often do not examine how this social category became "central to national storytelling" (Tsing 2003, 155) in Zimbabwe in such a way that being identified as "(former) farm workers" can mark their livelihood options. Even though the dissolution of domestic government as a mode of belonging on most farms means radical changes to the social relations, power relations, and forms of dependency informing farm labor, the social identity of "farm worker" still matters in these new agrarian landscapes where "politicised informalization" has "replaced older legal rights and regulations" (Hammar, McGregor, and Landau 2010, 274). People marked as (former) farm workers have often been discriminated against in terms of getting access to land and whose moral behaviour is questioned and doubted by others, which has shaped possibilities of livelihoods for them when displaced from the farms (e.g., Hartnack 2005).

For example, Godfrey Magaramombe (2010), who is the director of the Farm Community Trust of Zimbabwe and a scholar, estimates between 50 and 70 percent of the former farm workers up to 2009 were remaining in the Fast Track Land Resettlement (former commercial farming) areas. Yet, his studies and experience show that most of them live separately from the new settlers and any new farm workers they may have hired, maintaining what he calls "residential autonomy." The limited research available suggests that there has often been great distrust and conflict between the groups, with new settlers trying to remove former farm workers from their homes in the former farm compound and a number of disputes over access to land, water, and other natural resources as well as the labor of the former farm workers (e.g., Magaramombe 2010; Scoones, et al. 2010: passim; Matondi 2012, 183; Hartnack 2015).[1]

This research shows that these former farm workers are very much marked as a "represented community" by their association with the mode of belonging of domestic government, even though that form of power/sovereignty dynamic informing livelihood and residential possibilities has largely been dismantled. For example, Matondi suggests that most of the new settler farmers disdain ex-farm workers for several reasons, "including the behaviour of some of them during the land occupations (some supported white landowners) and cultural differences. The majority of people on the FTFs [Fast Track Farms, in the Mashonaland area of his study] are Shona and hold those who adopt 'external' cultural practices in low regard, while ex-farmworkers have cultural connections to Malawi and other countries as a result of labour migration during the colonial period" (2012, 233). He also gives the example of attitudes of a few settler farmers in his study who "alleged that farmworkers were immoral and promiscuous and changed partners every day. They accused them of being lazy and greedy" (2012, 222); it is important to note here that such essentializing appraisals of farm workers were also commonly held by white farmers (see Rutherford 2001a, passim). Magaramombe also observes very different accessibility to resources for the two distinct communities in his research area: "The new settler community is defined by its entitlements and privileges, while the worker community has been dispossessed and has few if any entitlements" (2010, 365).

To better understand these social dynamics, the precarious livelihoods of those involved with farm labor (as well as many others living in the new resettlement farms) and the continued valance of "farm worker" in marking hierarchies need to be situated within the emergent configurations of dependency ties, power relations, and subject positions through which people can seek to make claims on resources, including land and labor. My analysis of the Upfumi labor struggle sheds insight into these new dynamics, providing critical focus on the emergent modes of belonging on the farms, the particular struggles and social projects and how they may interact with electoral politics, which clearly plays an influential role in these spaces. Rather than hope that better policies or more active trade unions will improve the situation for those engaging in farm labor, I modestly suggest that one needs to examine the entanglements of livelihoods, power, and belonging in the new rural spaces. Such an analytic framing would provide insight into how such initiatives and programs would be understood and engaged with, given a particular concatenation of dependency ties and emergent but unstable modes of belonging that operate on the former commercial farms in particular areas. Let me also modestly propose that this form of an analysis can be applied to other labor struggles, as a way to understand the weight of representation and the configuration of power in particular places, which enable and constrain social mobilization and action.

Belongings: The Politics of Solidarities

If those that focus on sovereignty minimize the grounding of politics in places and livelihoods while those that emphasize livelihoods downplay the weight and influence of politics and power in much of the academic literature and media coverage concerning Zimbabwean rural areas since 2000, the heuristic of belonging enables one to examine both. It allows one to recognize how struggles for both redistribution and for human rights, for social justice and for democracy, must work through existing social relations, power relations, ties of dependency, and the cultural politics of electoral politics informing "specific criteria of belonging and exclusion" (Eckert 2011, 310) in different places at particular historical conjunctures. By doing so, one could better discern the possibilities, the channels, and the dangers for different groups and in different sites in one's analysis. Otherwise, if one simply focuses on rights or on social justice, one can miss how such political imaginaries are predicated on hierarchies of who "belongs" and who does not, and the significant consequences for livelihoods and decision-making at different scales of action that emerge from such valuations.

Such nuances often are lost in the work by activists, particularly as they may focus on, to borrow from Tsing (2003), what could be called "the allegories" of sovereignty or rights in their analyses, drawing out, for instance, evidence of the importance of "reclaiming national resources for the (indigenous) peoples" or "the abusive and unlawful use of power" in Zimbabwe to inspire mobilizations and solidarities elsewhere. Such translations across boundaries are common in activism as much as in international investment or humanitarian work (e.g., Tsing 1997, 2005; Bornstein 2005), and thus should not be viewed as inherently problematic. But they do not provide much insight into how such narratives are used by, and help to situate,

FARM LABOR STRUGGLES IN ZIMBABWE

different groups and locations in the specific place in question, such as Zimbabwe. Particular sets of metaphorical entailments of "Zimbabwe" may be inspirational to other social justice struggles over access to land (e.g., Hanlon, Manjengwa, and Smart 2012) or to campaigns against human rights abuses and political tyrannies (e.g., Power 2003). But they do not necessarily help one to understand the situations of former farm workers and those engaged in farm labor since 2000.

As I have endeavored to show and argue in this book, "farm workers" in Zimbabwe have not only been placed in disadvantaged positions by narratives and practices of sovereignty on the commercial farms and on the scale of the nation but they have also rarely been viewed as people who could advocate for their "rights." They have been characterized as "victims" (of white farmers, ZANU (PF), war veterans, etc.), whose main form of agency fits the narrow confines of such narratives (e.g., loyal workers, foreigners, nationalist Africans, etc.). In contrast, the struggle at Upfumi shows how a group of largely women farm workers were able to work through the hierarchies within the mode of belonging shaping their lives to engage in a lengthy labor struggle and to imagine themselves as part of a national scale struggle, largely due to its leadership connecting their demands through various networks interlinked with electoral political mobilizing and national and international scales of actions. Yet, it was not an unproblematic struggle, as its leadership resorted to its own use of masculinist authority and occasional violence, both in the waging of their labor "war" and against some of its supporters.

Initially, I was caught up in its extraordinary struggle, providing a bit of support where I could and offering some solidarity by listening to the accounts, complaints, and aspirations of many living in the *musososo* and beyond. For a long time, I missed how the practice of poritikisi in the struggle was viewed with ambivalence and at times fear by many of the fired workers, as much as they supported it as a weapon in their struggle. Moreover, it is important to note that my own relationships with many had contingent dependency relations, as a number saw my interest and presence as someone who could play a larger role in improving their material conditions (recall, for example, the rumors that I was going to help find a farm for them or invest money into the financial "project") than I actually did. Although I am sure my actions disappointed some, and likely have been the subject of different accounts and debates for some who were involved in the labor struggle, I have tried my best here to provide an analysis of the Upfumi struggle that gives some justice to providing a sense of its uniqueness in regard to farm workers in Zimbabwe and how to understand it in terms of much wider events and discursive framings of Zimbabwe.

Although I have aimed to unsettle some of the hegemonic narratives used to understand the agrarian struggles and changes in Zimbabwe (and elsewhere in the Global South), which deploy "sovereignty" or "rights" to overdetermine their analyses, any political ambitions in this book are quite modest. I am not investing policy-makers, technical experts, civil society organizations, black Zimbabweans, white farmers, farm workers, or foreign anthropologists with the burden of deciding a, or to bring some, future prosperity to those who engage in farm labor in Zimbabwe. Such political (even if called technical) prescriptions are seductive to many of us social scientists and they do often effectively hail and motivate certain audiences. But as I am not involved in any actualized relations of solidarity with different groups of Zimbabweans, or with those who are in dialogue (even if in unequal terms) with groups of Zimbabweans, such future-making pronouncements seem to me disingenuous, if not suspect. Like other ethnographies, my discursive authority rests on my presentation of "discourse—including quotations and eyewitness descriptions, that is, textual signs of presence—drawn from all the sites at which the constituent discourses are produced and received." Yet, as Charles Briggs (1996, 457–458) continues, recognizing one's place "in transnational political-economic relations—as based on race, class, gender, sexuality, nationality, and occupation—is crucial." As I am not positioned, for example, by activist ties working with a group of Zimbabweans (e.g., Hale 2006), my aim thus rests with troubling other accounts and putting forth some analytical heuristics that examine some of the forms of power governing rural struggles (and their representations) and the often contested words and actions of farm workers involved in this momentous labor struggle, rather than laying out blueprints for action.

I know *The Ground of Politics* is a very different book than what Tawonga would have written. The forced destruction of his manuscript motivated by fear of his association with me during the heightened uncertainties and anxieties of jambanja troubles me and unsettles any sense of complete discursive authority, at least for me. Tawonga would undoubtedly have different, if not richer, insights than I have provided and his book would have been subjected to very different responses given his own positioning in "transnational political-economic relations" compared to me. His location as a male member of the group of mainly women farm workers who engaged in the remarkable labor struggle at Upfumi, who still lives in the same farm area and is tied to considerably precarious livelihood practices and relations of dependency, form a very different location compared to what I face as a tenured professor at a Canadian university. This positioning does not mean Tawonga, let alone other current or former farm workers, lack a form of "agency." Rather, as I hope this book has demonstrated, they just have a very different set of possibilities and perils operating through the changing concatenation of social practices, dependencies and power relations.

For those who read this book, my imagined audience, I hope this contributes to a better understanding of some of the political and social projects and power relations that shaped the lives of these farm workers during a momentous period in Zimbabwean history and to encourage more critical attention to farm workers, labor struggles, ambitions, and oppressions ongoing in Zimbabwe and elsewhere. Reading this may play a small part in forming or reinforcing a recognition that historical shifts at various scales of action influence the configurations of power, livelihoods, and belonging in different places, leading to rural struggles for some form of rights and/or for some form of sovereignty, working through power relations and relations of dependency. Through recognizing such possibilities for altering the growing precariousness of rural—let alone, urban—livelihoods and the power relations that enable such conditions, one may find ways to work with others in such struggles.

NOTES

Introduction

1. All names of farm workers are pseudonyms, as I discuss later in this section.

2. Thanks to Willie Carroll, a Carleton University student in Geography and Environmental Studies, and his supervisor, Steve Prashker, for producing this map, which is based on ZSG (1998).

1. Oppression, Maraiti, and Farm Worker Livelihoods

1. In 1999, "DRC" in Zimbabwean parlance widely signified unending conflict. The camp took on this name after being established when the initial fifty or so of the already fired farm workers were evicted from the Upfumi farm compound in July 1999, as discussed in chapter 2.

2. There have been a number of great studies on these dynamics in different parts of South Africa, particularly in the Western Cape and Limpopo provinces. See, e.g., Du Toit 1993, 2004; Rutherford and Addison 2007; Addison 2013, 2014; Bolt 2012, 2013, 2015; Hall et al. 2013.

3. Most commercial farms were incorporated by the 1990s, but many of these corporations were in practice family-run farms that legally became incorporated for financial and tax reasons. Zimfarm and other large companies operating commercial farms are a different matter in terms of the emphasis on bureaucratic processes, positions, and typically more formal labor relations (Shadur 1994).

4. Communal lands are the former colonial native reserves, as discussed in the introduction.

5. The Zimbabwe secondary educational system has up to six "forms," or levels. Forms III and IV are directed toward writing exams in subjects for the "Ordinary" or "O" Levels; Forms V and VI are directed toward writing exams in subjects for the "Advanced" or "A" Levels. This school system bears a resemblance to that of Britain; in fact, until 2002, the "O" and "A" level exams were set and marked in conjunction with the University of Cambridge International Examination system.

6. Unless otherwise noted, the use of the "$" refers to Zimbabwean dollars, a currency that devaluated spectacularly in the 2000s until it was discontinued in January 2009.

7. There often were other factors that worked against the education of children living on commercial farms, including the fact that commercial farming areas had the fewest schools, particularly secondary schools, than any other land use areas in Zimbabwe; some farm workers could not pay for their children to continue with education because of relative costs or chose not to spend money on it because they did not see the benefits of formal education; others, for gendered reasons, did not want to further the education of their daughters (Save the Children [UK] 2000). Several women gave examples of the latter when explaining the ending of their own formal schooling. For example, Rita recalled, "I failed to go ahead with schooling because my father only respected the male children." Another woman said that when she finished Form III her father said he had no money for her to do Form IV as he wanted to save his money to educate his sons. She said "I was so mad. A girl must be sent to school as girls think about their parents more than boys! But nothing changed."

8. These reasons can include competition between land-giving authorities, the need to have people open up "virgin" land or, in some cases, people selling part of their land (e.g., Hughes 1999; Rutherford 2001a).

9. Steven Rubert (1998, 92ff.) observes that white farmers in Rhodesia adopted the "ticket system" from the mining industry in the early 1900s, in which each farm worker received a "ticket" with the numbers from one to thirty written on it. A number was stroked off after the farmer or boss-boy deemed the particular worker had successfully completed the day's task. After the thirtieth number was stroked off, which could take more than thirty days of work, the worker was paid.

10. This report will not be included in the Bibliography as a way to keep the name of the farm anonymous.

11. This was equivalent to around US$2 on the black-market exchange (for black-market foreign exchange rates at this time, I rely on Makochekanwa 2007, 10–11).

12. In Zimbabwe, "colored" is a racial category referring to children of "mixed race" couples, prototypically an African woman and a European man, who have faced their own specific forms of opportunities and discrimination based on how they have been emplaced in the hegemonic mode of belonging of the nation itself (Mandaza 1997; Muzondidya 2005).

13. A new army division comprised solely of ChiShona speakers and trained by the North Koreans and the CIO (Central Intelligence Organisation, the secret police) brutally persecuted ZAPU cadres and more broadly SiNdebele speakers from 1981 to 1987, leaving thousands killed and many more tortured and brutalized in southern and western Zimbabwe. This operation of terror code-named *Gukurahundi* (the early rains that blows away the chaff in the spring) was carried out in the name of crushing a small number of "dissidents" from ZIPRA (ZAPU's guerrilla army of the 1970s) who were carrying out random attacks in the region with support from apartheid South Africa (Catholic Commission for Justice and Peace and Legal Resources Foundation 1998). Gukurahundi clearly demonstrated for many Zimbabweans that the postcolonial state and ZANU (PF) was just as apt to use terror on certain members of its population as its colonial predecessor. In fact, the ZANU (PF) government maintained many of the same laws, state organizations, and some of the same personnel used for the state of emergency during the 1970s by the Rhodesian administrations before them (Hatchard 1993).

2. The Traction of Rights, the Art of Politics

1. This location is famously and tightly associated with the history of African nationalism in Zimbabwe and ZANU (PF)'s own history (Alexander 2000b; Scarnecchia 2008). Gwisai did not remain long as an MP as he was expelled by the MDC executive in April 2002 due, in part, to his critical comments concerning what he saw as MDC's rightward leanings. Gwisai subsequently lost his seat in a by-election to the new MDC candidate when he ran as an Independent.

2. Typically, the speaker starts with *"Pamberi ne/na"* ("Forward with") something (for example, "ZANU" or the name of a person, like "Mugabe"), while raising his or her right arm, fist clenched, while punching the air; a convention intended to elicit the same from the others in the meeting. This is followed by a *"Pasi na"* ("Down with") something, like *"mabhunu"* (derogatory name for whites) or even *"Udhakwa,"* (drunkenness), while bringing the arm down, fist clenched, again eliciting the same behavior from the crowd.

3. After the passing of the Public Order and Security Act in 2002, Section 16 of the act makes it a crime punishable by imprisonment to make statements construed as leading to feelings of hostility toward the president.

4. In 1998, this was worth approximately US$208.

5. Within a year, Chishiri was elected councillor in another ward in Goromonzi rural district council as that ward's incumbent had passed away.

6. This area is several hundred kilometers north-northwest of Harare in Mashonaland West province, next to the border with Zambia.

7. This included tents and other supplies to help protect the fired workers living in the muso-soso from the elements.

8. This was perhaps due to the intense disputes between rival leaders that ended up paralyzing this NGO at that time (Dorman 2003).

9. Later, Jerry Gotora became the president of the Association of Zimbabwe Rural and District Councils and then president of Wildlife and Environment Zimbabwe (formerly Zimbabwe Wildlife Society).

10. Solomon Mujuru was a significant political and business person in Zimbabwe. He was a former guerrilla leader and the first commander of the Zimbabwe Armed Forces. When he retired from the military, he became a major businessman in Zimbabwe, including having a number of commercial farms. He had been widely seen as leading one of the major factions within ZANU (PF) until he died suspiciously in a fire at his farmhouse in August 2011. Sydney Sekeremayi has been a minister in the ZANU (PF) governments since 1980 and a leading politician from Mashonaland East.

11. I made a copy of the letter, which is in my possession.

12. The chair of the Goromonzi council was referring to the farm occupations led by Svosve residents in Mashonaland East starting in June 1998, which started to get some support by the ZANU (PF) government to put pressure on donors during the negotiations over land reform (Alexander 2006; Sadomba 2011).

13. For instance, Chenjerai spoke to this tension by repeating a conversation he witnessed between a major MDC organizer and an ISO organizer. According to Chenjerai, the MDC official told the ISO official "to join the MDC structures. The ISO official replied that he would help organize the MDC but remain within ISO. The MDC man replied 'You internationals, you should think national for a change!'" The tension between MDC and ISO only increased after the parliamentary elections, after which Gwisai was tossed out of the MDC and lost his parliamentary seat.

14. Gwisai told me that since this was a tort—and not a labor issue—it would have to be fought in a different legal arena, and he did not have time to represent these workers in such a case.

3. The Drama of Politics

1. Such increasingly "informal" economic activities have become even more dominant Zimbabwe since 2000 (see Jones 2010).

2. The plastic containers that contain Chibuku beer, a sorghum beer brewed and sold by the national brewery company, were popularly called "scuds," named after Iraqi missiles used during the first Gulf War, when there was widespread anti-United States sentiment expressed in Zimbabwe.

3. *Kuchaya mapoto*, literally "beating the pots," was a common form of marriages for the farm workers and others (Rutherford 2001a, 177ff.; Jeater 1993). It simply meant living together without initiating any bridewealth payments or getting any legal or religious documents sanctifying the marriage.

4. As noted earlier, "DRC" refers to the Democratic Republic of Congo and was used as short-hand for a place of dispute.

5. The official criteria, albeit not necessarily followed even before 2000, included if the farm was adjacent to a Communal Land, if it was being underutilized, if the farmer owned more than one farm, etc.; see Chiremba and Masters 2003, 102–103.

6. This stood for Zimbabwe Foundation for Education with Production, an organization that, among other things, established eight primary and secondary pilot schools to provide educational experiments for ex-combatants; these schools integrated academic subjects with practical training (see Horst 1988).

7. Councillor Banda was a witness for the losing ZANU (PF) candidate, Chihota, in his successful petition to overturn the result. Banda testified that he had been assaulted by an MDC supporter while he was standing in a voting queue at another polling booth, and, thus, he was unable to vote.

4. Politics and Precarious Livelihoods during the Time of Jambanja

1. Councillor Banda had left his living quarters at the ZANU (PF) headquarters at the Goromonzi turnoff in 2001 for unclear reasons, though people of the Upfumi struggle suggested it was because of the tensions between him and some of his seniors in the ruling party.

2. Under the Land Acquisition Act, a "Section 8 is a compulsory acquisition order. It is a very unassuming piece of paper without letterhead or a stamp and is signed by the acquiring authority. In the act it gives the owner 45 days to stop all activities and a further 45 days to move out of his home from the date of service" (JAG 2002).

3. This was equivalent to around US$150 as in 2000 the exchange rate of the Zimbabwean dollar to the U.S. dollar was approximately sixty to one on the black-market, which everyone by then used as the most accurate barometer of the value of the Zimbabwean dollar; inflation was rapidly increasing, soon to be replaced by world-leading hyperinflation rates.

4. For similar arguments about women enjoying the "freedom" from patriarchal control for different places and time periods in Africa, see, e.g., White 1990; Schmidt 1992; Jeater 1993; Campbell 2003.

5. Whereas Rita and many of the women involved in such transactional sex saw it mainly in terms of economic contexts, as a way to maintain autonomy and support themselves and their children, it is important to note that the meaning of transactional sex differs in varied social contexts (Masvawure 2010).

6. In 2001, the brother sold the "Carl farm" to a University of Zimbabwe lecturer from West Africa who evicted the people renting huts on the farm and began producing crops for sale on the small plot.

7. The government designated 1471 commercial farms for compulsory purchase in 1997. However, most ultimately were delisted due to a variety of legal and political reasons (see Moyo 1998, 2000).

8. This was worth approximately US$15 in early 2002.

9. An article exploring the compensation issue in 2012 determined that "a total of 6,422 farms were acquired, of these 1,250 were valued and 4,962 farms are still to be valued. To date 210 farmers have been compensated since the FTLR [Fast Track Land Reform program]" (Sokwanele 2012).

10. Although a 2003 amendment sought to simplify the process for those whose foreign citizenship was within the Southern African Development Community, there was still much confusion in practice and a number of legal cases sought to clarify the amendment (see Research and Advocacy Unit 2008, 20ff.). The new constitution of 2013 clarified this confusion by conferring citizenship upon birth to those who were born in Zimbabwe and descended from SADC citizens, as long as they were ordinarily resident in Zimbabwe on May 23, 2013 (Veritas 2013).

11. In 2012, the MDC alleged the now-former Councillor Banda was doing the same thing, now in the role of the ZANU (PF) district coordinating commission chairperson (reference withheld).

12. For example, a reporter who characterized the dispute between workers and the farmer over compensation, wrote that the farmer "has been locked in his homestead for three days by his once-loyal workers" (Thornycroft 2002; see also Rutherford 2001c).

13. For instance, after the 2000 parliamentary election when the MDC won his constituency, the farmer posted a small sign outside his farm on the farm road declaring that "Seke will Never Be a Colony Again", a politicized play on the ZANU (PF) electoral slogan that "Zimbabwe will never be a colony again."

14. Iain Kay lost the parliamentary race in 2000 against ZANU (PF) minister Sydney Sekeremayi, though there were many allegations of intimidation and cheating. He and his family and their farm workers were threatened and evicted from the farm several times in the early 2000s (BBC 2003). Later he was elected for the MDC.

Conclusion

1. Parts of this paragraph and the following come from Rutherford 2014, 231–232.

BIBLIOGRAPHY

Abrahamsen, Rita. 2000. *Disciplining Democracy: Development Discourse and Good Governance in Africa*. London: Zed Books.

Adams, Mary. 2009. "Playful Places, Serious Times: Young Women Migrants from a Peri-urban Settlement, Zimbabwe." *Journal of the Royal Anthropological Institute* 15 (4): 797–814.

Addison, Lincoln. 2013. *Labor, Sex and Spirituality on a South African Border Farm*. PhD thesis, Rutgers University.

———. 2014. "Delegated Despotism: Frontiers of Agrarian Labour on a South African Border Farm." *Journal of Agrarian Change* 14 (2): 286–304.

Agamben, Giorgio. 2005. *State of Exception*. Translated by Kevin Attell. Chicago: University of Chicago Press.

ALB (Agricultural Labour Bureau). 1984. *Chairman's Report to the Commercial Farmers' Union Congress*. W. D. C. Reed, chairman. Harare: Agricultural Labour Bureau.

———. 1997. *Agricultural Labour Bureau Handbook*. Harare: ALB.

Alexander, Jocelyn. 2006. *The Unsettled Land: State-Making & the Politics of Land in Zimbabwe, 1893–2003*. Oxford: James Currey.

Alexander, Jocelyn, and JoAnn McGregor. 2013. "Introduction: Politics, Patronage, and Violence in Zimbabwe." *Journal of Southern African Studies* 39 (4): 749–763.

Alexander, Peter. 2000a. "Zimbabwean Workers, the MDC & the 2000 Election." *Review of African Political Economy* 27 (85): 385–406.

———. 2000b. "A Worker's Voice: Zimbabwean MP Munyaradzi Gwisai Interviewed." *Socialist Review* 244. Accessed February 5, 2007. http://pubs.socialistreviewindex.org.uk/sr244/alexander.htm#gwisai.

Amani Trust. 2002. *Preliminary Report of a Survey on Internally Displaced Persons from Commercial Farms in Zimbabwe*. A report prepared by the Mashonaland Programme of the Amani Trust. May 31. Harare: Amani Trust.

Amanor-Wilks, Dede. 1995. *In Search of Hope for Zimbabwe's Farm Workers*. Harare: Dateline Southern Africa and Panos Institute.

Andersson, Jens. 2001. "Mobile Workers, Urban Employment, and 'Rural' Identities: Rural-Urban Networks of Buhera Migrants, Zimbabwe." In *Mobile Africa: Changing Patterns of Movement in Africa and Beyond*, edited by M. De Brujin, R. van Dijk, and D. Foeken, 89–106. Leiden, Netherlands: Brill.

Armstrong, Alice. 1998. *Culture and Choice: Lessons from Survivors of Gender Violence in Zimbabwe*. Harare: Violence Against Women in Zimbabwe Research Project.

Auret, Diana. 2000. *From Bus Stop to Farm Village: The Farm Worker Programme in Zimbabwe*. Harare: Save the Children Fund (UK).

Auslander, Mark. 1993. "'Open the Wombs!' The Symbolic Politics of Modern Ngoni Witchfinding." In *Modernity and Its Malcontents: Rituals and Power in Postcolonial Africa*, edited by J. Comaroff and J. L. Comaroff, 167–192. Chicago: University of Chicago Press.

Bannerjee, Abhijit, Angus Deaton, Nora Lustig, and Ken Rogoff. 2006. *An Evaluation of World Bank Research, 1998–2005*. Washington, DC: World Bank.

Barchiesi, Franco. 2011. *Precarious Liberation: Workers, the State, and Contested Social Citizenship in Postapartheid South Africa*. Albany: State University of New York Press.

Barrientos, Stephanie, Catherine Dolan, and Anne Tallontire. 2003. "A Gendered Value Chain Approach to Codes of Conduct in African Horticulture." *World Development* 31 (9): 1511–1526.

BBC (British Broadcasting Corporation). 2003. "Forced to Flee." *BBC Correspondent*. Accessed March 18, 2014. news.bbc.co.uk/2/hi/programmes/correspondent/2758313.stm.

Beckman, Bjorn, Sakhela Buhlungu, and Lloyd Sachikonye, eds. 2010. *Trade Unions and Party Politics: Labour Movements in Africa*. Cape Town: HSRC Press.

Bhachi, Talent. 2011. "Illegal Abortion Horror." *The Zimbabwean*. Accessed December 11, 2011. www.thezimbabwean.co.uk/news/zimbabwe/54840/illegal-abortion-horror.html.

Blair, David. 2002. *Degrees in Violence: Robert Mugabe and the Struggle for Power in Zimbabwe*. London: Continuum.

Bolt, Maxim. 2012. "Waged Entrepreneurs, Policed Informality: Work, the Regulation of Space and the Economy of the Zimbabwean–South African Border." *Africa* 82 (1): 111–130.

———. 2013. "Producing Permanence: Employment, Domesticity and the Flexible Future on a South African Border Farm." *Economy and Society* 42 (2): 197–225.

———. 2015. *Zimbabwe's Migrants and South Africa's Border Farms: The Roots of Impermanence*. Cambridge: Cambridge University Press.

Bond, Patrick. 1998. *Uneven Zimbabwe: A Study of Finance, Development and Underdevelopment*. Trenton, NJ: Africa World Press.

Bond, Patrick, and Masimba Manyana. 2002. *Zimbabwe's Plunge: Exhausted Nationalism, Neoliberalism and the Search for Social Justice*. Scottsville, South Africa: University of Natal Press.

Bond, Patrick, and Richard Saunders. 2005. "Labor, the State, and the Struggle for a Democratic Zimbabwe." *Monthly Review* 57 (7):1–8.

Bornstein, Erica. 2005. *The Spirit of Development: Protestant NGOs, Morality, and Economics in Zimbabwe*. Stanford, CA: Stanford University Press.

Botchwey, Kwesi, Paul Collier, Jan Willem Gunning, and Koichi Hamada. 1998. *Report of the Group of Independent Persons Appointed to Conduct an Evaluation of Certain Aspects of the Enhanced Structural Adjustment Facility*. Washington, DC: International Monetary Fund.

Brand, C.M. 1977. "African Nationalists and the Missionaries in Rhodesia." In *Christianity South of the Zambezi*, vol. 2, edited by M. F. C. Bourdillon, 69–85. Gweru, Zimbabwe: Mambo Press.

Brett, E. A. 2005. "From Corporatism to Liberalization in Zimbabwe: Economic Policy Regimes and Political Crisis (1980–1997)." Working Paper no. 58, Crisis States Programme, London School of Economics and Political Science, London.

Briggs, Charles. 1996. "The Politics of Discursive Authority in Research on the 'Invention of Tradition.'" *Cultural Anthropology* 11 (4): 435–469.

———. 2004. "Theorizing Modernity Conspiratorially: Science, Scale, and the Political Economy of Public Discourse in Explanations of a Cholera Epidemic." *American Ethnologist* 31 (2): 164–187.

Buckles, Catherine. 2001. *African Tears: The Zimbabwe Land Invasions*. Johannesburg: Covos Day Books.

Burke, Timothy. 1996. *Lifebuoy Men, Lux Women: Commodification, Consumption, and Cleanliness in Modern Zimbabwe*. Durham, NC: Duke University Press.

Business Day. 2013. "'Showers of Blessings' as Mandela Memorial Service Starts." *BDlive*. Accessed March 17, 2014. www.bdlive.co.za/national/2013/12/10/showers-of-blessings-as-mandela-memorial-service-starts.

Campbell, Catherine. 2003. *"Letting Them Die": Why HIV/AIDS Intervention Programmes Fail*. Oxford: James Currey.

Carver, Richard. 2000. *Zimbabwe: A Strategy of Tensions*. UNHCR Centre for Documentation and Research, WRITENET Paper No. 04/2000. Accessed December 21, 2010. http://www.refworld.org/pdfid/3ae6a6c70.pdf.

Catholic Commission for Justice and Peace and the Legal Resources Foundation. 1998. *"Breaking the Silence, Building True Peace": A Report on the Disturbances in Matabeleland and the Midlands 1980–1988*. Harare: CCJP and LRF.

Centre for Democracy and Development. 2000. *Zimbabwe Constitutional Referendum: 12–13 February, 2000: The Report of the Centre for Democracy and Development Observer Mission*. London: Centre for Democracy and Development.

CFU (Commercial Farmers' Union). 2000. *Farm Invasions Update*. Accessed December 11, 2012. http://www.zimbabwesituation.com/jul29.html#link4.

Chambati, Walter. 2011. "Restructuring of Agrarian Labour Relations after Fast Track Land Reform in Zimbabwe." *Journal of Peasant Studies* 38 (5): 1047–1068.

Chambati, Walter and Sam Moyo. 2003. *Fast Track Land Reform and the Political Economy of Farm Workers in Zimbabwe*. Harare: AIAS.

Chan, Stephen. 2003. *Robert Mugabe: A Life of Power and Violence*. Ann Arbor: University of Michigan Press.

Chazan, May. 2015. *The Grandmothers' Movement: Solidarity and Survival in the Time of AIDS*. Montreal: McGill-Queen's University Press.

Cheater, Angela. 1984. *Idioms of Accumulation: Rural Development and Class Formation among Freeholders in Zimbabwe*. Gweru, Zimbabwe: Mambo Press.

———. 1986. *The Politics of Factory Organization: A Case Study in Independent Zimbabwe*. Gweru, Zimbabwe: Mambo Press.

Chimhowu, Admos and Phil Woodhouse. 2006. "Customary vs. Private Property Rights? Dynamics and Trajetories of Vernacular Land Markets in Sub-Saharan Africa." *Journal of Agrarian Change* 6 (3): 364–371.

———. 2010. "Forbidden but Not Suppressed: A 'Vernacular' Land Market in Svosve Communal Lands, Zimbabwe." *Africa* 80 (1): 14–35.

Chipunza, Paidamoyo. 2013. "Domestic Violence Cases Up." *The Herald.* Accessed October 9,
  2013. www.herald.co.zw/index.php?option=com_content&view=article&id=71651:do
  mestic-violence-cases-up&catid=37:top-stories&Itemid=130#.UccSuZywVeg.
Chiremba, Sophia, and William Masters. 2003. "The Experience of Resettled Farmers in
  Zimbabwe." *African Studies Quarterly* 7 (2–3): 97–117.
Clarke, Duncan. 1977. *Agricultural and Plantation Workers in Zimbabwe.* Gweru, Zimbabwe:
  Mambo Press.
Comaroff, John, and Jean Comaroff, eds. 1999. *Civil Society and the Political Imagination in
  Africa.* Chicago: University of Chicago Press.
Cooper, Fredrick. 1987. *On the African Waterfront: Urban Disorder and the Transformation of
  Work in Colonial Mombasa.* New Haven, CT: Yale University Press.
———. 1996. *Decolonization and African Society: The Labour Question in French and British
  Africa.* Cambridge: Cambridge University Press.
Daily News. 2000. "Police, Army Ignore Public Outcry over Joint Operation." *Daily News.*
  Accessed March 5, 2012. www.zimbabwesituation.com/jul14a.html#link7.
Das, Veena. 2004. "The Signature of the State: The Paradox of Illegibility." In *Anthropology
  in the Margins of the State,* edited by Veena Das and Deborah Poole, 225–252. Santa Fe,
  NM: School of American Research Press.
Dorman, Sara Rich. 2002. "'Rocking the Boat': Church-NGOs and Democratization in
  Zimbabwe." *African Affairs* 101 (402): 75–92.
———. 2003. "NGOs and the Constitutional Debate in Zimbabwe: From Inclusion to
  Exclusion. *Journal of Southern African Studies* 29 (4): 845–863.
Du Toit, Andries. 1993. "The Micro-politics of Paternalism: The Discourse of Management
  and Resistance on South African Fruit and Wine Farms." *Journal of Southern African
  Studies* 19 (2): 314–336.
———. 2004. "'Social Exclusion' Discourse and Chronic Poverty: A South African Case
  Study." *Development and Change* 35 (5): 987–1010.
Eckert, Julia. 2011. "Introduction: Subjects of Citizens." *Citizenship Studies* 15 (3–4):
  309–317.
Englund, Harri. 2004. "Introduction: Recognizing Identities, Imagining Alternatives." In
  Rights and the Politics of Recognition in Africa, edited by Harri Englund, 1–29. London:
  Zed Books.
———. 2006. *Prisoners of Freedom: Human Rights and the African Poor.* Berkeley: University
  of California Press.
The Farmer. 2001. "Rabble-Rousing Union." *The Farmer.* Accessed August 19, 2012. www
  .zimbabwesituation.com/july3_2001.html#link10.
———. 2002. "ALB Studies Government Decree on Farm Worker Benefits." *The Farmer.*
  Accessed April 30, 2011. www.zimbabwesituation.com/jan30_2002.html#link16.
FCTZ (Farm Community Trust of Zimbabwe). 2000. *Farm Worker Communities in the Fast
  Track Resettlement and Land Reform Programme 1980–Present.* December 18. Harare:
  FCTZ.
Ferguson, James. 1999. *Expectations of Modernity: Myths and Meanings of Modern Life on the
  Zambian Copperbelt.* Berkeley: University of California Press.
———. 2006. *Global Shadows: Africa in the Neoliberal World Order.* Durham, NC: Duke
  University Press.
———. 2013. "Declarations of Dependence: Labour, Personhood, and Welfare in Southern
  Africa." *Journal of the Royal Anthropological Institute* 19 (2): 223–242.

Fisher, Josephine. 2010. *Pioneers, Settlers, Aliens, Exiles: The Decolonisation of White Identity in Zimbabwe*. Canberra, Australia: ANU E Press.

Fisher, William F. 1997. "Doing Good: The Politics and Antipolitics of NGO Practices." *Annual Review of Anthropology* 26: 439–464.

Fontein, Joost. 2006. *The Silence of Great Zimbabwe: Contested Landscapes and the Power of Heritage*. London: UCL Press.

Foucault, Michel. 1979. *Discipline & Punish: The Birth of the Prison*. Translated by Alan Sheridan. New York: Vintage Books.

———. 1982. "The Subject and Power." Translated by Leslie Sawyer. In *Michel Foucault: Beyond Structuralism and Hermeneutics*, edited by Hubert Dreyfus and Paul Rabinow, 208–229. Chicago: Chicago University Press.

———. 1991. "Governmentality." Translated by Rosi Braidotti and Colin Gordon. In *The Foucault Effect: Studies in Governmentality*, edited by Graham Burchell, Colin Gordon, and Peter Miller, 87–104. Chicago: University of Chicago Press.

GAPWUZ (General Agricultural Workers Union of Zimbabwe). 2010. *If Something is Wrong: The Invisible Suffering of Farmworkers Due to 'Land Reform.'* Harare: GAPWUZ and Weaver Press.

Geschiere, Peter. 2009. *The Perils of Belonging: Autochthony, Citizenship, and Exclusion in Africa and Europe*. Chicago: University of Chicago Press.

Gibbon, Peter and Stefano Ponte. 2005. *Trading Down: Africa, Value Chains, and the Global Economy*. Philadelphia: Temple University Press.

Gibbon, Peter, Benoit Daviron, and Stephanie Barral. 2014. "Lineages of Paternalism: An Introduction." *Journal of Agrarian Change* 14 (2): 165–189.

Goebel, Allison. 2005. *Gender and Land Reform: The Zimbabwe Experience*. Montreal: McGill-Queen's University Press.

Grier, Beverley. 2006. *Invisible Hands: Child Labor and the State in Colonial Zimbabwe*. Portsmouth, NH: Heinemann.

Grillo, Ralph. 1974. *Race, Class and Militancy: An African Trade Union, 1939–1965*. London: Chandler.

Grobler, John. 2007. "'I was in a Zimbabwe death squad,'" *Mail and Guardian*. Accessed October 9, 2013. mg.co.za/article/2007-04-05-i-was-in-a-zimbabwe-death-squad.

Gulbrandson, Ørnulf. 2012. *The State and the Social: State Formation in Botswana and Its Precolonial and Colonial Genealogies*. Oxford: Berghahn.

Gwisai, Munyaradzi. 2000. "Challenges for the Working Class in the Year 2000." *Socialist Worker (Zimbabwe)*. Accessed May 7, 2000. www.voiceoftheturtle.org/iso/newspaper/jan%202000.pdf.

———. *Farm Workers Rights on Compulsory Land Acquisition*. Mimeo. An opinion piece prepared for GAPWUZ.

Hale, Charles. 2006. "Activist Research v. Cultural Critique: Indigenous Land Rights and the Contradictions of Politically Engaged Anthropology." *Cultural Anthropology* 21 (1): 96–120.

Hall, Ruth, Poul Wisborg, Shirhami Shirinda, and Phillan Zamchiya. 2013. "Farm Workers and Farm Dwellers in Limpopo Province, South Africa." *Journal of Agrarian Change* 13 (1): 47–70.

Hammar, Amanda, 2002. "The Articulation of Modes of Belonging: Competing Land Claims in Zimbabwe's Northwest." In *Negotiating Property in Africa*, edited by K. Juul and C. Lund, 211–246. Portsmouth, NH: Heinemann.

———. 2008. "In the Name of Sovereignty: Displacement and State Making in Post-independence Zimbabwe." *Journal of Contemporary African Studies* 26 (4): 417–434.

Hammar, Amanda, JoAnn McGregor, and Loren Landau. 2010. "Introduction. Displacing Zimbabwe: Crisis and Construction in Southern Africa." *Journal of Southern African Studies* 36 (2): 263–283.

Hanlon, Joseph, Jeannette Manjengwa, and Teresa Smart. 2013. *Zimbabwe Takes Back Its Land*. West Hartford, CT: Kumarian.

Hansen, Thomas Blom, and Finn Stepputat. 2005. "Introduction." In *Sovereign Bodies: Citizens, Migrants and States in the Postcolonial World*, edited by Thomas Hansen and Finn Stepputat, 1–38. Princeton: Princeton University Press.

———. 2006. "Sovereignty revisited." *Annual Review of Anthropology* 35: 295–315.

Hartnack, Andrew. 2005. "'My Life Got Lost': Farm Workers and Displacement in Zimbabwe." *Journal of Contemporary African Studies* 23 (2): 173–192.

———. 2014. "Whiteness and Shades of Grey: Erasure, Amnesia and the Ethnography of Zimbabwe's Whites." *Journal of Contemporary African Studies* 33 (2): 285–299.

———. 2015. *Cultivations on the Frontiers of Modernity: Power, Welfare and Belonging on Commercial Farms Before and After "Fast-Track Land Reform" in Zimbabwe*. PhD thesis, University of Cape Town.

Hartnack, Michael. 2002. "Mugabe Flexes His Muscles." *The Australian*. Accessed January 22, 2012. www.zimbabwesituation.com/dec2_2002.html#link4.

Hatchard, John. 1993. *Individual Freedoms and State Security in the African Context: The Case of Zimbabwe*. Harare: Baobab Books.

Hellum, Anne, and Bill Derman. 2004. "Land Reform and Human Rights in Contemporary Zimbabwe: Balancing Individual and Social Justice through an Integrated Human Rights Framework." *World Development* 32 (10): 1785–1805.

The Herald. 2000. "Group of Ex-combatants Invades Two More Farms." *The Herald*.

Hodgson, Dorothy, and Sheryl McCurdy. 2001. "Introduction: 'Wicked' Women and the Reconfiguration of Gender in Africa." In *"Wicked" Women and the Reconfiguration of Gender in Africa*, edited by Dorothy L. Hodgson and Sheryl McCurdy, 1–24. Portsmouth, NH: Heinemann.

Holtzclaw, Heather. 2004. *The Third Chimurenga? State Terror and State Organized Violence in Zimbabwe's Commercial Farming Communities*. PhD thesis, Michigan State University, East Lansing.

Horn, Nancy. 1994. *Cultivating Customers: Market Women in Harare, Zimbabwe*. Boulder, CO: Lynne Rienner.

Horst, Shannon. 1988. "Zimbabwe's Ex-combatants Test New Models for Education." *The Christian Science Monitor*. Accessed January 21, 2013. http://www.csmonitor.com/1988/0502/omap.html.

HRW (Human Rights Watch). 2009. *Crisis without Limits: Human Rights and Humanitarian Consequences f Political Repression in Zimbabwe*. New York: HRW.

Hughes, David McDermott. 1999. "Refugees and Squatters: Immigration and the Politics of Territory on the Zimbabwe–Mozambique Border." *Journal of Southern African Studies* 25 (4): 533–552.

———. 2005. "Hydrology of Hope: Farm Dams, Conservation, and Whiteness in Zimbabwe." *American Ethnologist* 33 (2): 269–287.

———. 2006. *From Enslavement to Environmentalism: Politics on a Southern African Frontier.* Seattle: University of Washington Press.

———. 2010. *Whiteness in Zimbabwe: Race, Landscape and the Problem of Belonging.* New York: Palgrave.

Hunter, Mark. 2010. *Love in the Time of AIDS: Inequality, Gender, and Rights in South Africa.* Bloomington: Indiana University Press.

International Bar Association. 2001. *Report of IBA Zimbabwe Mission 2001.* Accessed September 22, 2013. www.ibanet.org/Article/Detail.aspx?ArticleUid=05c3f170-e3ad-4e04-a952-511f6c28bba4.

IRIN. 2004. "Roadblocks Set-up to Search for Maize." *IRIN.* Accessed December 2, 2011. http://www.zimbabwesituation.com/sep17_2004.html#link4.

JAG (Justice for Agriculture). 2002. "The Land Acquisition Act–Questions & Answer." *Kubatana.net.* Accessed May 5, 2008. http://archive.kubatana.net/html/archive/agric/021212jag.asp?sector=AGRIC.

JAG and GAPWUZ (Justice for Agriculture and the General Agricultural and Plantation Workers of Zimbabwe). 2008. *Destruction of Zimbabwe's Backbone Industry in Pursuit of Political Power: A Qualitative Report on Events in Zimbabwe's Commercial Farming Sector since the Year 2000.* Harare: JAG.

Jeater, Diana. 1993. *Marriage, Perversion and Power: The Construction of Moral Discourse in Southern Rhodesia 1894–1930.* Oxford: Clarendon Press.

Jones, Jeremy. 2010. "'Nothing is Straight in Zimbabwe': The Rise of the *Kukiya-kiya* Economy 2000–2008." *Journal of Southern African Studies* 36 (2): 285–299.

Kalaora, Léa. 2011. "Madness, Corruption and Exile: On Zimbabwe's Remaining White Commercial Farmers." *Journal of Southern African Studies* 37 (4): 747–762.

Kaler, Amy. 1998. "A Threat to the Nation and a Threat to the Men: The Prohibition of Depo-Provera in Zimbabwe 1981." *Journal of Southern African Studies* 24 (2): 347–376.

Kanyenze, Godfrey. 2001. "Zimbabwe's Labour Relations Policies and the Implications for Farm Workers." In *Zimbabwe's Farm Workers: Policy Dimensions*, edited by Dede Amanor-Wilks, 86–114. Lusaka, Zambia: Panos Southern Africa.

Kelly, David, and Martha Kaplan. 2001. *Represented Communities: Fiji and World Decolonization.* Chicago: University of Chicago Press.

Kesby, Mike. 1996. "Arenas for Control, Terrains of Gender Contestation: Guerrilla Struggle and Counter-insurgency Warfare in Zimbabwe 1972–1980." *Journal of Southern African Studies* 22 (4): 561–584.

———.1999. "Locating and Dislocating Gender in Rural Zimbabwe: The Making of Space and the Texturing of Bodies." *Gender, Place and Culture* 6 (1): 27–47.

Kinsey, Bill. 1999. "Land Reform, Growth and Equity: Emerging Evidence from Zimbabwe's Resettlement Programme." *Journal of Southern African Studies* 25 (2): 173–196.

Kopytoff, Igor. 1987. "The Internal African Frontier: The Making of African Political Culture." In *The African Frontier: The Reproduction of Traditional African Societies*, edited by Igor Kopytoff, 3–83. Bloomington: Indiana University Press.

Kriger, Norma. 1992. *Zimbabwe's Guerrilla War: Peasant Voices.* Cambridge: Cambridge University Press.

———. 2003. *Guerrilla Veterans in Post War Zimbabwe: Symbolic and Violent Politics, 1980–1987.* Cambridge: Cambridge University Press.

———. 2005. "ZANU (PF) Strategies in General Elections, 1980–2000: Discourse and Coercion." *African Affairs* 104 (414): 1–34.

———. 2006. "From Patriotic Memories to 'Patriotic History' in Zimbabwe, 1990–2005." *Third World Quarterly* 27 (6): 1151–1169.

Ladley, Andrew, and David Lan, 1985. "The Law of the Land: Party and State in Rural Zimbabwe." *Journal of Southern African Studies* 12 (1): 88–101.

Lan, David. 1985. *Guns and Rain: Guerrillas & Spirit Mediums in Zimbabwe*. Oxford: James Currey.

Larmer, Miles. 2007. *Mineworkers in Zambia: Labour and Political Change in Post-colonial Africa*. London: Taurus Academic.

LeBas, Adrienne. 2011. *From Protest to Parties: Party-Building and Democratization in Africa*. Oxford: Oxford University Press.

Lentz, Carola. 2013. *Land, Mobility and Belonging in West Africa*. Bloomington: Indiana University Press.

Li, Tania Murray. 2007. "Governmentality." *Anthropologica* 49 (2): 275–294.

Loewenson, R. 1988. "Labour Insecurity and Health: An Epidemiological Study in Zimbabwe." *Social Science & Medicine* 27 (7): 733–741.

———. 1992. *Modern Plantation Agriculture*. London: Zed Books.

Lund, Christian. 2006. "Twilight Institutions: Public Authority and Local Politics in Africa." *Development and Change* 37 (4): 685–705.

Magaisa, Ishmael. 1999. *Prostitution in Zimbabwe: A Study of Black Female Prostitutes in Harare*. PhD thesis, University of Zimbabwe, Harare.

Magaramombe, Godfrey. 2010. "'Displaced in Place': Agrarian Displacements, Replacements and Resettlement among Farm Workers in Mazowe District." *Journal of Southern African Studies* 36 (2): 361–375.

Makochekanwa, Albert. 2007. "Zimbabwe's Black Market for Foreign Exchange." University of Pretoria, Department of Economics Working Paper Series. Accessed December 16, 2012. web.up.ac.za/UserFiles/WP_2007_13.pdf.

Mamdani, Mahmood. 1996. *Citizen and Subject: Contemporary Africa and the Legacy of Late Colonialism*. Princeton: Princeton University Press.

———. 2001. "Beyond Settler and Native as Political Identities: Overcoming the Political Legacy of Colonialism." *Comparative Studies in Society and History* 43 (4): 651–664.

Mandaza, Ibbo. 1997. *Race, Colour and Class in Southern Africa*. Harare: SAPES Books.

Mandaza, Ibbo, and Lloyd Sachikonye, eds. 1991. *The One-Party State and Democracy: The Zimbabwe Debate*. Harare: SAPES Books.

Manyukwe, Clemence. 2007. "Youth Service Report Opens Can of Worms." *Financial Gazette*. Accessed October 9, 2013. allafrica.com/stories/200705240672.html.

Marongwe, Nelson. 2004. *Fast Track Resettlement and Its Implications for the Wildlife Land-Use Option: The Case for Dahwye Resettlement Scheme*. ZERO Regional Environment Organisation. Harare: ZERO.

Masvawure, Tsitsi. 2010. "'I Just Need to Be Flashy on Campus': Female Students and Transactional Sex at a University in Zimbabwe." *Culture, Health & Sexuality* 12 (8): 857–870.

Matondi, Prosper. 2012. *Zimbabwe's Fast Track Land Reform*. London: Zed Books.

Maxwell, David. 1999. *Christians and Chiefs in Zimbabwe: A Social History of the Hwesa People c.1870s–1990s*. Edinburgh: University of Edinburgh Press.

Mbembe, Achilles. 2001. *On the Postcolony*. Berkeley: University of California Press.

McCandless, Erin. 2012. *Polarization and Transformation in Zimbabwe: Social Movements, Strategy Dilemmas and Change*. Durban, South Africa: University of KwaZulu-Natal Press.

McGregor, JoAnn. 2002. "The Politics of Disruption: War Veterans and the Local State in Zimbabwe." *African Affairs* 101 (402): 9–37.

———. 2009. *Crossing the Zambezi: The Politics of Landscape on a Central African Frontier*. Oxford: James Currey.

Mitchell, Timothy. 2002. *Rule of Experts: Egypt, Techno-Politics, Modernity*. Berkeley: University of California Press.

Moore, David. 1995. "Democracy, Violence, and Identity in the Zimbabwean War of National Liberation: Reflections from the Realms of Dissent." *Canadian Journal of African Studies* 29(3): 375–402.

———. 2004. "Marxism and Marxist Intellectuals in Schizophrenic Zimbabwe: How Many Rights for Zimbabwe's Left? A Comment." *Historical Materialism* 21(4): 405–425.

———. 2007. "'Intellectuals' Interpreting Zimbabwe's Primitive Accumulation: Progress to Market Civilization?" *Safundi* 8 (2): 199–222.

Moore, Donald. 2005. *Suffering for Territory: Race, Place, and Power in Zimbabwe*. Durham, NC: Duke University Press.

Moyo, Jonathan 1992. *Voting for Democracy: Electoral Politics in Zimbabwe*. Harare: University of Zimbabwe Press.

Moyo, Sam. 1995. *The Land Question in Zimbabwe*. Harare, Zimbabwe: SAPES Books.

———. 1998. *The Land Acquisition Process in Zimbabwe (1997/98)*. Harare: UNDP Resource Centre.

———. 2000. *Land Reform under Structural Adjustment in Zimbabwe*. Uppsala, Sweden: Nordiska Afrikainstitutet.

———. 2001. "The Land Occupation Movement and Democratization in Zimbabwe: Contradictions of Neoliberalism?" *Millenium: Journal of International Studies* 30 (2): 311–330.

———. 2011. "Three Decades of Agrarian Reform in Zimbabwe." *Journal of Peasant Studies* 38 (3): 493–531.

Moyo, Sam, John Makumbe, and Brian Raftopoulos. 1999. *NGOs, the State, and Politics in Zimbabwe*. Harare: SAPES Books.

Moyo, Sam, Blair Rutherford, and Dede Amanor-Wilks. 2000. "Land Reform and Changing Social Relations for Farm Workers in Zimbabwe." *Review of African Political Economy* 27 (84):181–202.

Moyo, Sam and Paris Yeros. 2005. "Land Occupations and Land Reform in Zimbabwe: Towards the National Democratic Revolution." In *Reclaiming the Land: The Resurgence of Rural Movements in Africa, Asia and Latin America*, edited by S. Moyo and P. Yeros, 165–205. London: Zed Books.

Moyo, Sam and Paris Yeros. 2007. "The Radicalized State: Zimbabwe's Interrupted Revolution." *Review of African Political Economy* 34 (111): 103–121.

MPSLSW (Ministry of Public Service, Labour and Social Welfare, Government of Zimbabwe). 2001. *Zimbabwe Farm Workers Survey – Land Reform: A Labour Perspective*. In collaboration with the Interntional Organization for Migration. September. Harare: MPSLSW.

Muckraker. 2000. "Zimbabwe: Moyo Buried under the Landslide." *Zimbabwe Independent.* Accessed March 19, 2000. http://allafrica.com/stories/200002180189.html.

Mugwati, Thokozani and Peter Balleis. 1994. *The Forgotten People: The Living and Health Conditions of Farm Workers and their Families.* Gweru, Zimbabwe: Mambo Press.

Munro, William. 1998. *The Moral Economy of the State: Conservation, Community Development and State-Making in Zimbabwe.* Athens, OH: Ohio University Press.

Muronzi, Chris. 2014. "Mugabe Estate in Sorry State." *Zimbabwe Independent.* Accessed March 19, 2014. http://www.theindependent.co.zw/2014/03/07/mugabe-estate-sorry -state/.

Muzondidya, James. 2005. *Walking a Tightrope: Towards a Social History of the Coloured Community of Zimbabwe.* Trenton, NJ: Africa World Press.

———. 2007. "Jambanja: Ideological Ambiguities in the Politics of Land and Resource Ownership in Zimbabwe." *Journal of Southern African Studies* 33 (2): 325–341.

Nyamnjoh, Francis. 2006. *Insiders and Outsiders: Citizenship and Xenophobia in Contemporary Southern Africa.* London: Zed Books.

Palley, Claire. 1979. *The Rhodesian Elections.* London: Catholic Institute for International Relations.

Palmer, Robin. 1990. "Land Reform in Zimbabwe, 1980–1990." *African Affairs* 89 (355): 163–181.

Pankhurst, Donna. 1991. "Constraints and Incentives in 'Successful' Zimbabwean Peasant Agriculture: The Interaction between Gender and Class." *Journal of Southern African Studies* 17 (6): 611–632.

Phimister, Ian. 1988. *An Economic and Social History of Zimbabwe, 1890–1948.* London: Longman.

Pilossof, Rory. 2012. *The Unbearable Whiteness of Being: Farmers' Voices from Zimbabwe.* Harare: Weaver Press.

Parliament of Zimbabwe. 2003. *Second Report of the Portfolio Committee on Lands, Agriculture, Water Development, Rural Resources and Resettlement.* Third Session—Fifth Parliament. Presented to Parliament on June 11.

Peace, Adrian, 1979. *Choice, Class and Conflict: A Study of Southern Nigerian Factory Workers.* London: Humanities Press.

Potts, Deborah. 2010. *Circular Migration in Zimbabwe and Contemporary Sub-Saharan Africa.* Woodbridge, UK: James Currey.

Power, Samantha. 2003. "How to Kill a Country: Turning a Breadbasket into a Basket Case in Ten Easy Steps—the Robert Mugabe Way." *The Atlantic* December: 86–94.

Raftopoulos, Brian. 1986. "Human Resources Development and the Problem of Labour Utilisation." In *Zimbabwe: The Political Economy of Transition 1980–1986*, edited by Ibbo Mandaza, 275–317. Dakar, Senegal: CODESRIA.

———. 2001. "The Labour Movement and the Emergence of Opposition Politics in Zimbabwe." In *The Labour Movement in Zimbabwe: Problems and Prospects*, edited by Brian Raftopoulos and Lloyd Sachikonye, 1–24. Harare: Weaver Press.

———. 2003. "The State in Crisis: Authoritarian Nationalism, Selective Citizenship and Distortions of Democracy in Zimbabwe." In *Zimbabwe's Unfinished Business: Rethinking Land, State and Nation in the Context of Crisis*, edited by Amanda Hammar, Brian Raftopoulos, and Stig Jensen, 217–241. Harare: Weaver Press.

———. 2006. "Reflections on Opposition Politics in Zimbabwe: The Politics of the Movement for Democratic Change (MDC)." In *Reflections on Democratic Politics in Zimbabwe*, edited by Brian Raftopoulos and Karin Alexander, 6–28. Cape Town: Institute for Justice and Reconciliation.

———. 2013. "An Overview of the GPA: National Conflict, Regional Agony and International Dilemma." In *The Hard Road to Reform: The Politics of Zimbabwe's Global Political Agreement*, edited by Brian Raftopoulos, 1–38. Harare: Weaver Press.

Raftopoulos, Brian, and Alois Mlambo, eds. 2009. *Becoming Zimbabwe: A History from the Pre-Colonial Period to 2008*. Harare: Weaver Press.

Raftopoulos, Brian, and Ian Phimister, eds. 1997. *Keep on Knocking: A History of the Labour Movement in Zimbabwe, 1900–1997*. Harare: Baobab Books.

———. 2004. "Zimbabwe Now: The Political Economy of Crisis and Coercion." *Historical Materialism* 12 (4): 355–382.

Raftopoulos, Brian, and Lloyd Sachikonye. 2001. *Striking Back: The Labour Movement and the Post-Colonial State in Zimbabwe 1980–2000*. Harare: Weaver Press.

Ranger, Terence. 1985. *Peasant Consciousness and Guerilla War in Zimbabwe: A Comparative Study*. London: James Currey.

———. 1993. "The Communal Areas of Zimbabwe." In *Land in African Agrarian Systems*, eds. Thomas Bassett and Donald Crummey, 354–385. Madison: University of Wisconsin Press.

———. 1995. *Are We Not Also Men? The Samkange Family & African Politics in Zimbabwe 1920–64*. London: James Currey.

———. 2002. "The Zimbabwean Elections: A Personal Experience." accessed May 8, 2010. http://cas1.elis.ugent.be/avrug/pdf02/ranger01.pdf.

———. 2004. "Nationalist Historiography, Patriotic History and the History of the Nation: The Struggle over the Past in Zimbabwe." *Journal of Southern African Studies* 30 (2): 215–234.

———. 2005. "The Rise of Patriotic Journalism in Zimbabwe and Its Possible Implications." *Westminster Papers in Communication and Culture* 2 (special issue): 8–17.

Ranger, Terence, and Ngwabi Bhebe, eds. 2001. *The Historical Dimensions of Democracy and Human Rights in Zimbabwe*, vol. 1. Harare: University of Zimbabwe Press.

Reeler, A. P. 2003. "The role of militia groups in maintaining ZanuPF's political power." Unpublished manuscript. Accessed October 11, 2012. kubatana.org/docs/hr/reeler _militia_mar_030331.pdf.

Research and Advocacy Unit. 2008. *A Right or a Privilege: Access to Identity and Citizenship in Zimbabwe*. Accessed May 22, 2012. www.researchandadvocacyunit.org/index. php?view=download&alias=292-a-right-or-a-privilege&category_slug=womens-programme-1&option=com_docman&Itemid=127. Harare: Research and Advocacy Unit.

Reuters. 2000. "Zimbabwe Labor Movement Calls for General Strike," *Reuters*. Accessed May 22, 2012. http://www.zimbabwesituation.com/jul29.html#link1.

Rubert, Steven. 1998. *A Most Promising Weed: A History of Tobacco Farming and Labor in Colonial Zimbabwe, 1890–1945*. Athens, OH: Ohio University Center for International Studies.

Rutherford, Blair. 1999. "To Find an African Witch: Anthropology, Modernity, and Witch-Finding in North-West Zimbabwe." *Critique of Anthropology* 19 (1):105–125.

———. 2001a. *Working on the Margins: Black Workers, White Farmers in Post-Colonial Zimbabwe*. London: Zed Books.

———. 2001b. "Farm Workers in Trade Unions in Hurungwe District in Post-Colonial Zimbabwe." In *Striking Back: The Labour Movement and the Post-Colonial State in Zimbabwe, 1980–2000*, edited by Brian Raftopoulos and Lloyd Sachikonye, 197–220. Harare: Weaver Press.

———. 2001c. "Commercial Farm Workers and the Politics of (Dis)placement in Zimbabwe: Liberation, Colonialism, and Democracy." *Journal of Agrarian Change* 1 (4):626–651.

———. 2002. "Not All Black and White." *Globe & Mail* (Canada).

———. 2004. "Desired Publics, Domestic Government, and Entangled Fears: On the Anthropology of Civil Society, Farm Workers, and White Farmers in Zimbabwe." *Cultural Anthropology* 19 (1):122–153.

———. 2008. "Conditional Belonging: Farm Workers and the Cultural Politics of Recognition in Zimbabwe." *Development and Change* 39 (1):73–99.

———. 2012. "Shifting the Debate on Land Reform, Poverty and Inequality in Zimbabwe: An Engagement with Zimbabwe's Land Reform: Myths & Realities." *Journal of Contemporary African Studies* 30 (1): 147–157.

———. 2013. "Electoral Politics and a Farm Workers' Struggle in Zimbabwe (1999–2000)." *Journal of Southern African Studies* 39 (4): 845–863.

———. 2014. "Organization and (De)mobilization of Farm Workers in Zimbabwe: Reflections on Trade Unions, NGOs, and Political Parties." *Journal of Agrarian Change* 14 (2):214–239.

Rutherford, Blair, and Rinse Nyamuda. 1999. "Learning About Power: Development and Marginality in an Adult Literacy Center for Farm Workers in Zimbabwe." *American Ethnologist* 27 (4):839–854.

Rutherford, Blair, and Lincoln Addison. 2007. "Zimbabwean Farm Workers in Northern South Africa: Transnational Strategies of Survival in an Ambivalent Border-Zone." *Review of African Political Economy* 34 (114):619–635.

Sachikonye, Lloyd. 2003. *The Situation of Commercial Farm Workers after Land Reform in Zimbabwe*. Unpublished report. London: Catholic Institute for International Relations.

———. 2011. *When a State Turns on Its Citizens: 60 Years of Institutionalised Violence in Zimbabwe*. Johannesburg: Jacana.

———. 2012. *Zimbabwe's Lost Decade: Politics, Development & Society*. Harare: Weaver Press.

Sadomba, Zvakanyorwa Wilbert. 2011. *War Veterans in Zimbabwe's Revolution: Challenging Neo-Colonialism, Settler and International Capital*. London: James Currey.

Sadomba, Zvakanyorwa Wilbert, and Kirk Helliker. 2010. "Transcending Objectifications and Dualisms: Farm Workers and Civil Society in Contemporary Zimbabwe." *Journal of Asian and African Studies* 20 (10): 1–17.

Saunders, Richard. 2000. *Never the Same Again: Zimbabwe's Growth Towards Democracy, 1980–2000*. Harare: ESP.

Saunyama, Jairos. 2015. "Children Selling Their Bodies to Earn a Living." *Nehanda Radio*. Accessed April 22, 2015. http://nehandaradio.com/2015/04/01/children-selling-their -bodies-to-earn-a-living/.

Save the Children (UK). 2000. *We Learn with Hope: Issues in Education on Commercial Farms in Zimbabwe*. Harare: Save the Children Fund.

Scarnecchia, Timothy. 1999. "The Mapping of Respectability and the Transformation of African Residential Space." In *Sites of Struggle: Essays in Zimbabwe's Urban History*, edited by Brian Raftopoulos and Tsuneo Yoshikuni, 151–162. Harare: Weaver Press.

———. 2006. "The 'Fascist Cycle' in Zimbabwe, 2000–2005." *Journal of Southern African Studies* 32 (2): 221–237.

———. 2008. *The Urban Roots of Democracy and Political Violence in Zimbabwe: Harare and Highfield, 1940–1964*. Rochester, NY: University of Rochester Press.

Schmidt, Elizabeth. 1992. *Peasants, Traders, & Wives: Shona Women in the History of Zimbabwe, 1870–1939*. Portsmouth, NH: Heinemann.

Scoones, Ian, Nelson Marongwe, Blasio Mavedzenge, Jacob Mahenehene, Felix Murimbarimba, and Chrispen Sukume. 2010. *Zimbabwe's Land Reform: Myths and Realities*. Oxford: James Currey.

Shadur, Mark. 1994. *Labour Relations in a Developing Country: A Case Study on Zimbabwe*. Aldershot, UK: Avebury.

Selby, Angus. 2006. *Commercial Farmers and the State: Interest Group Politics and Land Reform in Zimbabwe*. PhD thesis, University of Oxford.

Shamu, Simukai, Neemah Abrahams, Marleen Temmerman, and Christina Zarowsky. 2013. "Opportunities and Obstacles to Screening Pregnant Women for Intimate Partner Violence during Antenatal Care in Zimbabwe." *Culture, Health & Sexuality* 15 (5): 511–524.

Shutt, Allison. 2000. "Pioneer Farmers and Family Dynasties in Marirangwe Purchase Area, Colonial Zimbabwe." *African Studies Review* 43 (3): 59–80.

Sithole, Masipula. 2001. "Fighting Authoritarianism in Zimbabwe." *Journal of Democracy* 12 (1): 160–169.

Sokwanele. 2012. "The Significance of Land Compensation for Rehabilitation of Zimbabwe's Land Sector." *The Zimbabwean*. Accessed July 11, 2012. www.thezimbabwean.co.uk /news/zimbabwe/59149/the-significance-of-land-compensation.html.

Spierenburg, Marja. 2004. *Strangers, Spirits, and Land Reforms: Conflicts about Land in Dande, Northern Zimbabwe*. Leiden, Netherlands: Brill.

SPT (Solidarity Peace Trust). 2003. *National Youth Service Training–"Shaping Youths in a Truly Zimbabwean Manner": An Overview of Youth Militia Training and Activities in Zimbabwe, October 2000–August 2003*. Port Shepstone, South Africa: SPT.

Stewart, Julie. 1987. "Playing the Game: Women's Inheritance of Property in Zimbabwe." In *Women and Law in Southern Africa*, edited by Alice Armstrong, 85–104. Harare: Zimbabwe Publishing House.

Sylvester, Christine. 1991. *Zimbabwe: The Terrain of Contradictory Development*. Boulder, CO: Westview Press.

Tandon, Yash. 2001. "Trade Unions and Labour in the Agricultural Sector in Zimbabwe." In *The Labour Movement in Zimbabwe: Problems and Prospects*, edited by Brian Raftopoulos and Lloyd Sachikonye, 221–249. Harare: Weaver Press.

Tendi, Miles-Blessing. 2011. "Robert Mugabe and Toxicity: History and Context Matter." *Representation* 47 (3): 307–318.

Thompson, E. P. 1963. *The Making of the English Working Class*. Harmondsworth, UK: Penguin.

Thornycroft, Peta. 2002. "Zimbabwe Farmers Snared in Pay Revolt." *The Telegraph*. Accessed December 2, 2013. www.telegraph.co.uk/news/worldnews/africaandindianocean /zimbabwe/1403417/Zimbabwe-farmers-snared-in-pay-revolt.html.

Tom, Tom, and Maxwell Musingafi. 2013. "Domestic Violence in Urban Areas in Zimbabwe: A Case Study of Glen Norah (Harare)." *Research on Humanities and Social Sciences* 3 (3): 45–50.

Tsing, Anna. 1997. "Transitions as Translation." In *Transitions, Environments, Translations: Feminisms in International Politics*, edited by Joan Scott, Cora Kaplan, and Debra Keates, 253–272. New York: Routledge.

———. 2003. "Agrarian Allegory and Global Futures." In *Nature in the Global South: Environmental Projects in South and Southeast Asia*, edited by Paul Greenough and Anna Tsing, 124–169. Durham, NC: Duke University Press.

———. 2005. *Friction: An Ethnography of Global Connection*. Princeton: Princeton University Press.

Veritas. 2013. "The New Constitution & Citizenship." *Constitution Watch*. Accessed March 16, 2014. http://www.veritaszim.net/node/450.

Waeterloos, Evert, and Blair Rutherford. 2004. "Land Reform in Zimbabwe: Challenges and Opportunities for Poverty Reduction among Commercial Farm Workers." *World Development* 32 (3): 537–553.

Walters, William. 2012. *Governmentality: Critical Encounters*. London: Routledge.

Werbner, Pnina. 2014. *The Making of an African Working Class: Politics, Law, and Cultural Protest in the Manual Workers' Union of Botswana*. London: Pluto Press.

Werbner, Richard. 1998. "Smoke from the Barrel of a Gun: Postwars of the Dead, Memory and Reinscription in Zimbabwe." In *Memory and the Postcolony: African Anthropology and the Critique of Power*, edited by Richard Werbner, 71–102. London: Zed Books.

———. 2004. *Reasonable Radicals and Citizenship in Botswana*. Bloomington: Indiana University Press.

White, Luise. 1990. *The Comforts of Home: Prostitution in Colonial Nairobi*. Chicago: University of Chicago Press.

———. 2003. *The Assassination of Herbert Chitepo: Texts and Politics in Zimbabwe*. Bloomington: Indiana University Press.

Willems, Wendy. 2004. "Peasant Demonstrators, Violent Invaders: Representations of Land in the Zimbabwean Press." *World Development* 32 (10): 1767–1783.

———. 2005. "Remnants of Empire? British Media Reporting on Zimbabwe." *Westminster Papers in Communication and Culture* 2 (Special Issue): 91–108.

Worby, Eric. 1994. "Maps, Names, and Ethnic Games: The Epistemology and Iconography of Colonial Power in Northwestern Zimbabwe." *Journal of Southern African Studies* 20 (3): 371–392.

———. 1998. "Inscribing the State at the 'Edge of Beyond': Danger and Development in Northwestern Zimbabwe." *PoLAR: Political and Legal Anthropology Review* 21 (2): 55–70.

———. 2001. "A Redivided Land? New Agrarian Conflicts and Questions in Zimbabwe." *Journal of Agrarian Change* 1 (4): 475–509.

———. 2003. "The End of Modernity in Zimbabwe? Passages from Development to Sovereignty." In *Zimbabwe's Unfinished Business: Rethinking Land, State and Nation in the Context of Crisis*, edited by Amanda Hammar, Brian Raftopoulos, and Stig Jensen, 49–81. Harare: Weaver Press.

Zamchiya, Phillan. 2013. "The Role of Politics and State Practices in Shaping Rural Differentiation: A Study of Resettled Small-Scale Farmers in South-Eastern Zimbabwe." *Journal of Southern African Studies* 39(4): 937–953.

ZCDT (Zimbabwe Community Development Trust). 2003. *Report on Internally Displaced Farm Workers Survey: Kadoma, Chegutu and Kwekwe Districts*. February. Harare: ZCDT.

Zimbabwe Lawyers for Human Rights. 2004. "Africa Citizenship and Discrimination Audit." First draft. Open Society. Accessed January 22, 2014. www1.umn.edu/humanrts /research/ZLHR-citizenship.html.

ZINISA (Zimbabwe Network for Informal Settlement Action). 2001. *The Situation of Children on Commercial Farms in Mashonaland Central*. Harare: ZINISA.

ZSG (Zimbabwe Surveyor General). 1998. *Land Classification Map of Zimbabwe*, 2nd edition. Harare: ZSG.

INDEX

belonging, 16, 27–28, 59, 63, 106–107, 148, 194, 220, 242, 250–251. *See also* citizenship
Briggs, Charles, 77, 252

Central Intelligence Organization (CIO), 75, 127
citizenship, 9, 16, 43–46, 47–48, 147–148, 172, 221–222, 228. *See also* belonging
Constitutional Commission, 11–12, 147–148, 166

domestic government, 16, 32–36, 51, 63, 65–66, 86, 92, 96, 142–143, 165–166, 179, 185, 191–192, 200, 223, 225, 232–234, 235–238, 243, 249. *See also* relations of dependency
domestic violence. *See* violence against women

electoral politics. *See* poritikisi
ex-combatants. *See* war veterans

farm workers: citizenship, 9, 167, 221, 228, 249; constitutional referendum (2000), 12, 166–167; Economic Structural Adjustment Programme (ESAP), 10; labor relations, 60–68, 80–86, 99–105, 121–124, 140, 213–215, 224, 225–227; land redistribution, 9, 13, 48–49, 114, 147, 148, 174–175, 204, 221–223, 225–226, 248–249; leadership, 90–92, 99, 181, 197, 211; living conditions, 52–55, 137–138; national scale narratives (as portrayed in), 23–24, 30, 49, 59, 65, 166, 181, 243–244, 245–249; working conditions, 50–51, 139–140, 144–145, 199–200, 213–215, 217–219, 224, 247
Ferguson, James, 20–22, 50
Foucault, Michel, 17–18, 42

gender, 21, 37–39, 87, 88, 152
General Agricultural and Plantation Workers Union of Zimbabwe (GAPWUZ), 11, 60, 62–63, 65–67, 89, 92, 94–95, 96–97, 105–106, 117–120, 161, 162, 165–166, 196, 214–216, 224–226
Green Bombers. *See* National Youth Service
Gwisai, Munyaradzi, 75, 113, 117–118, 123–124, 150, 158, 161, 225, 256n1

HIV/AIDS, 56, 207, 209–210, 217, 229
horticultural sector, 38, 39, 71–73
human rights, 30–31, 146–147, 250; part of good governance promotion, 10–11; and ZANU (PF), 62. *See also* labor rights

International Socialist Organization (ISO) of Zimbabwe, 117–118, 121, 124, 150, 175, 257n13

jambanja, 13, 91, 128, 168–178, 184–188, 191–192, 238

labor relations (administrative and legal structures), 60–63, 96, 100, 102, 106, 147, 150–152, 156–158, 159, 160, 195
labor rights, 50, 82, 90, 95–96, 124, 133, 139–141, 148
land access, 47–49, 148–149, 174, 202–204, 222; vernacular market, 48, 203–204. *See also* land occupations
land occupations, 168–171, 174, 181–182, 184–188, 191, 194, 200–201, 213, 233
land resettlement, 8, 9, 48, 147, 170, 185, 190–191, 201, 228, 234–235
liberation war, 29, 168. *See also* war veterans

BLAIR RUTHERFORD is Professor of Anthropology in the Department of Sociology and Anthropology (cross-appointed to the Institute of African Studies, the Institute of Political Economy, and Department of Geography and Environmental Studies) at Carleton University in Ottawa, Canada.

Printed and bound by CPI Group (UK) Ltd, Croydon, CR0 4YY

23/04/2025

14661003-0002